R. Boulic and G. Hégron (eds.)

Computer Animation and Simulation '96

Proceedings of the Eurographics Workshop
in Poitiers, France,
August 31–September 1, 1996

Eurographics

SpringerWienNewYork

Dr. Ronan Boulic
Computer Graphics Laboratory, Swiss Federal Institute of Technology,
Lausanne, Switzerland

Dr. Gerard Hégron
Ecole des Mines de Nantes, Nantes Cedex, France

© 1996 Springer-Verlag/Wien

Typesetting: Camera ready by authors

Graphic design: Ecke Bonk

Printed on acid-free and chlorine-free bleached paper

With 152 partly coloured Figures

ISSN 0946-2767
ISBN-13: 978-3-211-82885-4   e-ISBN-13: 978-3-7091-7486-9
DOI: 10.1007/978-3-7091-7486-9

Preface

This volume contains research papers presented at the *Seventh Eurographics Workshop on Computer Animation and Simulation* which took place at Poitiers, France, August 31st-September 1st, 1996. In this preface we first outline the workshop reviewing process. Then we describe the scope of the present venue and show how the workshop WEB pages are useful even after the workshop. Finally we wish to acknowledge all the persons who dedicated their precious time helping us making 96 venue a success.

Process. This year's Call for Papers was publicized electronically more than ever before. The workshop WWW home page received a sustained rate of visitors as links and notifications were made at Eurographics'96, Eurographics Association, and at public or private servers. Thirty one full papers have been submitted. Each submitted paper has been reviewed by three members of the international program committee, namely:

Bruno Arnaldi	(IRISA / INRIA Rennes, France)
Norman Badler	(University of Pennsylvania, USA)
Michael Cohen	(Microsoft, USA)
Sabine Coquillart	(INRIA, France)
Marie-Paule Gascuel	(iMAGIS-IMAG, France)
Pedro Lopes	(INESC Multimedia Centre, Portugal)
Annie Luciani	(ACROE-IMAG, France)
Nadia Magnenat-Thalmann	(University of Geneva, Switzerland)
Kees van Overveld	(Eindhoven University of Technology, The Netherlands)
Demetri Terzopoulos	(University of Toronto, Canada)
Daniel Thalmann	(Swiss Federal Institute of Technology, Switzerland)
Michiel Van de Panne	(University of Toronto, Canada)
David Zeltzer	(Massachusetts Institute of Technology, USA)

Whenever necessary the senior reviewers have co-opted additional experts in the reviewing process. We are grateful to the following for accepting this task :

Pascal Becheiraz	(Swiss Federal Institute of Technology, Switzerland)
Pierre Beylot	(University of Geneva, Switzerland)
Mathieu Desbrun	(iMAGIS-IMAG, France)
Jean Loup Florens	(ACROE-IMAG, France)
Manuel Noronha Gamito	(INESC Multimedia Centre, Portugal)
Jean Marc Jot	(INA,France)
Prem Kalra	(University of Geneva, Switzerland)
Alexis Lamouret	(University of Toronto, Canada)
Jean Louchet	(INRIA, France)
Laurent Moccozet	(University of Geneva, Switzerland)
Hansruedi Noser	(Swiss Federal Institute of Technology, Switzerland)
Igor Pandzic	(University of Geneva, Switzerland)
Marcia Riley	(University of Geneva, Switzerland)
Jos Stam	(INRIA, France)

Based on the reviews, we selected fourteen papers for presentation at the workshop and invite the authors to prepare the final version for inclusion in this volume.

Scope. We are especially pleased with the scope, innovation and general quality of EGCAS'96. Important contributions cover three major research streams of Computer Animation and Simulation :

- *Real-Time Animation for 3D Interaction* : in this rapidly growing field the need for adaptive techniques is vital to ensure the animation at a minimum interactive frame rate. Original techniques have been proposed to update the visibility map, refine mass/Spring simulations and optimize the display of very large particle systems. Real-Time Performance Animation have also been explored for human motion capture.

- *Fast and Intuitive Animation Design Methodology* : One major problem in animation design is the compromise an animator is faced with when required to design a complex realistic motion. Simulation-based tools leave little room for creativity while keyframe-based systems require considerable experience to produce the illusion of reality (along with desired behavioral and emotional effect). Some articles presented in the presented here address the problem of motion reusability which includes motion database management and motion composition from desired high level input. One very interesting approach introduces the concept of plausible motion design.

- *Simulation of Complex and Dynamic Scenes* : the real world is complex but new models and animation methods help to represent it in very efficient way as demonstrated here for deformable objects, plants, fire, and even the human anatomy.

The proposed methodologies, some with prototype implementations, bring solutions to currently open issues and pave the way for the next generation of Animation softwares.

WWW. This year for the first time a WEB site has been setup to diffuse information about the workshop. As we discovered by the responses of contributors, the WEB is now the second means by which potential authors get to know the existence of the workshop (the first being the activity of program committee members and the workshop notoriety). Another important reason for maintaining such a site after the EGCAS'96 : providing links to authors pages and especially to the animation files they cannot show on a printed media. So the 96 workshop site now gathers all the WEB addresses mentioned in the articles under the keyword *Animation(s)*. As links may be a volatile information, the workshop site page is the best place to maintain up-to-date information. We hope that our informal approach becomes more stable with the help of the Eurographics association and the publisher. The workshop WEB address is:

http://ligwww.epfl.ch/~boulic/egcas96/egcas96.html

Acknowledgments. The workshop mostly owes its high quality to the careful and insightful work of all the reviewers. The local organizer, Michel Mériaux, of the University of Poitiers notably contributed to provide a harmonious environment including, among other strategic aspects, the two lunches. Our gratitude goes to the Eurographics Association and to Werner Hansmann of University of Hamburg, to Terry Hewitt of University of Manchester and especially to Werner Purgathofer of the Technical University of Vienna, for their support in publishing the workshop as a volume of the Springer-Verlag Eurographics Series. We thank Xaviar Pueyo of the University of Girona and Carlo Vandoni from CERN for helping in publicizing the workshop. We are grateful to Sabine Coquillart, of INRIA, for adding the workshop WEB link to Eurographics'96 WEB page and to Ivan Herman of the Research Center in Computer Science of Amsterdam, for the same precious update of Eurographics Association WEB page. Last but not least, we wish to thank Srikanth Bandi of EPFL for proof-reading this text.

We acknowledge financial support from the following funding agencies: Boulic was supported by the Swiss Federal Institute of Technology and the Swiss Foundation for Research. Hégron was supported by l'Ecole des Mines de Nantes and the French Ministry of Industry.

Ronan Boulic (Co-Chair)
Swiss Federal Institute of Technology
Lausanne, Switzerland

Gérard Hégron (Co-Chair)
Ecole des Mines de Nantes
Nantes, France

Contents

X

4. Plant Development

5. Motion Control and Motion Management

1

Adaptive Optimization Techniques

Incremental Update of the Visibility Map as Seen by a Moving Viewpoint in Two Dimensions

Sherif Ghali   A. James Stewart

Department of Computer Science
University of Toronto

Abstract. Consider the following problem: A viewpoint moves amongst a
set of line segments in the plane and it is desired to maintain the sequence
of lines visible from the viewpoint at every increment in its position. The
sequence of visible lines is identical for most increments in the position
of the viewpoint. It is different only when the viewpoint crosses a visual
discontinuity line. Our objective is to be able to quickly report whether
the sequence of visible lines needs to be updated and perform the update
quickly in that case. We propose an algorithm that satisfies both criteria
while using space linear in the number of visual discontinuity lines. This
last condition is important because constructing the arrangement of these
lines would take space quadratic in their number.
Keywords: animation, visibility maps, on–line algorithms, incremental
update, discontinuity lines.

1   Introduction

As a viewpoint moves along a trajectory in a static scene represented by a set
of line segments, we would like to compute the view at successive points along
that trajectory. This problem can be solved in two settings: off–line and on–
line. In the off–line version, we are given all of the trajectory as part of the
input whereas, in the on–line version, the position updates are only known as
they occur. Clearly, the on–line problem is the more interesting for interactive
systems (for example, those that control the viewpoint with a mouse or an
infrared tracking system).

The term *frame–to–frame coherence* refers to the similarity between consecutive frames in an animation. This similarity makes it wasteful to render
each frame from scratch, given that most of the information has already been
computed for the preceding frame. The attempts to take advantage of frame–
to–frame coherence fall into several camps:

The traditional solution to this problem is to preprocess the scene such that
the depth order can be computed for an arbitrary viewpoint. Binary Space
Partitioning, or BSP, is a popular technique in this category [6, 18]. The BSP
algorithm is run once for a static scene and produces a tree of size in $\Omega(n)$ and
$\mathcal{O}(n^2)$, where n is the size of the scene. For each rendered image, a painter type
algorithm traverses the tree. In a real–time system, the cost of this traversal is
prohibitive even if the size of the tree is linear in the size of the input.

Define a "plane of support" to be a plane that is tangent to two polyhedra in a scene. By generating these planes and testing whether any one of them is intersected by the viewpoint trajectory, it is possible to update the visibility map as seen by the viewpoint [12]. However, intersecting the viewpoint trajectory at each increment with all planes of support is too expensive.

If the flight trajectory is restricted to be a line segment and is given as part of the input (off–line version), it is possible to compute the locations on the line segment where the visibility map changes [2, 15]. This takes time between quadratic and cubic in the size of the input.

The BSP and the 5D ray classification [1] algorithms have been modified to take advantage of frame–to–frame coherence [25, 10, 26]. The painting step in a BSP–based algorithm is too time–expensive, though, and the tree stored by space partitioning algorithms for ray tracing needs large storage to be effective, which may not be practical for a large input scene.

In [20], an algorithm is presented that preprocesses a set of static objects of size n in $\mathcal{O}(n^2)$ storage and close to $\mathcal{O}(n^2)$ time to maintain the view from a given trajectory in $\mathcal{O}(\log n)$ per update (off–line version).

The algorithm presented in [4] avoids storing the complete set of visual discontinuities by storing only those that are in close proximity to the viewpoint. A hierarchical voxel subdivision of the scene is performed and the discontinuity surfaces intersecting the increasingly larger voxels surrounding the viewpoint are stored. When the viewpoint moves, the discontinuities intersecting the voxels from the new viewpoint position to the nearest ancestor between the old and the new positions need to be computed. A comparative discussion between the algorithms of Pocchiola [20], Coorg and Teller [4], and the algorithm described in this paper is provided in Section 5.

2 Outline of the approach

Consider the following problem. Preprocess a set of segments in the plane such that it it possible to efficiently determine which segments are visible from a moving viewpoint after computing the solution from an initial viewpoint. The output will be a *visibility cycle* describing the segments visible in radial order around the viewpoint. A special tag for a segment (or a line) at infinity will be used when no segment is visible in a certain interval [20].

In Fig. 1, the scene consists of three line segments. The dotted lines define the sites of visual discontinuities across which a viewpoint sees a change in the topological structure of the visibility cycle. For the trajectory shown, the viewpoint can only see line segment b until line l is crossed, at which point segment a becomes visible.

The three dimensional analog of these lines has been used in the computation of aspect graphs [19, 9, 8] and in the computation of discontinuity meshes for scenes illuminated by area light sources [11, 13, 5, 24].

To solve the problem, we take the following steps.

1. Build the visibility graph for the given n line segments. The nodes in

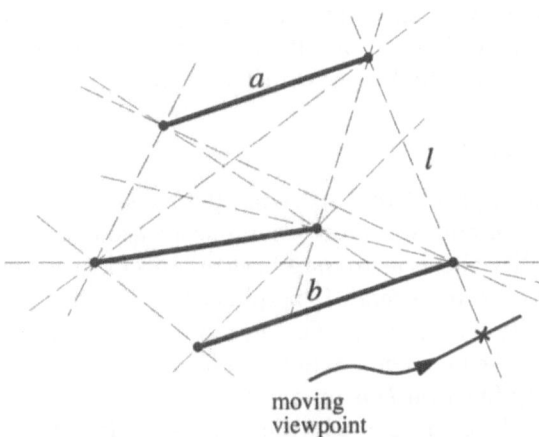

Fig. 1. The dotted lines connect each pair of mutually–visible endpoints. The scene visible from the moving viewpoint remains the same until the viewpoint crosses the line l.

the visibility graph are the endpoints of the line segments. Two nodes are joined by an edge if a line segment connecting the corresponding endpoints does not intersect any other line segment. This graph can be constructed in $\mathcal{O}(m \log n)$ time [17] for a graph with m edges.

2. Given a set of these discontinuities, preprocess it into a data structure that a viewpoint traversing the scene can query to determine whether any discontinuity has been crossed. This will be discussed in Section 3.

3. As long as no discontinuity is crossed, the viewpoint sees the same visibility cycle. If one is crossed, however, then an update needs to be performed on the cycle to reflect the features newly visible. This will be discussed in Section 4.

3 Efficiently Detecting the Intersection of the Flight Path with a Discontinuity Line

Imagine constructing the arrangement [22] of the m discontinuity lines which embed the pairs of mutually–visible endpoints in the visibility graph. As the viewpoint moves but remains inside one cell in the arrangement, the set of visible segments and their order around the viewpoint remains unchanged. We would therefore like to compute the description of the boundary of the current cell and intersect it with the path with each position increment. The obvious approach to do so is to compute the complete arrangement. The description of each cell will consist of the set of lines bounding it. Unfortunately, the size of the resulting arrangement will be in $\Theta(m^2)$. Given that the number of discontinuity lines is already between linear and quadratic in the number of input segments, we cannot afford to spend that much space for the arrangement. We attempt instead to form an implicit description of the cell the viewpoint is currently in. To do so, we review a tool that we shall use: geometric duality.

3.1   Geometric Duality

Geometric Duality is an old tool in classical Projective Geometry. In recent years, it has proved useful in solving a number of geometric problems (see, for example, [3]). Duality allows us to map a set of objects with which we have little intuition (e.g. lines, or, in general, hyperplanes) to another set about which we can think more easily (e.g. points). Furthermore, this mapping does not cost us anything: we simply reinterpret the data we have.

One such duality function D is to map a point (a, b) onto the line $ax + by = 1$ and vice–versa. Each of the line and the point is called the *dual* of the other. This mapping is a bijection. The plane where the original data sit is called the *primal plane* and the one to which they map is called the *dual plane*. Duality is *incidence preserving*: If a point P is incident to a line L in the primal plane then the dual of L, the point $L' = D(L)$ in the dual plane, is also incident to the dual of P, the line $P' = D(P)$.

Consider that a line L defines two open halfspaces: one that contains the origin (called L_1) and one that does not (called L_2). Duality is *sidedness preserving*: Point P lies in halfspace L_1 of a line L if and only if the dual point L' lies in halfspace P_1' of the dual line P'. In the next section we exploit this property.

3.2   Computation of the description of the current cell

We need to store the description of the set of lines bounding the cell in which the viewpoint lies in the arrangement of lines in the primal plane. Since computing the arrangement is too expensive, we take the following approach. Dualize (i.e. compute the dual) of the set of discontinuity lines S. Dualize the viewpoint V. Let the duals be $S' = D(S)$ and $V' = D(V)$. V' divides the dual plane and the set of points S' into two sets S_1' and S_2', the first lying on the same side of V' as the origin and the second on the opposite side. Construct C_1, the convex hull of S_1', and C_2, the convex hull of S_2'. See Fig. 2. It follows from the construction and from duality being sidedness preserving that the set of lines bounding the cell in which the viewpoint lies in the primal plane is a subset of the set of points on the two convex hulls C_1 and C_2.

As long as the viewpoint moves inside the current cell in the primal plane, the set of visible segments remains unchanged. As the viewpoint V gets closer to a line L on the boundary of the cell and becomes incident on it, the dual $V' = D(V)$ becomes incident on the dual of that line, $L' = D(L)$. When V crosses L in the primal plane, it enters another cell. This is reflected in the dual plane by the point L' crossing line V'. See Fig. 3. L' now has to be deleted from one convex hull and inserted into the other. In what follows, we discuss how to perform the insertion and deletion of points.

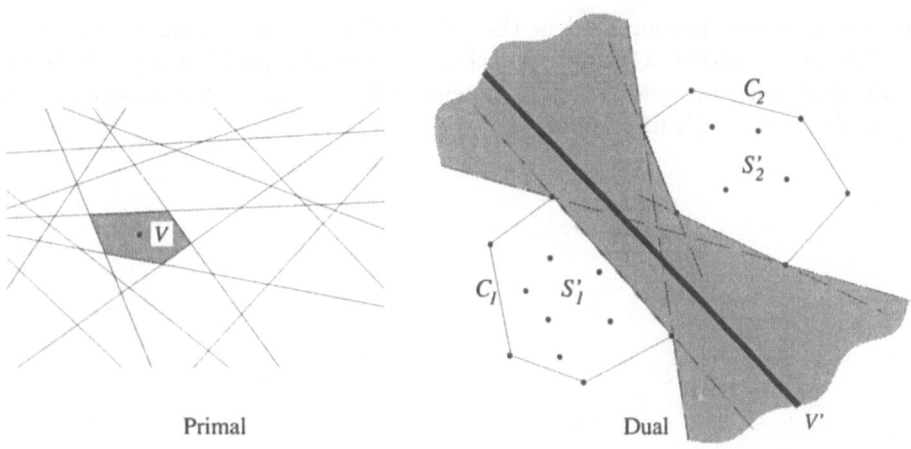

Primal   Dual V'

Fig. 2. The figure on the left shows the arrangement of the discontinuity lines. The set of points shown on the right is the set of dual points of these lines. All viewpoints in any one cell in the arrangement on the left have the same visibility cycle. When the viewpoint V moves in the shaded cell in the primal plane, its dual line V' also moves in the shaded region shown in the dual. The exit of V from the shaded cell in the primal is signaled in the dual by V' intersecting one of the two convex hulls C_1 or C_2.

3.3 Dynamic Maintenance of Convex Hulls

We need to maintain the convex hulls of two sets of points in the dual plane as points are deleted from one and inserted into the other. A lower bound of $\Omega(\log n)$ per insertion/deletion operation follows from the lower bound of the convex hull problem [22]. Currently, the best known algorithm achieves $\mathcal{O}(\log^2 n)$ time per operation [16]. It is an open problem whether an algorithm exists that can perform the updates in logarithmic time.

When inserting a point into a convex hull in the dual plane, the point is connected to the two common tangents between it and the hull. The points that disappear from the hull boundary correspond to the discontinuities in the primal plane that no longer bound the current cell. When deleting a point from a hull in the dual, an arbitrary number of points can appear on the hull boundary. These points correspond to the lines in the primal plane that bound the new cell the viewpoint enters.

The two convex hulls that we maintain in the dual plane give us a concise description of the discontinuities in the primal plane which, when crossed, may require an update of the visibility cycle. The hulls can be stored in space linear in the number of discontinuities. For every new position of the viewpoint V, the dual V' is computed and a test performed to see if any point on either of the two convex hulls in the dual plane has switched sides. If more than one point has switched sides, the distances separating the corresponding discontinuities from the old viewpoint is compared in the primal plane to determine which one is the first to be crossed. Comparing each new viewpoint position with all points on the two hulls can potentially be expensive but this is sufficient because few points lie on the hulls in practice.

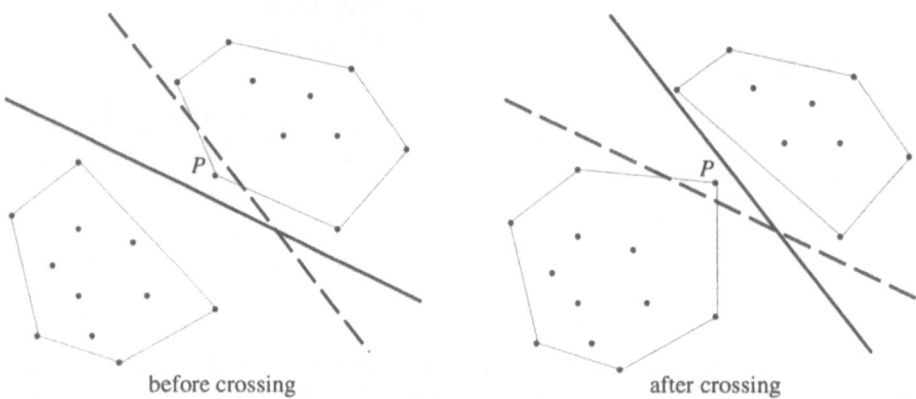

before crossing   after crossing

Fig. 3. The figure on the left (respectively, right) shows the configuration in the dual plane before (respectively, after) the discontinuity line is crossed. In both figures, the solid line is the dual of the current position of the viewpoint with the dashed line showing the position of the dual after (respectively, before) crossing. As the discontinuity point P is crossed, P is deleted from one set of points and inserted into the other, while maintaining the convex hulls of both sets of points.

Occasionally the viewpoint V will cross a discontinuity that is defined by two *hidden* endpoints (recall that the discontinuity lines embed two segment endpoints and extend to infinity). An endpoint is hidden if the line segment joining it to the viewpoint intersects a segment of the scene. A portion of a discontinuity is called a *true* discontinuity if the visibility cycle changes when the viewpoint crosses the discontinuity in that portion. It is called a *false* discontinuity if no change in the visibility cycle occurs. To determine whether a discontinuity crossing is a true or a false one, we store with each discontinuity the coordinates of the two endpoints that gave rise to it. Also, a small modification of the algorithm of Overmars and Welzl [17] allows us to identify the two edges (if any) that intersect each discontinuity line nearest to each of the two endpoints that gave rise to it. Even though a false discontinuity does not require a change to the visibility cycle, the convex hulls in the dual plane still need to be updated to maintain a current description of the cell the viewpoint is in.

We take advantage of the fact that the set of points to be maintained is static by the following simplification of the algorithm of Overmars and van Leeuwen [16] which lends itself to an easy implementation. The points are sorted in the x-direction and are stored at the leaves of a binary tree. See Fig. 4. Every node in the tree stores two convex hulls; the one above the dual V' of the viewpoint V and the one below it. Initially, each leaf node stores a variable to identify whether it is above or below V'. The two convex hulls at a node are constructed from its children's hulls by finding their upper and lower common tangents. When a point switches sides with respect to V', only those nodes that lie on the path from the corresponding leaf node to the root need be updated. If the number of points is n, there are $\mathcal{O}(\log n)$ nodes on that path and $\mathcal{O}(\log n)$ time needs to be spent at each node to compute the upper and lower common tangents for a total update time of $\mathcal{O}(\log^2 n)$. In practice, since the tree itself is static (but not the hulls stored at its nodes) a heap implementation suffices. To guarantee the bounds above for time but in particular for space, Overmars and van Leeuwen avoid duplicating the points on the convex hull at each level in the tree by storing only one copy of the convex hulls at the root node in concatenable queues. An update operation (either insert or delete) is performed by first descending down the tree on the path from the root to the leaf that needs to be updated and the concatenable queues are broken at each level into two halves. This is followed by a percolating step to reconstruct the hulls at each level from the leaf to the root. Given that the number of points on the convex hull is small in practice, our implementation stores the complete convex hulls at each level.

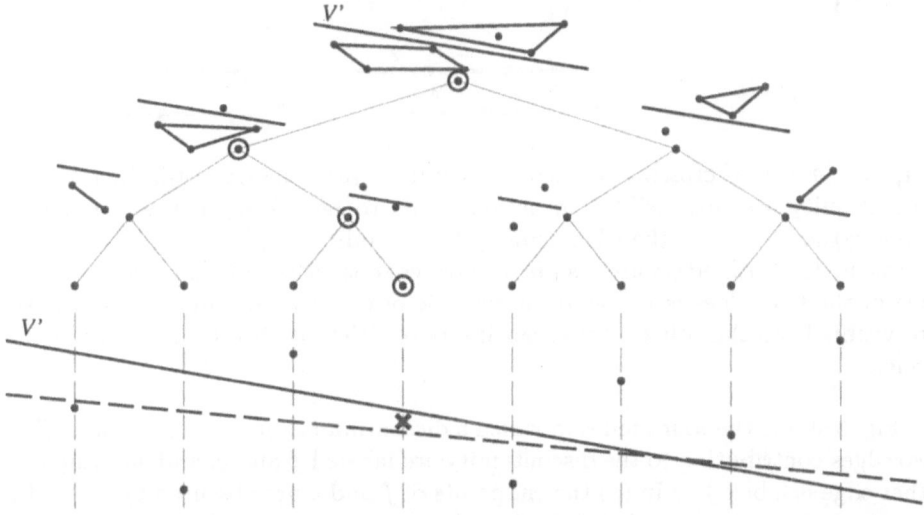

Fig. 4. The bottom half of the figure shows the points in the dual plane. These points are sorted by x-coordinate and stored at the leaves of the binary tree shown above. The dotted line is the dual of the previous position of the viewpoint. At every node in the tree, the convex hulls of the points that lie above and below the line are stored. After the point (shown in 'x') crosses the line, only the convex hulls at the nodes of the tree that lie on the path to the root need to be updated (nodes are circled in the figure).

4   Updating the Visibility Cycle

An initial view can easily be computed in $\mathcal{O}(n \log n)$ time by sweeping radially around the starting location of the viewpoint. The output will be a circular list of the visible segments. This list may need to be updated when the viewpoint crosses a discontinuity line. The problem of updates is well–studied in the computation of aspect graphs [19, 9] and in the computation of the visible portions of area light sources [24, 5]. The following presentation is the two–dimensional version of the problem and is similar to ideas presented in [27, 20].

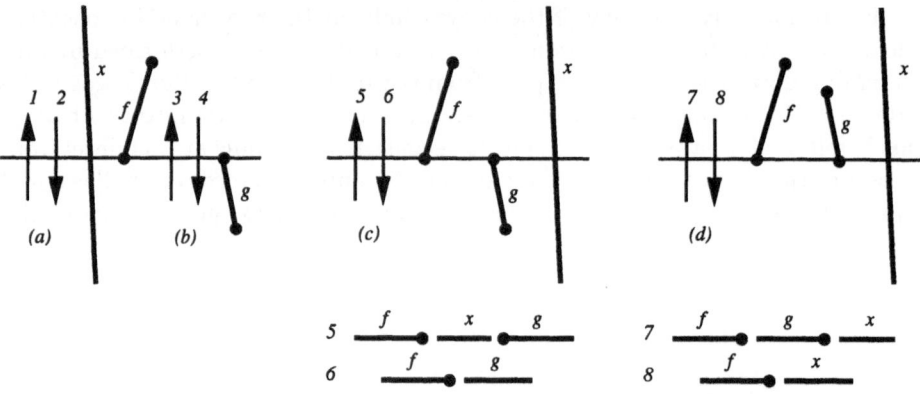

Fig. 5. Modes of crossing a discontinuity line: (a) Edges contributing to the discontinuity are not visible; no action needs to be taken. (b) Viewpoint is crossing the interior of the edge defining the visibility graph; no action needs to be taken. (c) Both edges are visible; a third edge is either added or deleted. (d) One of the two edges is visible from one side of the discontinuity line and both are visible from the other side; either insert or delete edge g from the visibility cycle.

Fig. 5 shows the four modes in which a discontinuity line can be crossed. The two edges contributing to the discontinuity are labeled f and g, and an arbitrary other edge is labeled x. In (a) the endpoints of f and g are obscured by x. In (b) the viewpoint crosses the interior of the line segment connecting the endpoints of f and g. No update is needed in either of these two cases. In cases (c) and (d) the visibility cycle needs to be modified. Underneath each of these cases a section of the cycle is shown. An endpoint is highlighted with a solid point if it is the actual endpoint of the segment. Non–highlighted endpoints refer to edges that are partially obscured by another edge. The section of the cycle where the two edges f and g occur is compared to each of the four transitions 5...8 and a simple update is performed on the cycle in each case.

5 Conclusion

An on–line algorithm to maintain the current cell in an arrangement of discontinuity lines has been implemented in C++. The implementation has been simplified by building it on the LEDA library [14]. Real–time tracking of the position of the viewpoint is performed as the mouse moves and the set of visible line segments is identified for each increment. An animation of this algorithm is available on video [7].

Note that the number of discontinuities is in $\Omega(n)$ and $\mathcal{O}(n^2)$ in a scene of n segments. Experimental results with random sets of line segments indicate that the number of discontinuities grows linearly with the number of segments. Intuitively, in a dense scene, each segment endpoint will tend to see a constant number of other segment endpoints.

Comparisons

In what follows, we compare the algorithm presented here with the one by Pocchiola [20]. There are two main advantages to our algorithm. The first is the ability to process queries on–line, which is important for interactive applications. The second is that we only spend time proportional to the number of edges in the visibility graph during preprocessing [17] whereas Pocchiola's algorithm needs time in $\Omega(n^2)$ for both time and storage. (Notice, however, that the number of edges in the graph can reach $\Theta(n^2)$, e.g. for a set of segments on a circle [27].) However, we spend time $\mathcal{O}(\log^2 n)$ per update whereas he only spends $\mathcal{O}(\log n)$ and can deal with more complex convex shapes than line segments.

Also, we use the dual plane to avoid having to compute the arrangement of lines in the primal plane whereas Pocchiola computes an arrangement of curves which takes $\Theta(n^2)$ space in a scene of n objects. Finally, the algorithm presented here has been implemented using simple data structures. A drawback in our approach, on the other hand, is that we keep the portions of the discontinuity lines that are not important (because a viewpoint crossing such a portion cannot see the the two endpoints that gave rise to the discontinuity). Pocchiola is able to remove the superfluous curved segments arising in his case during the preprocessing and thus does not get false signals to update the view during the processing of the trajectory.

It is more difficult to compare the algorithm presented here and that of Coorg and Teller [4] without empirical trials. The algorithm we propose is simple and is able to update the position of the viewpoint in polylog time in the number of discontinuities. The algorithm by Coorg and Teller suffers from the traditional problem of relying on a user–given parameter to perform the subdivision of the scene into voxels. In our approach, we don't compute the arrangement of the discontinuity lines since it has quadratic cost, but we spend time in the preprocessing step to compute the (full) visibility graph. Coorg and Teller, on the other hand, avoid the computation of the complete set of discontinuities (which could use space cubic in the size of the input for the 3D case) by only considering the interaction between the objects visible and the partition of the space that lie in their shadow volume with respect to the viewpoint. Of course, the algorithm of Coorg and Teller operates in 3D whereas ours is in the plane.

Problem in 3D

The obvious question is whether it is possible to scale upwards and solve the problem in three dimensions. Several complications arise in the 3D case that make this a non–trivial task. No algorithm is known that can compute the discontinuity surfaces in a scene in time proportional to the size of the output. Also, as is well known [23, 19, 9], *three* edges can construct a quadric surface. The arrangement of the discontinuity surfaces in the primal space would no longer be a planar arrangement. Quadrics would also add a difficulty since the dual of these surfaces is no longer a point. Finally, an insertion or deletion of a point to a convex hull of a set of discontinuities in the dual space can take linear time in the size of the hull, although we would expect this to be much less in practice.

References

[1] J. Arvo and D. B. Kirk. Fast ray tracing by ray classification. In Maureen C. Stone, editor, *Computer Graphics (SIGGRAPH '87 Proceedings)*, volume 21, pages 55–64, July 1987.

[2] M. Bern, D. Dobkin, D. Eppstein, and R. Grossman. Visibility with a moving point of view. In *Proc. 1st ACM-SIAM Sympos. Discrete Algorithms*, pages 107–117, 1990.

[3] B. Chazelle, L. J. Guibas, and D. T. Lee. The power of geometric duality. *BIT*, 25:76–90, 1985.

[4] S. Coorg and S. Teller. Temporally coherent conservative visibility. In *Proc. 12th Annu. ACM Sympos. Comput. Geom.*, pages 78–87, 1996.

[5] G. Drettakis and E. Fiume. A fast shadow algorithm for area light sources using backprojection. *Computer Graphics Proceedings, Annual Conference Series 1994*, 28:223–230, August 1994.

[6] H. Fuchs, Z. M. Kedem, and B. Naylor. On visible surface generation by a priori tree structures. *Comput. Graph.*, 14(3):124–133, 1980.

[7] S. Ghali and A. J. Stewart. Maintenance of the set of segments visible from a moving viewpoint in two dimensions. In *Proc. 12th Annu. ACM Sympos. Comput. Geom.*, pages V3–V4, 1996.

[8] Z. Gigus, J. Canny, and R. Seidel. Efficiently computing and representing aspect graphs of polyhedral objects. *IEEE Trans. PAMI*, 13(6):542–551, 1991.

[9] Z. Gigus and J. Malik. Computing the aspect graphs for line drawings of polyhedral objects. *IEEE Transactions on Pattern Analysis and Machine Intelligence*, 12(2):113–122, February 1990.

[10] E. Groller and W. Purgathofer. Using temporal and spatial coherence for accelerating the calculation of animation sequences. In Werner Purgathofer, editor, *Eurographics '91*, pages 103–113. North-Holland, September 1991.

[11] P. Heckbert. Discontinuity meshing for radiosity. *Third Eurographics Workshop on Rendering*, pages 203–215, May 1992.

[12] H. Hubschman and S. W. Zucker. Frame-to-frame coherence and the hidden surface computation: Constraints for a convex world. *ACM Transactions on Graphics*, 1(2):129–162, 1982.

[13] D. Lischinski, F. Tampieri, and D. Greenberg. Discontinuity meshing for accurate radiosity. *IEEE Computer Graphics & Applications*, pages 25–39, November 1992.

[14] K. Mehlhorn and S. Näher. LEDA: a platform for combinatorial and geometric computing. *CACM*, 38:96–102, 1995.

[15] K. Mulmuley. Hidden surface removal with respect to a moving point. In *Proc. 23rd Annu. ACM Sympos. Theory Comput.*, pages 512–522, 1991.

[16] M. H. Overmars and J. van Leeuwen. Dynamically maintaining configurations in the plane. In *Proc. 12th Annu. ACM Sympos. Theory Comput.*, pages 135–145, 1980.

[17] M. H. Overmars and E. Welzl. New methods for computing visibility graphs. In *Proc. 4th Annu. ACM Sympos. Comput. Geom.*, pages 164–171, 1988.

[18] M. S. Paterson and F. F. Yao. Efficient binary space partitions for hidden-surface removal and solid modeling. *Discrete Comput. Geom.*, 5:485–503, 1990.

[19] H. Plantinga and C. R. Dyer. Visibility, occlusion, and the aspect graph. *Internat. J. Comput. Vision*, 5(2):137–160, 1990.

[20] M. Pocchiola. Graphics in Flatland revisited. In *Proc. 2nd Scand. Workshop Algorithm Theory*, volume 447 of *Lecture Notes in Computer Science*, pages 85–96. Springer-Verlag, 1990.

[21] M. Pocchiola and G. Vegter. The visibility complex. In *Proc. 9th Annu. ACM Sympos. Comput. Geom.*, pages 328–337, 1993.

[22] F. P. Preparata and M. I. Shamos. *Computational Geometry: an Introduction*. Springer-Verlag, New York, NY, 1985.

[23] D. M. Y. Sommerville. *Analytical Geometry in three dimensions*. Cambridge University Press, 1934.

[24] J. Stewart and S. Ghali. Fast computation of shadow boundaries using spatial coherence and backprojections. *Computer Graphics Proceedings, Annual Conference Series 1994*, 28:231–238, August 1994.

[25] E. Torres. Optimization of the binary space partition algorithm (BSP) for the visualization of dynamic scenes. In C. E. Vandoni and D. A. Duce, editors, *Eurographics '90*, pages 507–518. North-Holland, September 1990.

[26] D. Tost. An algorithm of hidden surface removal based on frame-to-frame coherence. In Werner Purgathofer, editor, *Eurographics '91*, pages 261–273. North-Holland, September 1991.

[27] E. Welzl. Constructing the visibility graph for n line segments in $O(n^2)$ time. *Inform. Process. Lett.*, 20:167–171, 1985.

Adaptive sampling for very large particle systems using an incremental self-organizing feature map: an application in molecular dynamic

Laurent Balmelli
Laboratory for Audio-Visual Communications
Swiss Federal Institute of Technology, Lausanne, Switzerland

Abstract. this paper describes an improvement of the self-organizing feature map (SOFM) obtained with the Kohonen neural network. The ameliorations are dedicated to its usage in computer graphics and mainly in animation of particle-based systems. We show its application in the context of the visualization of molecular dynamic systems. Comparison with other works based on particle systems is then made. Finally, we propose some possible extensions to this work.

Animations: http://lcavsun6.eplf.ch/EGCAS96

1 Introduction

The visualization of molecular dynamic systems can be achieved with several graphic techniques. In this paper, we consider a polygon-rendering method, which consists of displaying each atom with a sphere. Property mapping is then applied on the spheres, by colouring them using the temperature of the corresponding atom. If animated visualization is needed, this method is suitable as long as the system size is small (500-2000 atoms). For large system ($10^6 - 10^7$ atoms), this technique becomes unusable, as the scene complexity is too high for today's machines. This paper proposes a method for animated visualization of large molecular dynamic (MD) systems by reducing the amount of information (essentially the set of atom coordinates) and keeping the main interesting features: the system organization and the properties (like temperatures) distribution. This technique can be applied in several other applications based on particle systems. Suggestions are made in Section 4 to include it in other models. Comparisons are made with a crowd visualization model, a model for human hair structure and finally with a model for the visualization of water flow. Certainly a lot of extensions could be applied to this work, and some are detailed in Section 5. These are focused on the improvement of discretization performances on complex models and on the enhancement of animation capacities when using different levels of discretization.

2 Background

2.1 Molecular dynamic

A molecular dynamic problem consists of the physical simulation of a set of atoms. Each atom is considered as a point mass and Newton's equations are integrated to calculate its motion. In the basic model, electronic interactions are not taken into account. This model is however sufficient to simulate substances like gas, fluids (in [7], a simple MD model to simulate water is given), solids...etc. In this paper, we consider the issue of the visualization of a large set of atoms, where one wants to observe macro-phenomenons like aggregations, micelles or simply global system evolution.

A solution for visualizing and animating efficiently a very large MD system would be to discretize it according to its topology and its distribution, each discrete value representing a local density of atoms - in [1], the inverse problem is related, where the authors propose to simulate large particle sets using density functions based on the evolution of smaller sets -. This operation can be performed using a SOFM like the *Kohonen neural network*. To obtain the property distribution of the system, property mapping can be applied on the discrete representation. This technique can also be used to enhance the discrete model, as the network convergence quality depends heavily on the shape of the system.

To produce an animation of the system, a more efficient discretization method has to be defined such as one which considers the slow convergence of the Kohonen network. For this reason, an incremental algorithm is proposed to update the discrete representation. The advantage of having the possibility to quickly recalculate the discrete model from a previous configuration is that an animation can be produced with it. Visualization could even be achieved while the system is effectively computed using molecular dynamic algorithms, assuming that those are effective enough to not slow down the frame rate of the animation. This feature would allow us to study MD systems in "real-time". More simply, visualization can be achieved with sets of pre-computed data which in this case are atom positions at successive time steps.

2.2 Neural nets and the Kohonen network

This section presents the basic of neural networks and more details can be found in [2]. The mathematical neuron model is an information-processing unit. Three basic elements can be distinguished:

- A set of *synapses* (inputs), each of which is characterized by a weight of its own. A weight is positive if the associated synapse is excitatory, else the synapse is inhibitory.
- An *adder* for summing the input signals, weighted by the respective synapses of the neuron.
- An *activation function* for limiting the amplitude of the neuron output. Typically, the normalized amplitude range of the output belongs to the closed interval [0:1] or [-1:1].
- A *threshold* that has the effect of lowering the net input of the activation function.

A neuron is defined by the following pair of equations (1) and (2):

$$u_k = f_k(x_1, ..., x_p) \tag{1}$$

where f_k is a fixed arbitrary function, k is the neuron index and p is the number of synapses (In the basic neuron model described in [2], f_k is a weighted summation).

$$y_k = \varphi(u_k - \theta_k) \tag{2}$$

where u_k is the *adder* output, θ_k is the *threshold* and y_k is the output signal of the neuron. The activation function φ in can be any "useful" function, depending on the usage context.

In Figure 1, $w_{k,j}$ is the weight of neuron k on *synapse j*, x_j is the input value on *synapse j*.

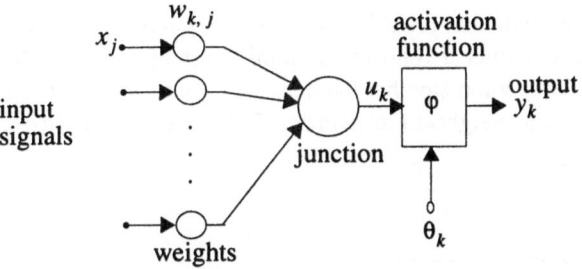

Fig. 1. Basic neuron model

The Kohonen network is composed of a set of neurons, usually organized as a 2D mesh (see Figure 2). The input is propagated to all neurons and each of them computes the output according to its characteristics. Neurons are only differentiated by their weight values. They all compute the same function.

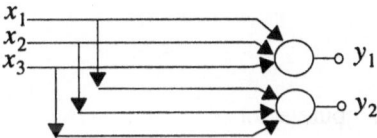

Fig. 2. Example of a two neurons network

Assuming that the network input is a tridimensional vector $\vec{x}$, the first feature of the Kohonen network is that each neuron k simply computes the Euclidean distance between the input and its weights. In this model, θ_k is null and φ is the identity function.

$$y_k = \sqrt{(x_1 - w_{k,1})^2 + (x_2 - w_{k,2})^2 + (x_3 - w_{k,3})^2} \tag{3}$$

The *winner neuron* is defined as the closest neuron from the input (see Figure 4).

The second feature is that a static neighborhood is initially defined between the neurons of the network. Every neighbouring neurons are linked together by a line for representation. Figure 3 shows a tridimensional cubic neighborhood between the neurons of the network.

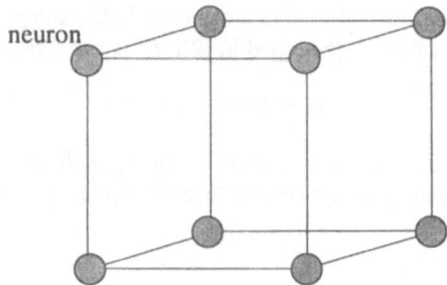

Fig. 3. Example of a 3D neighborhood in the Kohonen network

We now present an algorithm for a Kohonen network having a 3D input (each neuron has 3 synapses). The inputs are chosen randomly in the input space to obtain a *feature of generalization*. One could say that the network "learns" the distribution of the input space by modifying the weights of its neurons. This concept is discussed in more details in [2].

Initialization

- input: $(\vec{x_1}, \vec{x_2}, ..., \overrightarrow{x_{n-1}}, \vec{x_n})$ a set of n 3D vectors.

- set $\vec{w_k}$ to random values for each neuron

- define a static neighborhood between the neurons of the network.

- α is a learning factor, $0 < \alpha \leq 1$.

- V_k is a set of neighbours for neuron k.

- t=0

Algorithm

1. Pick randomly an input vector
2. Search the *winner neuron.*
   The winner neuron (i.e the closest neuron) is defined as the one with
   $y_k = min_{1...p}(y_l)$, where p is the number of neurons and
   $y_l = \left\| \vec{w_l} - \vec{x_i} \right\|$.
3. For this neurone k and $V_k(t)$, do update
   $\vec{w_j} = \vec{w_j} + \alpha(t) \cdot (\vec{x_i} - \vec{w_j})$ where $j \in \{k, V_k(t)\}$
4. t=t+1, update α and V_k for the next iteration.
5. return to step 1 until the network has converged.

The complexity of the weight update depends directly on the chosen network topology. The level of convergence of the network can hardly be evaluated and the convergence speed depends of the chosen parameters for the algorithm. One can say that the network converges when it presents an organization (this term will be clear with the following examples). It is very important to note that the neuron weights are initialized to random values. These values have to be uniformly distributed in a bounding box enclosing the MD system. After having randomly chosen an input, the *winner neuron* and its neighbours are approached from it using a displacement vector proportional to a α factor and to the distance they are separated by. Figure 4 illustrates this operation.

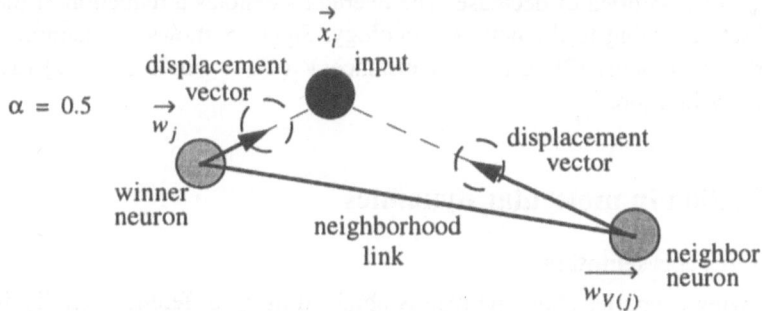

Fig. 4. Illustration of the Kohonen algorithm

This operation is performed by the Kohonen algorithm in each iteration.

The learning factor α is continuously decreased during the iterations. The chosen decreasing function is

$$\alpha(t+1) = \alpha(t)\left(\frac{1}{1+\Phi \cdot \alpha(t)}\right)$$

where $\alpha(t)$ is the value at iteration t and Φ is an increment set by the user. For instance, a common value for $\alpha(0)$ is 0.9. The value $\alpha(t)$ is updated after every T_α time interval. Initially, it is better to artificially extend the neighborhood for each neuron to the complete network, and decrease it during the iterations.

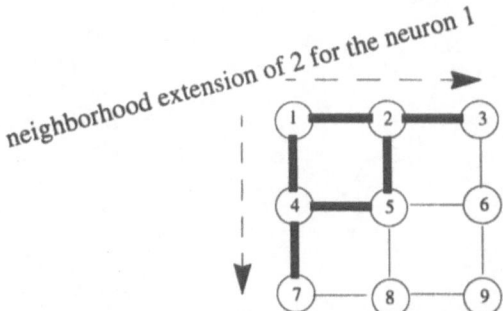

Fig. 5. Illustration of an extended neighborhood

The extended neighborhood is not used for the graphic representation and only direct neighbours are linked.

In the example of Figure 5, the initial neighborhood of neuron 1 is extended to neurons within a distance of 2. In this case $V_1(0) = \{2, 3, 4, 5, 7\}$. The neighborhood decreasing function is then

$$V_k(t+1) = \begin{cases} V_k(t) - 1 & \text{if } t \bmod T_v = 0 \text{ and } (V_k \notin \varnothing) \\ V_k(t) & \text{else} \end{cases} \tag{4}$$

where T_V is the interval of decrease. The operator - denotes a reduction of the neighborhood set according to the network topology. Figure 5 shows an example of a 2D neighborhood topology (2D grid). For instance, $V_1(0) - 1$ would be $\{2, 4\}$ (according to the indices in figure 5).

3 Application in molecular dynamics

3.1 Discrete representation

The following examples show the results obtained using different atom distributions. Some ranges for the algorithm parameters according to the system size and distribution are given in [9]. The chosen neighborhood topology is a 3D grid, whose size is given by three integers, *(nx,ny,nz)*, representing the number of neurons in each dimension.

In the first example, the system size is 250000 atoms and their distribution is approximately uniform. The network convergence is obtained using the parameters [$\alpha(0) = 0.9$, $T_\alpha = 1000$, $\Phi = 1$, $T_v = 2500$, $\delta = 6$, $nx = 6$, $ny = 6$, $nz = 6$] after 20000 iterations of the Kohonen algorithm.

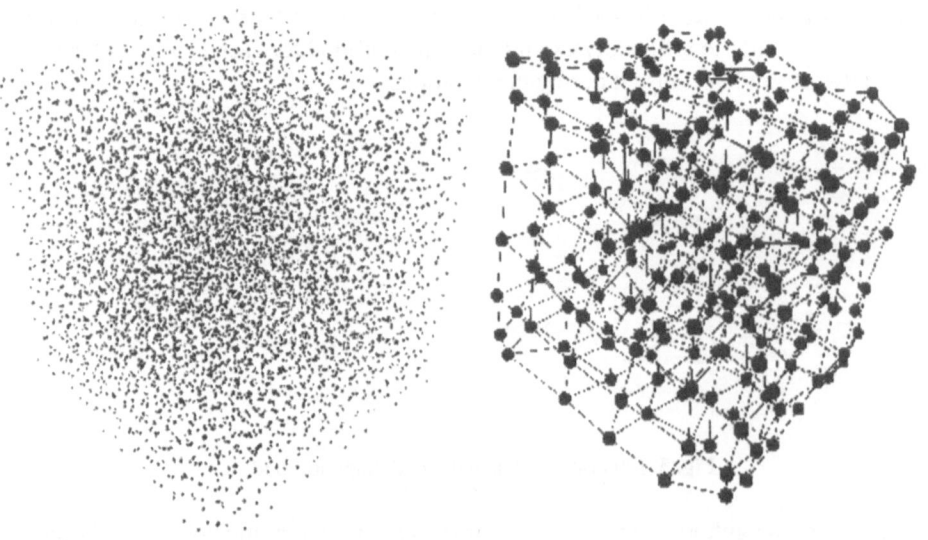

Fig. 6. Discretization of a system of 250000 atoms

One can see that the neuron distribution is an approximation of the system distribution. One obtains high quality convergence (i.e approximation) on continuous distributions of atoms for both uniform or non-uniform distributions. On detached distributions - when the system have more than one separated region where atoms are located- the convergence is harder, because of the regular structure of the network. This case is illustrated below.

In the next example, the system size is 170000 and the atoms are quite uniformly distributed in each of the boxes 1 and 2 (see configuration scheme on Figure 7), but the density of atoms in box 2 is half of the density in box 1. A network with a neighborhood configuration of [nx=5, ny=5, nz=6] was used. A neighborhood extension was made along dimension nz where the system was extended by box 2. The parameters used were [$\alpha(0)$ =0.9, T_α =1000, Φ = 1, T_v =2500, δ = 6, nx=5, ny=5, nz=6] and 20000 iterations of the Kohonen algorithm were performed.

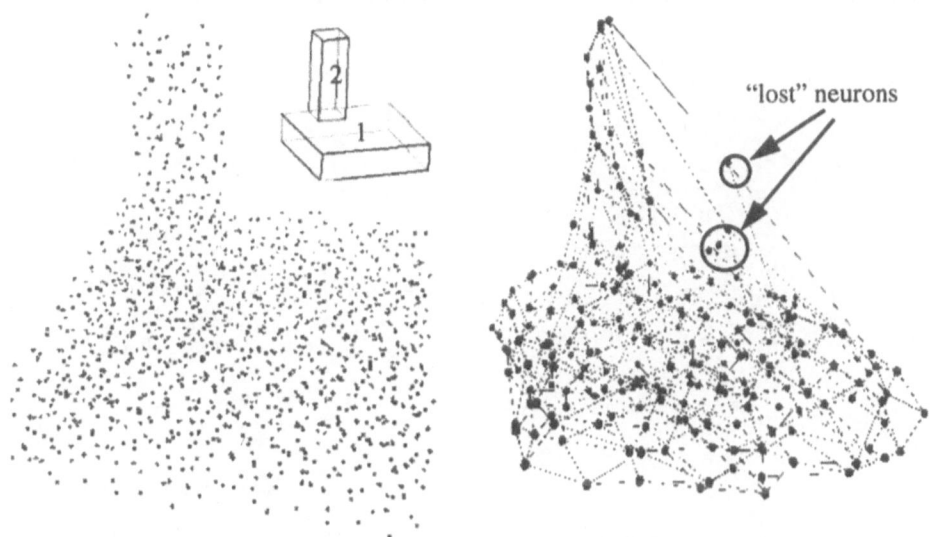

Fig. 7. Discretization of a detached MD system

In this case, convergence quality is lower and one can see that some neurons appear in locations where no atoms are present in the original system. We call these neurons *"lost" neurons*. This is due to the chosen neighborhood topology for the neural net. The neurons emphasized on the illustration have neighbours in both regions represented with boxes 1 and 2 and are "lost" between these. In Section 3.2, a technique is described to improve visualization of such discrete systems.

3.2 Property mapping

Each neuron (after convergence) can be coloured using information such as the average temperature of the surrounding atoms.

The property function applied to the neuron i is

$$p_i = \frac{1}{n_i} \sum_{j=1}^{n_i} T_j \tag{5}$$

where n_i is the number of atoms surrounding this neuron and T_j is the temperature of atom j. Other functions for p_i could be used to filter atom properties, and thus enhancing visualization in some applications.

The property mapping on the neural net must be applied after convergence because of the random initialization of the neuron weights. The neurons will then "travel" in the discrete space before reaching their final location. After convergence and for each atom of the original system, the winner neuron is searched. Then, the atom property is added to the neuron property. Finally, the final neuron property is the average of the properties which were added to it. The next illustrations show the results obtained using this technique. The MD systems are the same as those used in the previous examples.

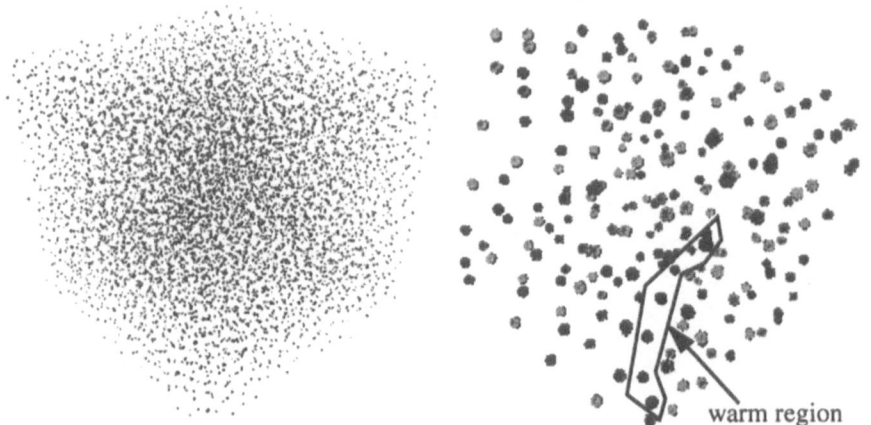

warm region

Fig. 8. Property mapping example

In Figure 8, the warm neurons (high average temperature p_i in (5)) are coloured in black in the discrete model. A color representation is available in the appendix.

With this result, one can see that in the discrete model the user can track more efficiently the properties of the system. Information that are not visible in the real system, due to the too great amount of data, can now be observed. The region emphasized on the discrete model shows a warm region of atoms which is not discernable in the real system. If after the property mapping operation some neurons were never "hit" by atoms (this will be the case for the lost neurons), they will be deleted from the representation. In the second example, property mapping on the detached distribution used in a previous example is applied.

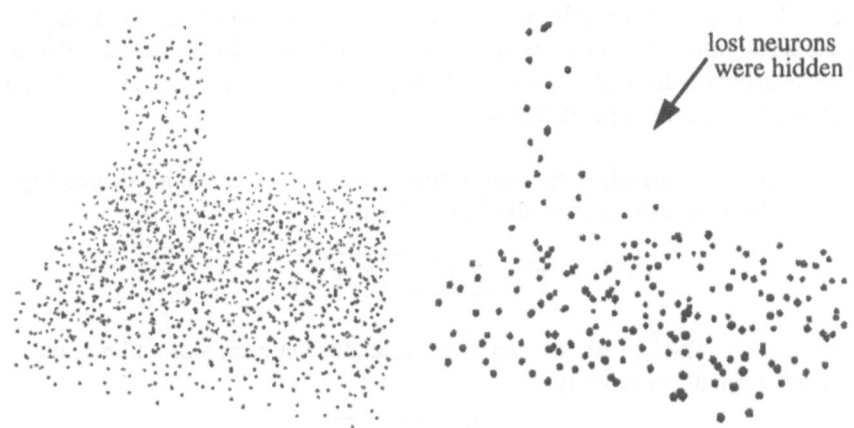

Fig. 9. Hiding of neurons using property mapping

As shown in Figure 9, The "lost" neurons are successfully hidden and the visualization of the discrete system has been enhanced. A color version of Figure 9 can be found in the appendix.

3.3 Adding an incremental mechanism

We call an incremental algorithm a method which allows, from an initial network configuration (defined by a set of neuron weights), to find the resulting network configuration after having modified the input space used for the previous network convergence. The construction of such an algorithm is possible for two reasons:

- Because of the very small time step used, the atoms in the MD system move slowly. Then, the values of the set of atom coordinates obtained at one iteration is not very different from the ones obtained at the next iteration.
- The values of a set of successive locations of an atom are correlated during the simulation.

The issue is that some atoms in the system move faster than others, and those ones ought to influence more the network, as the difference between their previous locations and the new ones is greater than that of the other atoms. For this reason, we propose a mechanism for choosing randomly these "interesting atoms" more often than the ones whose position do not vary greatly. The core of the incremental algorithm relies on this idea.

The velocity of an atom determines its activity. This value can be used to assign a probability to each atom for the random selection. A probability mass function can then be constructed for the whole system. Even if the network have previously converged before using the incremental algorithm, the atoms still have to be chosen randomly for the following reason: the Kohonen network gives an approximation of the distribution of its input and has a *feature of generalization,* and by choosing with a higher probability the fast atoms, the discrete model will reproduce more faithfully the system motion. This insight allows the network to be modified on only a small random subset of the database (the atom coordinates) and not the complete set, and thus lower the number of necessary iterations to obtain the network update. A simple and efficient algorithm for the random selection of the atoms is given below.

The first task is to normalize the atom velocities and to sort them in a decreasing order. The normalization is done using the value Γ, where

$$\Gamma = \sum_n \sqrt{v_{x,i}^2 + v_{y,i}^2 + v_{z,i}^2} \tag{6}$$

where $v_{x,i}$, $v_{y,i}$ and $v_{z,i}$ are the velocities of atom i on each axis and n is the system size. Each normalized velocity

$$\frac{v_i}{\Gamma} = \frac{\sqrt{v_{x,i}^2 + v_{y,i}^2 + v_{z,i}^2}}{\Gamma} = \bar{v}_i \tag{7}$$

is $0 \leq \bar{v}_i \leq 1$. Finally, by simply generating a random number in the range $[0 \ldots 1]$ and using the following algorithm, an atom can be chosen according to its assigned probability $\bar{v}_i$:

Initialization:

- $\left[\bar{v}_1^{a_1}, \ldots, \bar{v}_n^{a_n}\right]$ is the sorted velocity vector, where a_i corresponds to the atom index.

- initialize i to 0

Algorithm
1. generate a random number $0 \leq \xi \leq 1$

2. i=i+1, $c = \sum_{j=1}^{i} \bar{v}_j^{a_j}$ and *index*=a_i

3. if $\xi \leq c$ then take the atom *index* else return to 2

The great advantage of sorting the normalized atom velocities in a decreasing order is that one can minimize the number of steps of this algorithm for finding the chosen atom.

Initially, the non-incremental algorithm (see Section 2.2) is used to obtain an initial state for the incremental algorithm. During the incremental modification only a few iterations are sufficient to update the network (usually 5-10% of the number of iterations necessary for convergence when using the non-incremental algorithm), but this depends on the system shape and the topology of the network. This makes this method suitable for animation. To keep a fine discrete representation of the system, it is very important to have a very small learning value (computed by the $\alpha(t)$ function) and to have a 0-extended neighborhood, meaning that an input modifies only the winner neuron.

In the following example, a MD system containing 2000 atoms has been discretized using a 4x4x4 Kohonen network. The system has been simulated using molecular dynamic algorithm during 100 time steps. After computing each time step, the network has been incrementally updated using the new atom coordinates. Figure 10a shows the initial system state, figure 10c shows the MD system after 100 timesteps. Figure 10b shows the neural net obtained with the initial discretization. The result of this computation is taken as the initial network state by the incremental algorithm. Figure 10d shows the resulting incrementally modified network.

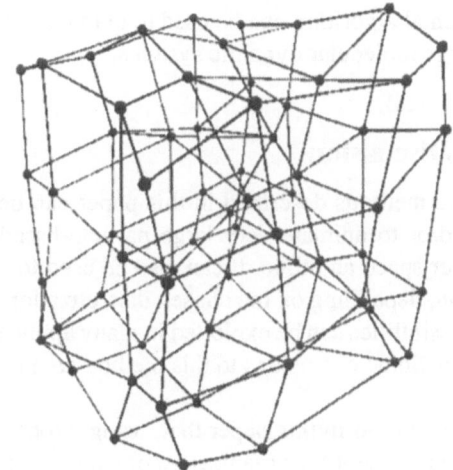

Fig. 10 a. Initial MD system   **Fig. 10 b.** Initial discretization

Fig. 10 c. MD system after 100 timestep   **Fig. 10 d.** Incremental discretization

One can observe in this example that the system begins to burst after some timesteps. The network tries to follow this motion and is heavily modified by the atoms "escaping" the system. In this kind of simulation, no boundaries for the MD system has been simulated. This is definitely the worse case for the incremental modification as the network structure cannot burst. No test has been made using solid boundaries for the MD system, but those cases should be easier to discretize as the system do not expand infinitely but stay located in a definite region.

The incremental mechanism added to the Kohonen algorithm is the key to obtain animated visualization of large systems because of the low number of iterations necessary to obtain the network update. This feature allows visualization of an MD system while this one is computed. In the case where the user works on pre-computed data, the incremental algorithm can be used to obtain a sufficient frame rate for the animation of very large molecular dynamic systems.

4 Discussion

The methods described in this paper can be used to improve rendering performances and/or to animate very large particle-based systems having drastic density variation over space and time. It can also be used to visualize them at different levels of resolution, depending on the chosen discretization level (i.e the values (nx,ny,nz)). These new possibilities can be exploited in many applications and some examples are presented below. Some extensions to this method are proposed in the Section 5.

We showed in this paper that, using a topological and adaptive sampling method, one can represent the organization of a molecular dynamic system with less information. In the example of Figure 8, one can see that the system is represented with 1000 times less information (if we consider the factor between the amount of atom coordinates and the amount of neuron weights). Animation of very large system can be thus performed. A multi-resolution concept can be introduced with the following example (this concept will be discussed in Section 5). Assuming that an user wants to initially visualize the organization and behaviour of a 10^6 atoms system by representing each atom with a sphere, then zooming into the "interesting" parts of the system to observe phenomenons like aggregation or micelles. Obtaining an animation with a sufficient frame rate with such a great amount of information is still a challenge in computer graphics, even when using level of details. This can be achieved by animating a discrete representation of the system. Zooming into the system will reduce the size of the visible scene. So discretization can be targeted on the observed sub-system, improving resolution of the discrete scene. One can obviously represent the real system when the scene complexity is sufficiently low, depending on the hardware used.

Assigning properties to the components of the discrete system is done with the property mapping process. Each discrete value characterizes its surrounding environment. We have also shown that the property mapping technique on the discrete system can also be useful to observe phenomenons that cannot be seen in the real system, because of the great quantity of information. This remark is illustrated by Figure 8.

In [3], a crowd in a virtual building is simulated using a model in which each individual is an independent entity. To optimize the position of signs, the corridors dimensions or the location of emergency exits, the pedestrian flow is visualized by representing each person with a geometric model. To prevent graphic bottlenecks, several levels of details are defined for those models, allowing faster animations when large crowd are visualized. An alternative to this graphic representation would be to discretize crowd before representation, as only global movement tendencies want to be observed. This approach would allow the simulation of a much bigger crowd. Geometric models should then be designed to represent groups of people instead of individuals. According to the chosen discretization level, our method would allow us to observe the evolution of crowd flows at different levels of resolution.

There is very little literature which directly concerns the simulation of human hair structure using particle systems. Particle systems have been previously used by Reeves [4] to model fire and by Reeves and Blau [5] to represent tree and grass. The application of our method is exposed for human hair representation, but can also be applied to those former works. Usual hair structure of a human is composed of ~100000 to 200000 strands of hair, whose diameter ranges from 40 to 120 μm. In [6], Rosenblum, Carlson and Tripp proposed a method in which each strand is represented using a series of connected straight strand segments. Each strand segment is rendered as a fixed width line and its position is determined by a simple dynamic simulation. Each strand structure is static, preventing the animation of large hair structures in case where many virtual humans are represented. Using our method, a entire hair structure could be discretized with a level of resolution depending on the distance to the viewpoint. This could be used to model a crowd of virtual humans. The discretization level could be adapted according to the distance from which the observation is made, or according to the graphic capabilities of the system used. To have a realistic motion of the hair structures, physical equations would need to be solved for the total number of strands in the scene and visualization would be achieved using the discrete systems, with an appropriate geometric model for each discrete value. Obviously, in the case where many humans, i.e many hair structures, are modelled, an equivalent number of neural net would have to be used. Discretization can still be done even when the observation of the hair structure is made at a close distance as the neuron-hiding capability of our method can be used to "erase" neurons not converging on a hair strand.

The visualization of water currents can also be efficiently achieved with particle-based techniques. In [7], Chiba and al. propose to model water using a set of imaginary particles called "water-particles". To generate images, they determine the water surface with a scalar field $F(x, y, z)$, using a sum of Gaussian density distribution (one for each water particle). The equation $F(x, y, z) - c = 0$ is then solved using an algorithm proposed by Doi and Koide [8]. This equation becomes complex when large expanse of water are modelled. Rendering can thus be improved by initially discretizing the set of water particles, which will obviously reduce the scalar field complexity. Our discretization method is convenient in this case, as the density of water particle is not necessary uniform, especially when simulating waves.

5 Future Works

There are many directions for future improvement, including:

Multi resolution mechanism. To allow switching dynamically from a level of discretization (for example, using a (x_d, y_d, z_d) network topology) to another (coarser, like $(x_d/2, y_d/2, z_d/2)$, or finer like $(x_d \times 2, y_d \times 2, z_d \times 2)$), a hierarchical data structure (like a tree structure) should be maintained for the network, where each level of the tree represents a level of discretization. At the present state of the method presented in this paper, if changing the level of discretization is needed, it has to be done "from scratch" meaning that the non-incremental algorithm has to be used to obtain a new initial state for the incremental algorithm. This extension would allow to switch from one data representation to another with a low computational cost (the cost for switching from a level of the tree structure to another). This feature would open new possibilities in animation using discrete systems, as levels of discretization could be interactively changed while zooming. The refinement of the discretization could also be done locally on the network. For example, in the application described in [6], this will allow an efficient refinement of the hair structure, making multiple levels of resolution available.

Arbitrary network topology. To improve convergence on arbitrary shapes, the network topology could be adapted to it. This can be achieved by maintaining an arbitrary linked data structure where each element represents a neuron. Finer convergence can be then obtained on complex shapes, minimizing the appearance of "lost" neurons (see Figure 7).

6 Acknowledgments

This work has been realized during a project at Silicon Graphics, Cortaillod in Switzerland with the collaboration of the Computer Graphics Lab at EPFL Lausanne, Switzerland. The project topic was to visualize large atoms systems simulated using parallel algorithm on SGI SMP machines. We greatly appreciate Silicon Graphics for providing an exciting environment in which this research was conducted. We also thank Prof. Daniel Thalmann of the Computer Graphics Lab at EPFL Lausanne for the coordination between EPFL and SGI. Last but not least, we would like to thank Ronan Boulic and Tolga Capin from the Computer Graphics Lab at EPFL Lausanne for their great advice, support and discussions and Grace Chang for her final review.

References

[1] A. Luciani, A. Habibi, A Vapillon, Y. Duroc: A physical model of turbulent fluids. Computer Animation and Simulation 95, D. Terzopoulos, D.Thalmann (eds.), Springer

Computer Science. ISBN 3-211-82738-2.

[2] Simon Haykins: Neural nets, a comprehensive foundation. IEEE Computer Society Press. ISBN 0-02-35761-7.

[3] Eric Bouvier, Pascal Guilloteau: Crowd simulation in immersive space management. 3rd EUROGRAPHICS Workshop on Virtual Environments, Monte Carlo (1996)

[4] William T. Reeves: Particle systems, a technique for modelling a class of fuzzy objects. Computer Graphics 17, (3), 359-376 (1983).

[5] William T. Reeves and Ricki Blau: Approximate and probabilistic algorithms for shading and rendering structured particle systems. Computer Graphics 19, (3), 313-322 (1985).

[6] R.E Rosenblum, W.E Carlson and E.Tripp III: Simulating the structure and dynamics of human hair: modelling, rendering and animation. The Journal of Visualization and Computer Animation, Volume 2 Number 4 October-December 1991.

[7] N. Chiba, S. Sanakanishi, K. Yokoyama, I. Ootawara, K. Muraoka and N. Saito: Visual simulation of water currents using a particle-based behavioural model. The Journal of Visualization and Computer Animation, Volume 6 Number 3 July-September 1995.

[8] A Doi and A. Koide: An efficient method of triangulating equi-valued surfaces by using tetrahedral cells. IEICE Trans. E74, (1), 214-224 (1991).

[9] Laurent Balmelli: Parallel algorithms for computation and visualization of molecular dynamic simulations. Diploma work (1996), Computer Science Dept., Swiss Institute of Technology, Lausanne, Switzerland.

Editors' Note: see Appendix, p. 215 for colored figures of this paper

Adaptive Refinement for Mass/Spring Simulations

Dave Hutchinson, Martin Preston, Terry Hewitt
Computer Graphics Unit, Manchester Computing,
University of Manchester, Manchester, M13 9PL, United Kingdom.
Email : {*Dave.Hutchinson | preston | hewitt*}*@mcc.ac.uk*
WWW : *http://info.mcc.ac.uk/CGU/*

Abstract. Mass/Spring networks are commonly used to produce simulations of deformable bodies for computer animation. However, such an approach can produce inaccurate results if too coarse a discretisation is employed, and so many animators use excessively large (and slow) networks. In order to remove the 'guesswork' from such an approach this paper presents a mechanism for adaptively refining portions of such systems to a required accuracy, thereby producing more pleasing results at a reduced computational cost. Following a discussion of the use of such an approach in simulating a deformable sheet, we present several characteristic examples to demonstrate its suitability.

Keywords: *Computer Animation, Simulation, Deformable Bodies, Spring-Mass Approximations, Adaptive Refinement.*

Animations: *http://info.mcc.ac.uk/CGU/research/animation/defrm.html*

1 Introduction

Keyframing techniques have been used for many years in the animation of deformable bodies [13, 3]. However, the realism of such an approach is heavily reliant on the skills of the animator, and so several researchers have adapted dynamic simulation to this area in the hope of reducing the burden on animators. Two fundamental solutions have been proposed, both of which discretise the body being simulated into finite elements, but which differ in the simulation model being employed.

The first group requires the derivation of differential elasticity equations, which are then integrated through time. Terzopoulos, Platt, Barr & Fleischer's [15] technique has since been extended to allow areas of rigidity in the bodies to be comfortably modelled [16], and for inelastic deformation to be simulated [14]. The second group disregards physical theory and employs a simulation method based on discretising the body into a number of masses, or particles [8], whose connectivity is maintained through constraint forces (usually generated from a damped spring abstraction). Systems of this nature have been used to simulate flesh around rigid bodies [6], the behaviour of cloth-like sheets [1, 12, 7], decomposable solids [4], fluids [9], and even worms [10].

The second group is most commonly used for two principal reasons: it is easier for the animator to integrate this approach with simulations of rigid bodies and it is far easier to implement. However, the strategy of approximation used in mass/spring networks only leads to plausible results if the *correct* granularity is chosen, and for practical cases this granularity is not obvious. If too coarse an approximation is employed then an incorrect animation will be generated, but unfortunately the animator will often have no way of knowing how 'right' this solution is. Conversely, if too fine a network is employed then a more correct answer *may* emerge, at the expense of increased computation. Consequently animators are often forced to either tinker with the model, or endure inaccurate results (thereby negating the advantages of dynamic simulation). Thingvold & Cohen [17] attempted to address this by employing a B-spline representation of the sheet being simulated, which could be refined in response to detected inaccuracy. However, the tensor nature of the surface meant that it was impossible to concentrate effort in particular regions (entire bands of the surface must be refined at once), so the technique has a tendency to produce excessively complicated, and slower, simulations.

This paper addresses that problem by presenting a mechanism for adaptively refining the network of spring/masses to concentrate effort *only* where it is needed. Using this system the animator defines an initially coarse approximation, and additionally a measure which indicates the accuracy required for this case. The system then proceeds to simulate the body in the normal way, but where potential inaccuracies are detected the body is refined only in the affected region, and then simulation may proceed. Whilst such an approach could be employed in the animation of either sheets or volumes, this paper concentrates on an implementation of adaptively refined sheets, though the extension to the simulation of volumes is discussed briefly in Section 7.

This approach has the advantages of:

- No longer requiring the animator to guess the discretisation required.

- Concentrating effort only where it leads to a more accurate solution, thereby producing the result more quickly than previous refinement techniques [17].

- Retaining the advantages of spring/mass networks (ease of both implementation and integration with the simulation of other bodies).

The rest of the paper is structured as follows. Section 2 describes existing deformable body techniques. Section 3 outlines our approach, with particular reference to the manner in which the animator can select the required accuracy (the refinement conditions). Following this Section 4 presents the implementation of this technique in detail. Such an adaptively refined body may be used in the simulation of a larger virtual world, and so in Section 5 we identify the considerations required to include collision detection and response. Section 6 presents results and timings for a number of characteristic cases, before Section

7 identifies the advantages, disadvantages and future work suggested by this approach.

2   Related Work

As described earlier two families of solution have been proposed for deformable body simulation, both of which rely on discretising the body into a finite number of components. The first group, proposed by Terzopoulos *et. al.* [15], deforms these finite elements using elasticity theory which works by recognising that the force applied to an element is (in varying proportions) absorbed or passed onto its neighbouring elements in a manner governed by its elasticity. Using a series of equations (based on Lagrange's ordinary differential equation) we can integrate through time to discover the forces caused, and hence the motion. Multigrid methods can be used to solve these sets of equations. This approach was extended to allow rigidity to be simulated (by incorporating a rigid "reference component") [16], and also to model inelastic deformations (so the body won't necessarily return to its original shape if stretched) [14]. These elaborations improve the original model, but Gascuel and Puech [5] noted that a remaining weakness is the difficulty of determining the spatial discretisation for non-trivial bodies. Palazzi and Forsey [11] described a multilevel approach to surface deformation which enables an animator to control the flexibility of a deformable object. External forces may have local or global effects on the surface depending on which levels of the multi-resolution representation they are applied to.

The second family of solutions employ a form of dynamic simulation which disregards the physics of object deformation, preferring instead to concentrate on a method which produces plausible, rather than thoroughly accurate results. By splitting the body into a network of masses connected by constraint forces, which behave like damped springs, a very simple integration process can be used to simulate the forces moving through the body, indirectly leading to visible deformations. Such a system suffers from numerous problems: sensitivity to integration step size, instability of solids simulated in this way (as springs operate only in one dimension it is possible for elements to invert themselves) and high computational cost for large networks. However, this approach is widely used largely because it is trivial to implement.

Thingvold & Cohen [17] improved on this model by representing this network as a B-spline surface, where particles corresponded to control points. Where the simulation detected problems (such as excessive stress) a region was refined [2]. However, the tensor nature of the surface meant that bands of the surface must be refined together. In many cases, such as when modelling wrinkling at the ends of sheets, the entire surface must be refined considerably. Whilst this implementation approach often leads to slow simulations, the application of dynamic refinement was shown to lead to more accurate results without the guesswork required in conventional particle systems.

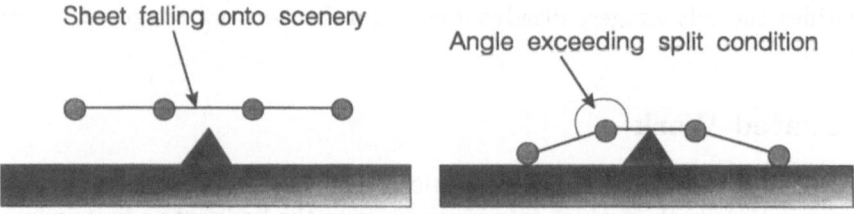

Figure 1: When the springs entering a mass point become non-planar, a discontinuity is detected

3 Outline of Technique

In this section we present an overview of the mechanisms used to improve the accuracy of spring/mass networks for simulating sheets before section 4 presents a practical implementation. In 3.1 we discuss the principal reasons for the inaccuracy of coarse networks, and identify the metric that an animator can use to guide refinement in our technique. In 3.2 we consider the response to any inaccuracies, i.e., how we refine portions of the network by adding new masses & springs without changing the properties of the sheet.

3.1 Detection of Inaccuracy

Networks of masses, connected by damped springs, attempt to approximate the behaviour of deformable bodies using a primitive model for the transmission of energy. The popularity of this model is primarily due to the pleasing nature of the results for very simple simulations. However, the difficulty of using measured physical properties means that significant inaccuracies appear in the result. Unfortunately, because these simulations are used in cases where the animator knows few of the true physical properties of the sheet, we cannot easily detect where these inaccuracies are. The 'success' of one of these simulations is instead related to the visual properties of the surface when rendered, and so we must concentrate our efforts on making the result *look* acceptable.

When coarse approximations of sheets are simulated the most visible errors occur when the surface creases. As the network may only bend on predefined lines (where the springs lie) these straight lines are frequently visible. Whilst spline surfaces can be passed through the point masses to mask the worst effects of this [17], they cannot cater for all situations. Therefore we will use, as our measure of inaccuracy, the presence of unsightly (and inaccurate) discontinuities.

Creases occur at mass points when opposite springs connecting neighbouring point masses become non-planar, as shown in Figure 1. Here the neighbouring masses have been moved out of the plane, but as the springs must operate in straight lines, a discontinuity appears. The angle at which this crease becomes excessive is related both to the rendering technique, and the situation, so it would be unwise to develop an automatic tolerance algorithm. Instead our technique relies on the animator specifying an angle which governs the accuracy he or

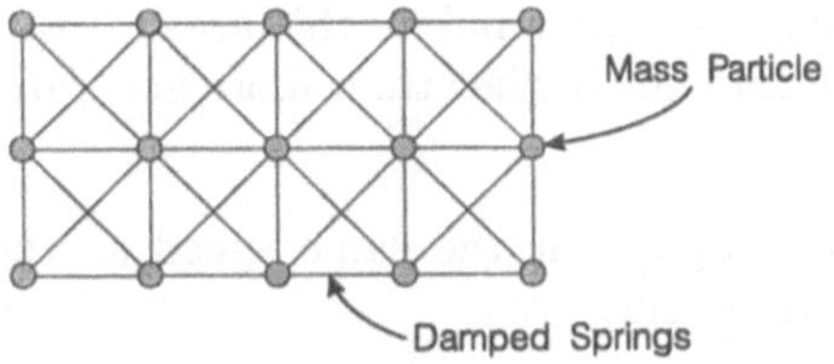

```
for(u=0; u < nU; u++)
  for(v=0; v < nV; v++)
    simulate_point(u,v,dt)

void simulate_point(u,v,dt) {
  find forces caused \
    by connecting springs and
    external influences;
  calculate new acceleration, \
    velocity and position;
}
```

Figure 2: a. Sheets are split into a number of discrete masses connected by damped springs in the vertical, horizontal and diagonal directions, and the simulation algorithm for this sheet is shown on the right.

she requires in the finished animation. Our 'inaccuracy' test can therefore be termed:

Split condition : If the angle between two springs joining a mass from opposite directions exceeds a specified tolerance S (in either direction), then we would produce an unacceptable simulation, and so must concentrate effort on refining this area of the model.

Our response to a split condition is to back the simulation up to a point at which it was acceptable (normally the previous time step), introduce more masses around the crease point, and then re-run that portion of the simulation to see whether we are now simulating to an acceptable degree of accuracy. Before we go on to discuss the mechanics of this (in section 3.2) we must also identify how this 'split tolerance' changes with the coarseness of the simulation. If the sheet is being approximated coarsely, then the animator will probably wish to remove *any* creases. However, if the surface has been refined considerably, then any minor discontinuities will be less obvious. To cater for this we also introduce a delta-angle δS, which is the angle added to the tolerance with the addition of each area of refinement. So, an initial refinement is caused when neighbouring springs exceed S, and a further refinement will be made if the angle exceeds $S + \delta S$. Finally we also employ a maximum level control, which an animator can employ to restrict the degree to which a sheet will refine in extreme cases.

3.2 Refinement

Our response to the detection of inaccuracy is the addition of masses and springs around the area where a discontinuity has occurred. However, in order to ensure that such a refined area continues to respond in the correct manner, we must maintain three constraints:

1. Every particle in our network must behave in the same way. If this is not so then the response of a particular mass to other forces may become unpredictable.

2. A given portion of the sheet must *behave* as though it has constant mass, independent of the number of particles used to simulate this area. If this is not the case then we will produce different, rather than more accurate, results using a refined network.

3. Forces must move across the refined portion at the same speed as the unrefined areas, otherwise shearing will occur.

Before discussing the approach taken to meet these conditions it is helpful to identify how they are catered for in the conventional uniform sheet. Figure 2 shows a sheet along with the simulation algorithm which is normally used. Here, at each time step, we iterate across the sheet and for each point calculate the forces affecting it due to connecting springs, the change in acceleration, and finally the new positions after the time step. If a force is applied at one end of the sheet during a simulation, it takes n time steps to reach a mass point n springs away. The effect of collisions with the environment is determined by calculating the mass of the portion of the sheet which is in collision. As the conventional network has uniformly spaced, and identical, masses this can be achieved by summing the effect of the relevant particles.

In order to refine the mass/spring network we need to add extra masses and springs. However, if we add masses to the system we run the risk of altering the properties of the sheet, and so we must pay special attention to ensuring the first two properties have been maintained. Thingvold & Cohen [17] did this by adding particles of lesser mass (thereby meeting the second constraint), but had difficulty satisfying the first, i.e., as we deal with single particles on each time step, the reduced mass particles would react differently to those present in the initial sheet.

We adopt the following approach: when we add particles we always use the same consistent mass (thereby meeting the first constraint), and we modify the simulation process to meet the remaining two constraints, i.e., to preserve the behaviour of the newly refined sheet.

To support this we employ a non-uniform representation of the sheet, and a form of simulation which deals with refined regions using different time step sizes. This new representation can be *thought of* as a multi-level or 'hierarchical sheet', and in this section we will discuss the simulation process as though we implement the data structure in a hierarchical fashion, before introducing the more optimal (yet similar) structure used in our implementation in Section 4.

At the beginning of the simulation we begin with a conventional m by n grid of points, at level 0. When we detect inaccuracies we generate mass points and springs in the level above, where *the mass of each new point is exactly the same as those in the level below.* At this new level, as shown in Figure 3, masses are spaced twice as finely. Upon refinement we generate 8 new points, (shown as filled circles in Figure 3), which surround the discontinuity point. For

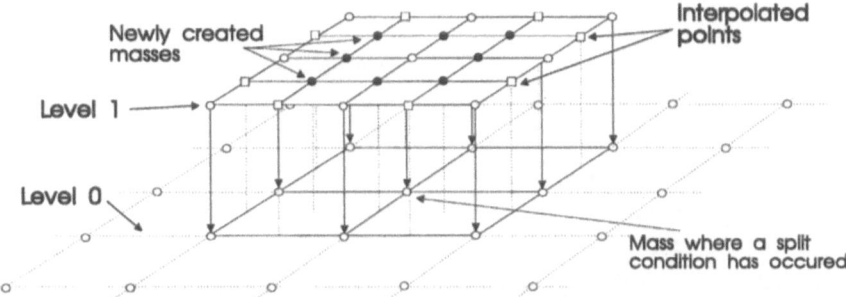

Figure 3: The sheet is modelled as a hierarchy of mass/spring networks. Here we show a single refinement around a point (note that the bend of the sheet is not shown)

these masses to be able to contribute to the behaviour of the sheet we must also connect them by springs.

Some of the points we connect these springs to exist in this new level, but some of them do not (as they will be related to mass points which haven't been refined). These different points can be grouped into 2 categories: those that correspond to mass points in the level below (shown as unfilled circles in Figure 3), and those which have no counterpart in the previous level (shown as unfilled squares). During the simulation of this level (which we discuss in greater detail below) we deal with these 'non-existent on level n' points specially. Where the point corresponds to a mass on level $n-1$, we use that point (i.e., we traverse the data structure). Where the point doesn't correspond we generate the point dynamically (by examining the points adjacent to it on level $n-1$, and finding the mid-point).

For this data structure to work we also need to make some changes to the simulation represented by the function `simulate_point()`. The principal differences are the addition of a level parameter to indicate which level the points are on, and the response to a refined area. If the function detects a refined area, i.e., the particle it is currently concerned with is present on the next level, then it initiates another loop across the points in the next higher level, which matches the loop executes at level 0. However, at this level the time step used is proportionally smaller.

This system achieves our conditions in the following ways:

1. The particles have uniform mass, so respond to forces in the normal way.

2. The stiffness of a spring doubles for each level of refinement to prevent regions of increased mass behaving differently. This increases the stability of the model, and allows the magnitude of forces passing through different refinement levels to be maintained. It also ensures that different refinement levels behave in a similar manner.

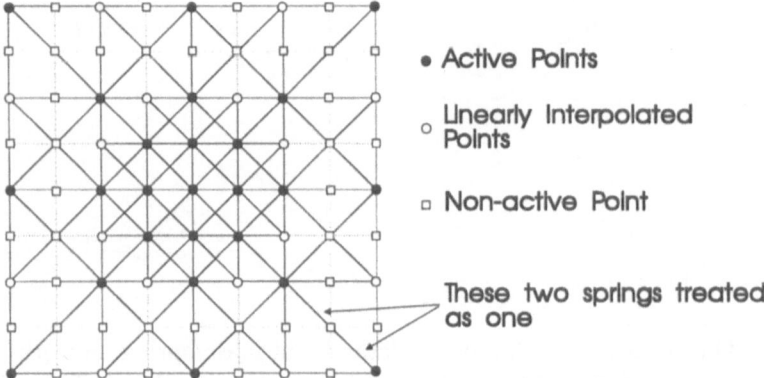

Figure 4: We flatten the sheet, storing the mass points on a uniform grid. The portion shown here corresponds to that shown in Figure 3.

3. The response of the body due to its mass is governed by the time in which it is allowed to respond, and the magnitude of that mass. By employing smaller step sizes for those points which correspond to smaller regions of the sheet, we achieve the same effect as a proportionally smaller mass would [17], as we employ Euler integration. We must, however, take care to account for transfer of momentum between objects, so that they respond in a predictable way, and this is discussed further in Section 5. The success of these modifications is demonstrated further in section 6.

4. The smaller step size for higher levels also allows us to ensure ripples pass across the surface at uniform speeds. The new version of `simulate_point()` achieves this by executing refined portions in the same time step as the unrefined portions.

4 Implementation of Adaptive Refinement

The previous section described in outline form how we refine the sheet network to cope with inaccuracies, using a hierarchical data structure which models the network at different levels of refinement, and a recursive process which simulates refined portions at the same speed as unrefined ones. In this section we now discuss the practical issues involved with implementing this approach, with Section 4.1 presenting the form of implementation used, and Section 4.2 discussing the manner in which we handle refinement in this new structure.

4.1 The Flattened Data Structure

Although traversing the hierarchical data structure in a recursive manner works well, it is by no means the most efficient method. Such a system requires repeatedly recursing up and down the hierarchy and redundancy is introduced when neighbouring regions are visited several times. Consequently we have developed a more optimal implementation method, where the simulation is performed within one loop and the data structure is effectively flattened into one level, as shown in Figure 4. We generate this 'flattened' representation by creating a new grid whose resolution matches the finest refinement possible of the sheet, for example if we are simulating a sheet which at level 0 is $5x5$, but which contains only one patch refined to 2 more levels, then the flattened sheet would consist of $17x17$ points. Whilst we could generate this flattened sheet statically (using the animators selected maximum refinement), we have instead chosen to begin with a sheet of a predefined refinement (2 levels), which is regenerated if further refinement is required (as this reduces the amount of memory consumed for the average case).

The simulation process works as follows. During each timestep T (which corresponds to t at level 0 in Section 3) of the simulation we iterate over the flattened sheet several times (in order to achieve the same effect as the recursive simulation), each time simulating the sheet for a 'sub-time-step' t. This smaller step size is calculated to correspond to the finest dt used in the hierarchical structure. So if the system has been refined only once then the small time step will be $T/2$, and for a system that has been refined to n levels then each step will be $T/(2^n)$.

For each t we must determine the behaviour of each mass point. As this is an optimisation of the hierarchical structure, we must be careful to ensure that we produce the same effects. We achieve this by storing, in the flattened sheet, a record of which hierarchical level each point is a member of. When we are on a sub-time-step which would correspond to moving a particular point in the hierarchical structure, then we perform conventional simulation (and also keep a record of the velocity calculated for this point), but where the point would not feel a change in acceleration the point mass is moved according to its previously calculated velocity (i.e., constant velocity, disregarding the effects of any connecting springs).

For example, if a system has been refined in some region once then $t = T/2$. Those points that are refined will feel forces from their neighbours on every time step t, whereas the unrefined regions only feel a force once over the whole time T. In general, for n-level refinements, if a point is at a time step where it doesn't feel a force then it is assumed to have constant velocity, the value of which will have been calculated during the last time step in which it felt a force.

This method affects only those points that are active at some level in our logical hierarchical structure. However, the flattened sheet is also likely to contain a large number of inactive points, who are present only in case of later refinement. These masses play no part in the simulation, but could incur a performance penalty as each of them must be examined at each t step. To avoid this penalty when the maximum refinement level is high, we optimise the loop by maintaining a binary tree of active points alongside the main structure, so that we do not need to step through the entire structure each time step. There is also a small overhead required for calculating which particles affect each other depending on the level they are at. This is because a particle at level three may have spring connections to particles at level 2,1 or 0. In our simulations this has proved to have a negligible effect on performance.

4.2 Refining the Flattened Structure

When a region is refined, we must activate some of the masses in the flattened structure, and velocities and positions must be assigned to them. These could be obtained by averaging the positions and velocities of surrounding particles. Unfortunately this does not always give good results because if a region is being refined, then an *inaccuracy* has occurred, and any averages are also likely to be misleading. Consequently, when we detect an inaccuracy around a single particle, we perform the following process

1. Back the simulation up a single t for the inaccurate particle, and all those immediately neighbouring it which would effect it on this t step. To find this set of points we examine those springs which connect to this mass, and follow them to those points which are active on this step.

2. Introduce the new masses by activating those points in the uniform sheet (as shown in Figure 4) which surround the inaccurate particle.

3. Calculate the position & velocity of these points by averaging the properties of the neighbouring mass point. As we have backed the simulation up for these particles these new averages will be accurate.

4. Re-run that t step for both the new points, and those which we have backed-up, in order to determine the new position of the sheet.

5   Collision Response for Refined Bodies

The detection of collisions between a sheet which is composed of a large number of polygons, and the environment, is aided by the use of adaptive refinement, as fewer polygons will be required. However, as we are using a complicated representation the calculation of the response caused by collisions is more complicated. Because our refined sheet contains a larger number of masses, any moving object colliding with it will experience a different effect depending on the amount of refinement and therefore number of masses it interacts with. This can be overcome in the following way.

We want an unrefined section of the sheet to react in the same way to collision with a moving object as a refined section would and also that a moving object will receive the same momentum change from a refined section as an unrefined one. If we know what percentage of the sheet is in collision with a moving object, then given that we also know the mass of the whole sheet (before any refinement), it is easy to calculate the mass m_a of the touching section of the sheet (that is the mass of the unrefined sheet which is in contact with the colliding object). The mass m_m of the points in the touching region may exceed m_a (as in our model refined masses are the same as unrefined), and so we must scale the momentum transfer between the two objects by the ratio of the mass in the

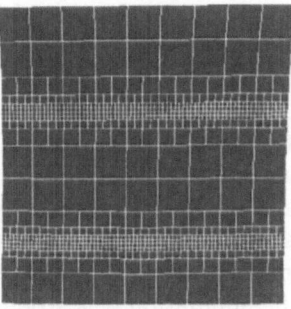

Figure 5: a. Unrefined sheet hanging.　b. Same sheet with two bands of refinement.

touching region and the actual mass of the sheet. The effect of this is to increase any momentum transfer to particles in the sheet by m_m/m_a, and to decrease the total momentum transfer from masses in the sheet to the moving object by m_a/m_m.

This means that any object colliding with a refined portion of the sheet will interact in the same way as a collision with an unrefined section.

6　Results & Discussion

To demonstrate the advantages of adaptively refined mass/spring networks this section presents three representative case studies. The algorithm described in Section 4, was implemented on a HP 9000/735 workstation, using a distributed graphics framework (HEDGE). The force exerted by springs due to deformation was proportional to the extension length, and damping was introduced as being proportional to the *rate* of extension. The sample implementation employs the technique discussed in section 4. At each time step an Euler integration process is used to determine the response of each particle to the relevant forces. Collision detection was performed using a simple and accurate, but inefficient algorithm which enabled us to model the response of the sheet to the environment. Self-collision was not detected, but the authors feel that Volino and Thalmann's technique [18] would be suitable for this technique. A primitive friction model was employed, so none of these examples include the effect of the sheet sliding across the scenery.

The first example, shown in Figure 5, is included to demonstrate how our non-uniform sheet representation preserves the properties of the more conventional uniform network. Two sheets were initially placed flat in the scene, one of which consisted of 10x10 masses, and the second had two bands of high refinement. One side of each sheet was clamped to a particular height, and then both sheets were allowed to drop in response to gravity. During the simulation both sheets retained the same dimensions, thereby demonstrating the mass preserving property of our algorithm. Note that, in order to achieve these results, considerable attention was paid to numerical accuracy. The refined sheet requires more calculation, and this runs the risk of introducing inaccuracies into the result, and so we employ increased precision when storing each attribute of the sheet.

The second and third examples are included to demonstrate both the ability of the adaptive refinement technique to identify areas of interest, and to considerably reduce the computation required. Each sheet initially consisted of 10x10 mass points, and had the maximum refinement degree set to prevent the sheet refining beyond 73x73. For each we set S to 25° and δS to 15°. The second animation consisted of dropping a sheet onto a polygonal model of a coffee cup. The third animation involved dropping the sheet over 4 poles. After a number of time steps the simulation was stopped, and the results examined. The state of the animation after 100 time steps for the cup animation is shown in Figure 6, and after 170 steps of the pole animation the sheets position in shown in Figure 7. The full animations are available on the accompanying web page (http://info.mcc.ac.uk/CGU/research/animation/defrm.html). Each picture shows both the refinement map, which identifies the nature of the network, and a shaded representation of the surface, which shows what a user of this technique would actually see.

The simulation of the sheet falling over the cup clearly demonstrates the ability of our adaptive refinement technique to detect where inaccuracy is caused by edges in the scenery, and the response caused (increasing the number of mass points in these regions). Note that, as the model of the cups' handle is extremely primitive, and has a square cross section, the network hasn't had to refine a great deal to accurately follow it.

The sheet hanging over the poles shows the detection of the scenery, but also indicates where creases and folds have been identified by the algorithm. This is clearly visible at the corners of the sheet, where the material falls back, causing a fold. Our primitive friction model is also causing creasing between the poles, as the sheet quickly reaches maximum extension in the mass/springs directly between the poles, but the neighbouring particles have greater freedom. A sequence of pictures taken from the animation is also shown in the colour plate in the Appendix.

Table 1 shows the measured execution times for these two examples. Without adaptive refinement an animator would have to employ a very fine network, so to compare the improvements we also performed simulations for the maximum 73x73 grid. The bulk of computation for the cup example is consumed by the collision detection, however it is clear that the refined sheet reduces this considerably (as there are fewer polygons in the sheet). The proportion of the computation caused by dynamic simulation is also considerably lower, and the extra load caused by detecting, and backing up the simulation to accommodate refinement, makes little difference. The full 73x73 grid sheet required ~18 hours of computation to reach this state, while the adaptive sheet needed ~1 hour.

The pole example does not suffer from such a severe collision detection cost, but the improvement due to adaptive refinement is still considerable. With the full case requiring $1\frac{1}{4}$ hours of computation, and the refined sheet needing only ~12 minutes to execute 170 time steps. Both of these examples clearly show the advantage of using an adaptive refinement technique which concentrates

Example	Cup 73x73	Cup Adaptive	Poles 73x73	Poles Adaptive
Num. Steps	100	100	170	170
Collision Detection	64319	3929.2	3580	687.0
Dynamic Simulation	474	16.3	669.8	76.3
Backing up	0.0	0.78	0.0	0.29
Refinement	0.0	0.71	0.0	1.2
Total	64793	3947.0	4598	764.79

Table 1: Sheet Statistics (all times measured in seconds)

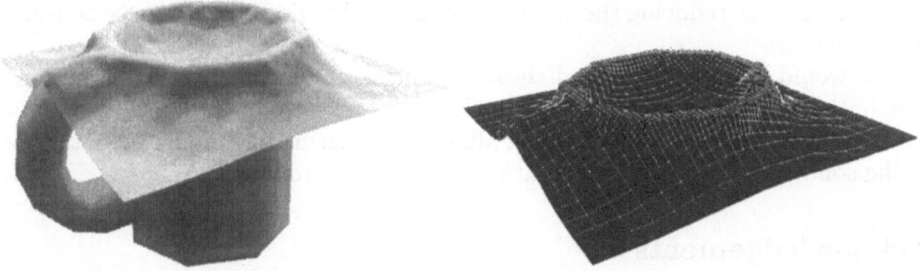

Figure 6: a. Rendered sheet over a mug   b. Refinement map.

effort only where required; if the same examples were simulated using a B-spline network (as per. [17]) the entire sheet would require refinement, and so would require computation closer to the maximum 73x73 sheet.

7   Conclusions

We have presented a method for adaptively refining spring/mass networks, which has the advantages of both optimising the simulation of such systems and adapting the amount of refinement required for a particular environment without prior knowledge of it. We have shown that this system can produce the same visually

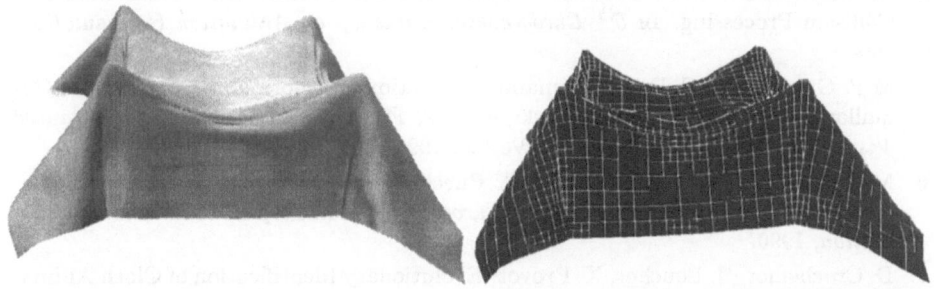

Figure 7: a. Rendered sheet over 4 poles (not shown) b. Refinement map.

pleasing result for less computational cost than a fine uniform discretisation. Although this method shares the weakness of ordinary particle systems (principally physical inaccuracy) a mechanism of adaptive refinement goes some way to ameliorating the worse effects of these inaccuracies.

We intend to concentrate our further work in two principal areas. Firstly we would like to develop more optimal schemes for implementing adaptive sheets. An unsplitting system (which detects planarity and responds by removing masses) is currently being developed. Special attention must be made to removing masses only where planarity is likely to be sufficient for more than a few steps (otherwise too much time will be spent refining again). We also plan to investigate the use of a non-rectangular grid which will then allow us to perform a discontinuity meshing (thereby reducing the complexity required to drape sheets over non-axis aligned edges).

We would also like to extend these techniques to the simulation of volumes. Our initial work in this area is concerned with developing a robust hypercube data structure for the volume, which allows us to accurately model indentations in the solid when it comes into contact with the environment.

Acknowledgements

The authors would like to thank all the staff and students at the Computer Graphics Unit for their help and encouragement. Dave Hutchinson would like to thank the Engineering and Physical Sciences Research Council for their financial support during this work.

References

1. D. E. Breen, D. H. House, and M. J. Wozny. Predicting the Drape of Woven Cloth Using Interacting Particles. In *Proceedings of SIGGRAPH '94*, pages 365–372, 1994. In Computer Graphics proceedings, Annual Conference Series.

2. E. Cohen, T. Lyche, and L. L. Schumaker. Algorithms for Degree Raising of Splines. *ACM Transactions on Graphics*, pages 171–181, July 1985.

3. S. Coquillart and P. Jancène. Animated Free-Form Deformation: An Interactive Animation Technique. *Computer Graphics*, 25(4):23–26, July 1991.

4. M. Desbrun and M-P. Gascuel. Highly Deformable Material for Animation and Collision Processing. In *5th Eurographics workshop on Animation & Simulation*, 1994.

5. M-P. Gascuel and C. Puech. Dynamic Animation of Deformable Bodies. In S. Coquillart, W. Straßer, and P. Stucki, editors, *From Object Modelling to Advanced Visual Communication*. Springer–Verlag, 1994.

6. M-P. Gascuel, A. Verroust, and C. Puech. Animation with Collisions of Deformable Articulated Bodies. In *1st Eurographics workshop on Animation & Simulation*, 1990.

7. D. Crochemore J. Louchet, X. Provot. Evolutionary Identification of Cloth Animation Models. In D. Terzopoulos and D. Thalmann, editors, *Computer Animation*

and Simulation '95 (Proceedings of 6th Eurographics Workshop on Animation & Simulation), pages 30 – 43. SpringerWien, 1995.

8. A. Luciani, S. Jimenez, J. L. Florens, C. Cadoz, and O. Raoult. Computational Physics : A Modeler-Simulator for Animated Physical Objects. In *Proceedings of Eurographics '91*, 1991.

9. G. Miller and A. Pearce. Globular Dynamics : A Connected Particle System for Animating Viscous Fluids. *Computer and Graphics*, 13(3):305–309, 1989.

10. G. S. P. Miller. The Motion Dynamics of Snakes and Worms. *Computer Graphics*, 22(4):169–178, August 1988.

11. L. F. Palazzi and D. R. Forsey. A Multilevel Approach to Surface Response in Dynamically Deformable Models. In *Computer Animation '94*, 1994.

12. X. Provot. Deformation Constraints in a Mass-Spring Model to describe Rigid Cloth Behaviour. In *Proceedings of Graphics Interface '95*, 1995.

13. T. W. Sederberg and S. R. Parry. Free Form Deformation of Solid Geometric Models. *ACM SIGGRAPH Computer Graphics*, 20(4):151–160, Aug 1986.

14. D. Terzopoulos and K. Fleischer. Modeling Inelastic Deformation: Viscoelasticity, Plasticity, Fracture. *Computer Graphics*, 22(4):269–278, August 1988.

15. D. Terzopoulos, J. Platt, A. Barr, and K. Fleischer. Elastically Deformable Models. *Computer Graphics*, 21(4):205–214, July 1987.

16. D. Terzopoulos and A. Witkin. Physically Based Models with Rigid and Deformable Components. *IEEE Computer Graphics & Applications*, pages 41–51, November 1988.

17. J.A. Thingvold and E. Cohen. Physical Modeling with B-Spline Surfaces for Interactive Design and Animation. In *1990 Symposium on Interactive Computer Graphics*, pages 129–137. ACM SIGGRAPH Computer Graphics, 1990.

18. P. Volino and N. M. Thalmann. Efficient Self-collision Detection on Smoothly Discretized Surface Animations Using Geometrical Shape Regularity. *Computer Graphics Forum* (Proceedings of Eurographics '94), 13(3), 1994.

Editors' Note: see Appendix, p. 216 for colored figure of this paper

2

Animation of Deformable Objects

A Fire Model for 2-D Computer Animation

Jinhui Yu & John W. Patterson

Glasgow Interactive Systems cenTre
Department of Computing Science
University of GLASGOW
G12 8QQ

Abstract: In this paper we present a model for fire in 2-D animation. Here the emphasis is on a stylistic representation of fires and the
flames which arise from the bodies of such fires. We show how to devise
a skeleton framework for generating animation sequences which match
the hand-drawn series, and in particular how to match the flame orientations, shapes, and the connection curves, as required by the simulated
style, between them. The parameters associated with these skeletons,
flame types and connection curves are brought together into a matrix
tableau for the particular representation of the fire base in the model.
The model for the flames at the top of the fire are made up from of three
simple sub-models. By stochastically varying the parameters the model
can generate plausible looking sequences of animated fire and include
the effects of wind straightforwardly.

Keywords: fire model, cartoon animation, computer animation.

1 Introduction

Animated effects like fire and water can add realism, drama, and atmosphere
to animation, and are thus important elements for an animator to master. In
a fire the movements of flames are governed by the movements of air currents
above the fire. The hottest part of a fire is in the centre and from this hot air
rises upwards. As it rises it is replaced by colder air rushing inward from the
sides. This air in turn is heated and rises in a continuous process. The flow of
air usually sculpts the flames to a roughly conical shape, with a succession of
cut-outs representing eddies of cold air, and starts at the base of the fire before
moving inwards and upwards. With this in mind, an animator can draw a fire
series like the one shown in Figure 1 [5]. With the usual studio limitations on
time and budget, drawings like those in Figure 1 are usually used as a cycle and
this means repeated cycles are required to produce animation for the required
length of time. Because of this, the effect usually looks mechanical.

In recent years methods of depicting gaseous phenomena, such as haze, fog,
clouds, dust, smoke and flames, have been studied by many workers. However,
most of them have aimed at realistic representation of the phenomena, and there

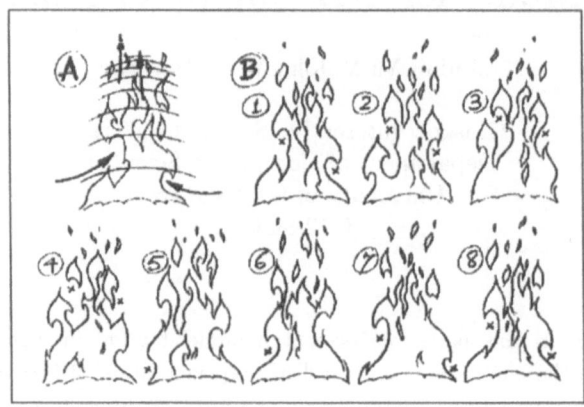

Figure 1: A hand drawn fire cycle

are have been few results relevant to the line drawing representation of fire in the conventional styles of 2-D animation. Reeves and Sims simulated firework effects by using particle systems [11]. Perlin generated a solar corona using a turbulence function [10]. MIRALab implemented more general fire functions using the same approach [15]. Inakage presented a technique based on a physical model of combustion, and succeeded in the photo-realistic representation of the flames of a candle and a Bunsen burner [6]. Ohshima and Itahashi [9]presented a simulation method employing 2D fractal texture and other processing techniques for generating animations of flames such as in a bonfire and in candle flames. Augui, Kohno and Nakajima [1] proposed cellular automata with simple state transition rules for simulating flames like those of an alcohol lamp. Gardner [4] modeled fire with fractal ellipsoids. Sakas [13] [12] proposed simulation methods based on the spectral theory of turbulence. Nishita *et al.* presented a display method for producing a still image of smoke [8] [7]. Chiba *et al.* simulated 2-D flames and smoke by visualizing turbulence [3]. Stam and Fiume used diffusion processes to animate fire and other gas phenomena [14].

In this paper we present a fire model which aims not at the photo-realistic representation of fire, but cartoon fire and giving it the same style as in some traditional animation. At present, the way of dealing with this problem in a computer-aided animation system like ANIMO [2] is to scan the hand drawn fire cycles into the system, which at best only preserves the level of quality of hand drawn animation. With the computer model, however, we can introduce stochastic controls with which the model can be made to generate different frames all the time. Thus we can avoid using repeated cycles and as a result improve the quality of the effect over hand drawn animation. Additionally we can simulate the effects of wind on the model.

Our model can be expressed as a hierarchical structure:

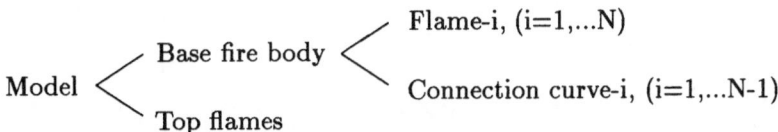

where N is the number of flames arising out of the body of the fire. The flames from the fire body are controlled by position skeletons and shape skeletons. Indices here have been assigned from left-to-right in the fire body. We construct a matrix out of all the parameters we have associated with the skeletons to represent the model of the base fire body. Top flames are controlled by another model which is related to the base fire model by additional parameters.

In this paper, we first describe how to construct the fire body model and the model for flames coming out of the top of the fire. Next, we analyze the parameters of the matrix in which we can control stochastically. Finally, we describe how to generate wind effect based on the foregoing model, and show examples of the relevant cases.

2 Fire flame model

In Figure 1 we see that the fire body is composed out of several flames of different shapes which form a fan connected by curves of a specific nature. From this we can separate out the fire body into the following parts:

1. Flames positions,

2. Flame shapes,

3. Connection curves.

For each part we define matching parameters which are used to build the fire body.

2.1 Flame position skeleton

The flame position skeleton is used to control flame positions, and is composed of a number of vectors, originating from the centre of the fire base and pointing to the positions of the flames. The end-points are derived from guide lines drawn in Figure 1(a) which govern the flame movements. Since the movements of air currents play an important role in the movements of the flames, especially those at the sides, it is important to ensure these flames are positioned as indicated by the crosses in Figure 1(b).

2.2 Flame skeleton

The flame shapes shown in Figure 1, suggest that it is natural to use a triangle as the skeleton of the flame, as shown in Figure 2. For each triangle we first define the coordinates x_f, y_f which serve as the reference point of the

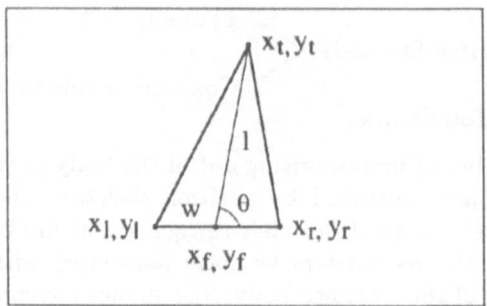

Figure 2: Flame skeleton

skeleton and determine the position of the flame. Then we define the parameters of length l, width w and the angle θ which are sufficient to define a triangle, see Figure 2. It is easy from the figure to calculate the coordinates of the triangle vertices, i.e,

$$
\begin{aligned}
x_t &= x_f + l * cos(\theta), \\
y_t &= y_f + l * sin(\theta), \\
x_l &= x_f - w, \\
y_l &= y_f, \\
x_r &= x_f + w, \\
y_r &= y_f.
\end{aligned}
\tag{1}
$$

where x_t, y_t refer to the coordinates of the top vertex, x_l, y_l and x_r, y_r refer to that of the left and right vertices respectively.

Skeleton types

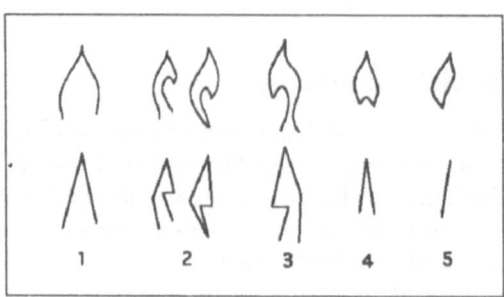

Figure 3: Skeleton types

Analysis of Figure 1 shows that flames have varying shapes, so it is necessary to define different types of skeletons to match different flame shapes. In our model we use $FlameType = i, (i = 1,...5)$ to define five types of skeletons which are shown in Figure 3. The first three are used for the fire body and the last two are used for individual flames at the top of the fire. In Figure 3 there are two skeletons associated with $FlameType$ 2. This is because the two are similar and we use one parameter to define their types and an additional flag *open* to indicate whether the skeleton keeps open or not. From the figure we can see that $FlameType$ 2 and 3, 1 and 4 are also similar, but we define them differently because they represent different shapes and their shapes are determined according to their $FlameType$ values. From the figure it is not difficult to calculate the coordinates of the skeleton.

Skeleton symmetry

Flames on the left and right side can be derived from the same skeleton if symmetry to the central vertical line on the fire body is taken into account. Here we define $FlameType$ as positive when it corresponds to the left side and negative when for the right side, to carry the symmetry information.

2.3 Flame shape

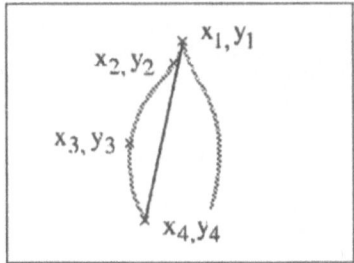

Figure 4: Flame shape

From the skeleton it is quite easy to generate flame shapes. We take $FlameType$ 1 as an example, as in Figure 4. Using the coordinates of the two extreme points x_1, y_1, x_4, y_4 which coincide with xt, yt and xl, yl in Figure 2 respectively, we can calculate the other two intermediate points x_2, y_2, x_3, y_3:

$$
\begin{aligned}
&fap_1 = 0.2, \\
&x_2 = x_1 + fa_1 * (x_4 - x_1) + \Delta x_2, \\
&y_2 = y_1 + fa_1 * (y_4 - y_1), \\
&fap_2 = 0.45, \\
&x_3 = x_1 + fa_2 * (x_4 - x_1) + \Delta x_3, \\
&y_3 = y_1 + fa_2 * (y_4 - y_1).
\end{aligned}
\tag{2}
$$

where fap_2 and fap_3 are position parameters which control the positions of the intermediate points, Δx_2 and Δx_3 are parameters related to the width of the skeleton and determine the shape of the flame. We take these points as control points and then interpolate them by a spline to get the final curve that draws flame shape. Similarly we can generate flame shapes corresponding to the right side of the skeleton.

From the foregoing process we can see the shape information is determined by control points which are related to skeletons derived from simple models. These models are accessed through parameter $FlameType$, and because this parameter is closely related to the flame shape we use $FlameType$ rather than $SkeletonType$ in section 2.2.1.

The foregoing method can generate a perfect, symmetric flame shape, but in Figure 1 we see that flames are not strictly symmetric, for example the first flame in frame 1, where the left side curve is longer and the right side curve is shorter. To deal with this problem we encode another parameter with the $FlameType$, in the form, for example $FlameType = 15$, where the first number 1 indicates the flame type as previously defined, and the second serves as a control parameter which becomes 0.5 after decoding and controls the length of the flame side curve.

2.4   Connection of flames

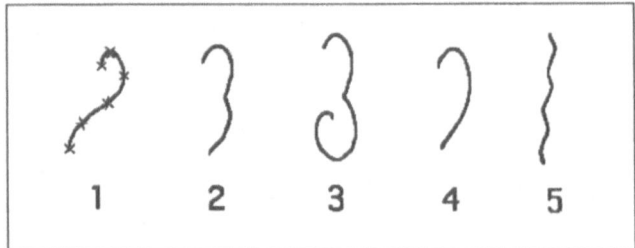

Figure 5: Connection types

Once flames are generated, we need to connect them in series to complete the drawing of the fire body. After the flame skeletons are placed in their proper positions, we note the coordinates of two terminal points of the flame skeleton x_l, y_l, x_r, y_r, which are now used for connection. From Figure 1 we can see that connection curves also have different shapes. Similar to flame types, we also define connection curve types by $ConnectType$. In our model we define five connection types and their corresponding shapes are shown in Figure 5.

Here we describe only how to generate connection curves of type 1. Similarly to generating the flame shape, we introduce four points between the two extreme points to control the shape of the connection curve, as indicated by the cross in

Figure 5. From the figure we can calculate their coordinates as follows:

$$x_3 = x_1 + lft * wd,$$
$$y_3 = y_1,$$
$$x_2 = x_1 + 0.5 * (x_3 - x_1),$$
$$y_2 = y_1 + 0.5 * wd,$$
$$x_4 = x_3 + fap1 * (x_6 - x_3) + lft * 0.2 * wd,$$
$$y_4 = y_3 + fap1 * (y_6 - y_3),$$
$$x_5 = x_3 + fap2 * (x_6 - x_3) - lft * 0.3 * wd,$$
$$y_5 = y_3 + fap2 * (y_6 - y_3),$$

$$(3)$$

where x_1, y_1 and x_6, y_6 coincide with the right and left terminal points of the two successive flames respectively, $fap1 = 0.2$ and $fap2 = 0.5$ are positional parameters which control positions of the relevant points, wd is a parameter related to the width of the skeleton, lft is a parameter related to the orientation of the skeleton with a value of 1 or -1 corresponding to the sign of the parameter $FlameType$. We take these points as control points and then interpolate them with a spline to get a connection curve of type 1.

Like flame symmetry, the connection curves can also be used symmetrically, and we use the same method to indicate the direction of the connection curve, i.e, define $ConnectionType$ as positive on the left and negative on the right.

With the foregoing method we can generate all types of connection curves but one, which needs to be dealt with differently. Looking at connection curves between the third and fourth flame (the second and third flame overlap each other partially) in frame 1, this in fact is composed of two connection curves of types defined previously. To generate this connection curve we set $ConnectionType$ to 9. When the model interprets this it generates another point x_d, y_d between the right extreme point of the third flame and the left extreme point of the fourth flame and below both of them, and we then take this point and the right extreme point of the third flame as a pair to generate the first connection curve (of type 1 in the case of frame 1), finally we take this point and the left extreme point of the fourth flame as a pair to generate the second connection curve (of type 5 in the case of frame 1).

2.5 Construction of the Matrix

The foregoing described how to generate flame and connection curve shapes. We can assign parameters to each step which can be expressed as a matrix with elements $p_{i,j} = P_{i,j}(FlameType, x, y, l, w, \theta, ConnectType)$ which represents the base fire model, where i represents ith frame which is related to time t, and j represents the jth frame in the fire body when indexed from the left side in one frame.

2.6 Top flames

Modeling top flames is more difficult than it looks. Flames at the top of the fire body consist mainly of flames of type 4 and 5, and occasionally of type 2 where some flames in the middle of the fire body are small. The movements of those flames are also governed by the guide-lines shown in Figure 1(a). Here we divide top flames into three parts: left, middle and right, then we detect the lowest flames on the base fire body (they are in the different frames for the left, middle and right parts), take them as the reference positions, and then generate corresponding vertical positions of the flames which are proportional to time t. Sizes and widths of the flames are controlled with a stochastic function, i.e, they decrease with time t and small random components are added to them.

2.7   Structure of the model

The structure of the model can be expressed by the following:

Step 1: Base fire body

1. Specify the matrix $MP(i, j) = p_{i,j}$;

2. Read parameters $x_{i,j}, y_{i,j}, l_{i,j}, w_{i,j}, \theta_{i,j}, lft_{i,j}, FlameType_{i,j}$ from the matrix;

3. Decode $FlameType_{i,j}$ to get direction flag and original $FlameType_{i,j}$ value;

4. Generate flame shape according to corresponding $FlameType_{i,j}$ value;

5. Save coordinates of two extreme points of the flame skeleton xl_j, yl_j and xr_j, yr_j;

6. Read xr_{j-1}, yr_{j-1} and xl_j, yl_j;

7. Read $ConnectType_{i,j}$ from the matrix;

8. Decode $ConectType_{i,j}$ to get direction flag and original $ConnectType_{i,j}$ value;

9. if $ConnectType_{i,j}$ does not equal to 9 then generate connection curve according to corresponding $ConnectType_{i,j}$ value;

10. if $ConnectType_{i,j}$ equals to 9, then generate another point xd, yd, and then generate connection curves between xr_{j-1}, yl_{j-1} and xd, yd, xd, yd and xl_j, yl_j respectively.

Step 2: Top flames

1. Detect the lowest positions of the flames on the base fire body for the left, middle and right top flames, take down their coordinates $xlmin, ylmin, xmmin, ymmin, xrmin, yrmin$ as reference positions;

2. Generate vertical positions of top flames by linear interpolation between trier corresponding reference positions and the highest position $ymax$ which is specified in advance ($ymax$ is the maximum value for the fire amplitude from the base to the top flames);

3. Repeat 1 and 2 in this step to generate second layer of top flames.

3   Analysis of parameters

We are able to adjust the parameters defined above to change the flame shapes until the they are comparable to hand-drawn shapes. This means that the parameters we defined for the model are sufficient to control the flame shapes.

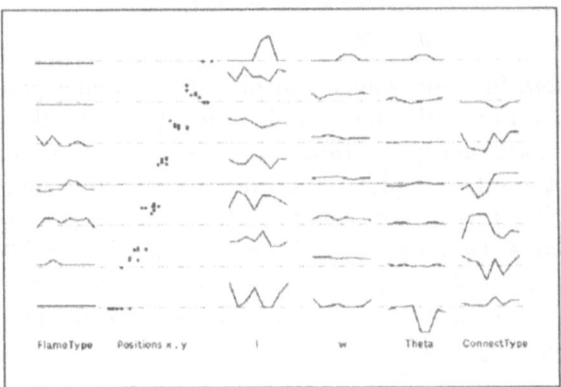

Figure 6: Parameters associated with the model

Figure 6 shows parameters associated with the model. The horizontal axis corresponds to time t and the vertical axis corresponds to amplitudes of the parameters for flames counted form the left to the right side in the base fire body. Horizontal dot lines represent zero value of amplitude for most of parameters of each flame with an exception for the parameter θ where they represent 0.5π radians. It is clear from the figure that these parameters vary irregularly with time t but their values are limited to certain ranges, only in the first, sixth and seventh flames the corresponding *FlameType* always stays as 1 or -1. This means that flames situated at the two bottom sides of the base fire body always consist of the same type. Also the y coordinate for the first and seventh flame stays as zero, and the x coordinate plus the value of w are constant thus ensuring the two extreme points at the base of the fire body stick to the predefined points (in other word, these two points should always be the same regardless of the variation in width of the flames). Since fire involves random movements it is natural for us to add some random control into the model. With the exception of the first and seventh flames, almost all parameters for other flames could be controlled stochastically. Also it is possible to control some parameters stochastically in the previous formulae, for example, to calculate the coordinates of the skeleton (see Figure 2), we can use the following formulae:

$$
\begin{aligned}
x_t &= x_f + (l + \Delta_l)cos(\theta), \\
y_t &= y_f + (l + \Delta_l)sin(\theta), \\
x_l &= x_f - (w + \Delta_w), \\
y_l &= y_f + \Delta_y, \\
x_r &= x_f + (w + \Delta_w), \\
y_r &= y_f + \Delta_y.
\end{aligned} \tag{4}
$$

where Δ is random function which controls corresponding parameters varying within a certain range. We should point out that not all parameters allow random control, particularly for those of the first, second, sixth and seventh flames. Because those flames play important role for animating fire effect, some parameters associated with those flames such as $FlameType$ and $ConnectType$ should stay the same. However, we still can vary their l, w and θ to some degree. With stochastic control of the relevant parameters the model can generate flames which change in shape all the time, we can thus avoid using repeated cycles and animate fire for as long as we wish.

4   Coloring

In comparison with shape, color is less important for the flame movements. This is true when we see early black and white animation. Even line drawn sequences by themselves can produce the illusion of movements, but coloring does improve the visual quality of the animation. Since the hottest part of the fire is in the centre and the fire is surrounded by cold air at the sides, we use a color gradient which varies from yellow in the hottest part to red representing the coolest part in the flame colors, and the visual effect seems satisfactory.

5   Simulation of wind effect

Simulation of the effects of wind on flames can make animation vivid and this can be achieved just by adding one parameter to our model. When a fire body is blown by wind from the side, flames are moved toward the other side but the bottom of the fire remains fixed, in effect flames look "bent". If we can generate a "bent" fire body then we can simulate the effect of wind. This is done by introducing an angle parameter $\Delta\theta$ which represents the angular amount changed compared with original "still" (i.e. no side wind) flames. The "bent" flames are derived in the following two steps:

1. Calculate the displacements for the reference points of the skeletons by the following formula,

$$
x' = x + ymax * tang(\Delta\theta) * (1 - cos(fa * 0.5 * \pi)) \tag{5}
$$

   where x, y are original position parameters specified in the matrix, and x' is the new parameter for x, $\Delta\theta$ is an angular value which controls the bending degree of the fire, the nonlinear coefficient $(1 - cos(fa * 0.5 * \pi))$ makes flame bends look more natural and $fa = y/ymax$,

2. Calculate the displacements of control points in a flame with the same formula as before, but with x and y replaced by the coordinates of the respective control points .

The results of computer generated fire frames for both "still" and wind effect are shown at the end of the paper (see Appendix). Since the degree of fire bending is controlled by $\Delta\theta$, this parameter can also be used as a interpolation variable to animate the process of fire moving from being in still air to being blown about by the wind. If, further, we modulate this parameter with a sinusoidal function in time t, then the model can generate the effect of a swaying fire. It should be pointed out that our model is devised from line drawing pictures rather than being physically based, so the simulation of wind effects is limited to small values of $\Delta\theta$. A serious distortion will arise if we allow $\Delta\theta$ to become too big. With this limitation our model can only simulate light winds but, even so, this is a significant improvement because it is so difficult for traditional animators to create this effect.

6 Conclusion

In this paper we present a cartoon fire model for 2D computer animation. The present model can be used directly for representing bonfires, torches etc, and the animated effect looks correct when we play back fire series generated by our model. We hope the model could be extended to some other situations such as objects burning, fire spreading *et al* and this is a topic for a future work.

References

[1] Agui T., Kohno Y. and Nakajima M., "Generating 2-dimensional flame images in computer graphics", *Trans. IECE of Japan*, vol 2 (1991), pp.184–189.

[2] *animo: USER'S GUIDE* (1995).

[3] Chiba N., Muraoka K., Takahashi H. and Miura M., "Two dimensional visual simulation of flames, smoke and the spread of fire", *Visualization and Computer Animation*, vol. 5 (1994), pp.37–53.

[4] Gardner G., "Fractal ellipsoid fire", *SIGGRAPH video Review*, vol. 14 (1992), pp.184–189 Issue 81.

[5] Harold W., *Timing for Animation*, Focal Press Limited, London, 1981.

[6] Inakage M., "A simple model of flames", *CGI'90*, (1990), pp.71–81.

[7] Nishita T. and Miyawaki Y. and Nakamae E., "A shading model for atmospheric scattering considering luminous intensity distribution of light sources", *Computer Graphics*, vol. 21 (1987), pp.303–310.

[8] Nishita T. and Nakamae E., "A display method of uniform particles in the atmosphere", *Proc. 35th Annual Convention IPS Japan*, (1987), pp.2307–2308.

[9] Ohshima T. and Itahashi S., "Texture animation", *Proc. NICOGRAPH'88*, (1988), pp.110–119.

[10] Perlin K., "An image synthesizer", *Computer Graphics*, vol. 19 (1985), pp.278–296.

[11] Reeves W. T., "Particle system- a technique for modeling a class of fussy objects", *Computer Graphics*, vol. 17 (1983), pp.358–376.

[12] Sakas G., "Modeling and animating turbulent gaseous phenomena", *The Visual Computer*, vol. 9 (1993), pp.200-212.

[13] Sakas G. and Gerth M., "Sampling and anti-aliasing of discrete 3-D volume density textures", *EUROGRAPHICS'92*, (1992), pp.107–117.

[14] Stam J. and Fiume E., "Depicting fire and other gaseous phenomena using diffusion", *Computer Graphics*, (1995), pp.129-136.

[15] Thalmann N. M. and Thalmann D., *Image synthesis*, Springer-Verlag, 1987

Editors' Note: see Appendix, p. 217 for colored figures of this paper

Smoothed Particles: A new paradigm for animating highly deformable bodies

Mathieu Desbrun   Marie-Paule Gascuel

iMAGIS* - GRAVIR / IMAG
BP 53, F-38041 Grenoble cedex 09, France

Abstract

This paper presents a new formalism for simulating highly deformable bodies with a particle system. Smoothed particles represent sample points that enable the approximation of the values and derivatives of local physical quantities inside a medium. They ensure valid and stable simulation of state equations that describe the physical behavior of the material.

We extend the initial formalism, first introduced for simulating cosmological fluids, to the animation of inelastic bodies with a wide range of stiffness and viscosity. We show that the smoothed particles paradigm leads to a coherent definition of the object's surface as an iso-surface of the mass density function. Implementation issues are discussed, including an efficient integration scheme using individually adapted time steps to integrate particle motion. Animation requires a linear complexity in the number of particles, offering reasonable time and memory use.

1 Introduction

Modeling and simulating deformable bodies has attracted a lot of attention in Computer Graphics. Elastic materials that recover their rest shape after any deformation are generally simulated with finite-difference [TPBF87] or finite-element [GMTT89, PW89] methods. Nevertheless, these approaches, which approximate the body by a mesh of nodes of fixed topology, are not adapted to the animation of substances able to undergo large inelastic deformations. In this case, the use of particle systems is more appropriate. These systems are unstructured in the sense that interactions between point masses do not depend on a specified graph of connections, but on distance. Consequently, particle systems seem the easiest approach for modeling large changes in shape and in topology.

---

*iMAGIS is a joint project of CNRS, INRIA, Institut National Polytechnique de Grenoble, and Université Joseph Fourier.

1.1 Previous approaches

Particle systems were first defined in Computer Graphics as sets of moving points, without interaction between them [Ree83]. More recently, particles systems have been widely used for simulating inelastic deformations and even fluids [MP89, TPF89, LJR+91, Ton91, DG95, LP95, LHVD95, GLG95]. Most methods developed so far use different simplified versions of the same attraction-repulsion force for modeling interactions between particles. This force derives from the Lennard-Jones potential, proposed for modeling pairwise microscopic interactions between atoms in a liquid. Animating n particles amounts to calculating at each time step the n^2 interaction forces, and then integrating the equations of motion for each particle to obtain its speed and position. To allow better performance, interaction forces are clamped to zero at a cutoff radius, reducing the number of interacting neighbors.

Despite many advantages such as the simplicity of implementation, the practical use of particle systems gives rise to a variety of problems. First, the parameters of Lennard-Jones interaction forces are not easy to manipulate. Finding values that will result in a desired global behavior is quite difficult. This may be related to the fact that Lennard-Jones forces come from microscopic observations, and here are applied on a totally different scale.

Time integration is also an important source of problems. As no stability criterion is provided, the integration time step is very difficult to handle. Even at rest positions (when particles are supposed to freeze), forces must be either integrated carefully or modified to avoid oscillations [LP95]. For all these reasons, small time steps seem inescapable.

A last problem, quite important in Computer Graphics applications, is the lack of definition of the surface surrounding the object. Providing such a surface is essential for interfacing particles with other models. A solution for computing a smooth surface from particles consists in using an iso-surface of some "implicit function" controlled by the particles [MP89, Ton91]. The resulting implicit surface can be used for collision and contact processing between the body and its environment [Gas93, DG95]. However, coating particles with an arbitrary implicit function introduces large volume variations. This problem should not occur if a coherent definition of the surface can be found since particles mimic a material that is supposed to keep its volume nearly constant.

1.2 Overview

This paper presents a new paradigm for simulating highly deformable substances with particle systems. We extend the Smoothed Particle Hydrodynamics (SPH) approach used by physicists for cosmological fluid simulation. The smoothed particles we define can be viewed either as matter elements, or sample points scattered in a soft substance. Each of them represents a small volume of inelastic material that moves over time. In practice, smoothed particles are used to approximate the values and derivatives of continuous physical quantities, such as local mass density or pressure, that need to be computed during the simulation. Smoothed particles ensure valid and stable simulation of a state equation describing the physical behavior of the material. We also use them for defining the surface of the substance in a coherent way using the level sets of the mass density function. Implementation issues are discussed, and, in particular, an efficient integration scheme with adapted time steps for each particle is presented.

2 Smoothed Particle Hydrodynamics

The Smoothed Particle Hydrodynamics (SPH) formalism was introduced by physicists for accurate simulation of fluid dynamics [Mon92]. Simulating a fluid consists in computing the variations of continuous functions such as mass density, speed, pressure, or temperature over space and time. Standard finite element techniques in hydrodynamics use an Eulerian approach: they consist of dividing space into a fixed grid of voxels, and then studying what flows in or out of each voxel. However, this kind of approach requires the division of huge empty volumes and is not intuitive for flows. SPH belongs to an alternative approach, called the Lagrangian approach, that consists of following the evolution of selected fluid elements over space and time. We describe in this section the fundamentals of this formalism as it provides sound bases for simulation, with simple implementation.

2.1 Discrete formulation of continuous fields

In SPH, the fluid is sampled by a set of elements called *particles*. A particle j has a fixed mass m_j, a position $\mathbf{r}_j$, a velocity $\mathbf{v}_j$, and a mass density ρ_j depending on the local density of particles. As a sample point, it can also carry physical field values like pressure or temperature. Then in a way very similar to Monte-Carlo techniques[PTVF92], these fields and their derivatives can be approximated by a discrete sum. To achieve this, particles are supposed to be smeared out in space according to a smoothing kernel W_h. This normalized kernel (i.e., the value of its integral is one) gives the spatial mass distribution profile over a smoothing length h. Then the smoothed values and derivatives of a continuous field f known only at particle locations can be approximated by:

$$< f(\mathbf{r}) > \quad = \quad \sum_j m_j \frac{f_j}{\rho_j} W_h(\mathbf{r} - \mathbf{r}_j) \tag{1}$$

$$< \nabla f(\mathbf{r}) > \quad = \quad \sum_j m_j \frac{f_j}{\rho_j} \nabla W_h(\mathbf{r} - \mathbf{r}_j) \tag{2}$$

where f_j denotes $f(\mathbf{r}_j)$, i.e. the value of f at particle j. Mathematical justification of the integral expressions we approximate by discrete sums can be found in Appendix A. These equations are the basis of the SPH formalism.

An immediate result gives a smoothed value of the mass density, defined everywhere by:

$$< \rho(\mathbf{r}) > = \sum_j m_j W_h(\mathbf{r} - \mathbf{r}_j). \tag{3}$$

2.2 Pressure forces

Equations (1) and (2) can be applied to derive smoothed versions of the hydrodynamical conservation laws, producing simple equations of motion for the particles. From here on, we will no longer distinguish between a function and its smoothed approximation. Thus the density ρ_i of a particle i is computed by the equation (3).

If the pressure P_i is known at each particle i, forces due to differences of pressure can be approximated. As these forces are locally proportional to the gradient of the pressure, Appendix B demonstrates that a symmetric expression of the pressure force on particle i can be written:

$$\mathbf{F}_i = -m_i \sum_{j \neq i} m_j \left(\frac{P_i}{\rho_i^2} + \frac{P_j}{\rho_j^2} \right) \nabla_i W_h^{ij} \tag{4}$$

where the notation $\nabla_i W_h^{ij}$ denotes the gradient of $W_h(\mathbf{r}_i - \mathbf{r}_j)$.

The value of pressure in equation (4) is computed from a state equation describing the simulated fluid. For instance, an ideal gas satisfies $PV = k$ where V is the volume of the fluid and k a given constant. It results in purely repulsive forces between particles, accounting for the fact that an ideal gas tends to expand in free space.

2.3 Viscosity

SPH most commonly expresses viscosity by adding a damping force term to the equation of motion of a particle:

$$\mathbf{D}_i = -m_i \sum_{j \neq i} m_j \Pi_{ij} \nabla_i W_h^{ij} \tag{5}$$

where:

$$\Pi_{ij} = \begin{cases} \dfrac{-c\mu_{ij} + 2\mu_{ij}^2}{\overline{\rho}_{ij}} & \text{if } \mu_{ij} < 0 \\ 0 & \text{if } \mu_{ij} \geq 0 \end{cases} \qquad \mu_{ij} = h\frac{\mathbf{v}_{ij} \cdot \mathbf{r}_{ij}}{\mathbf{r}_{ij}^2 + h^2/100}$$

$$\mathbf{v}_{ij} = \mathbf{v}_i - \mathbf{v}_j \qquad \mathbf{r}_{ij} = \mathbf{r}_i - \mathbf{r}_j \qquad \overline{\rho}_{ij} = (\rho_i + \rho_j)/2$$

The constant c is the *speed of sound* of the simulated fluid, which represents the fastest velocity of a wave front propagating in that medium. It indicates at which speed a deformation will be transmitted to the whole material. But it does not mean that particles cannot go faster than c: if external forces make them move faster, a shock wave occurs.

The first term in the expression of Π_{ij} is analogous to a shear and bulk viscosity. The second one, comparable to the Von Neumann-Richtmyer artificial viscosity used in grid-based methods, prevents particle interpenetration at high speed. We can note that the viscosity vanishes for rigid body motion and conserves linear and angular momenta as it depends on relative speeds of particle pairs.

3   Simulating highly deformable bodies with smoothed particles

The SPH approach provides a robust and reliable tool for fluid simulation, and has been widely used for simulating complex phenomena in astrophysics. However, although the smoothed particles paradigm is general, SPH does not directly apply to Computer Graphics. We no longer want to accurately simulate fluids, but rather to animate a wide range of inelastic deformable bodies. Several additions and modifications to the initial approach need to be defined.

3.1   Interaction Force Design

An important aspect of smoothed particles is that it derives local forces between pairs of neighbors particles from a global state equation. Such an equation describes how the physical variables evolve in the simulated material.

Pressure and cohesion forces

In SPH, the expression of pressure used in equation (4) resulted in positive, i.e., purely repulsive, forces expressing the natural expansion of the fluid. In astrophysics applications, pressure forces were often combined with gravitational forces balancing the expansion phenomenon.

In contrast, we would like to animate materials with constant density at rest. Consequently, the material should exhibit some internal cohesion, resulting in attraction-repulsion forces as in the Lennard-Jones model. To keep density at ρ_0, we replace the ideal gas state equation by:

$$P = k(\rho - \rho_0) \tag{6}$$

which is another expression of: $(P + P_0)V = k$, where $V = 1/\rho$ is the volume per unit mass, and $P_0 = k\rho_0$. Equation (6), designed to maintain density close to a constant value, has a double advantage. First, if particles have the same mass they will tend to be evenly distributed inside the object. This is essential since we are using them as sample points for approximating continuous functions. Moreover, constant density results in a constant volume. The material will then tend to naturally come back to its initial volume after a deformation.

Replacing P by its value in equation (4) leads to:

$$\mathbf{F}_i = -km_i \left[\frac{(\rho_i - \rho_0)}{\rho_i^2} \sum_{j \neq i} m_j \nabla_i W_h^{ij} + \sum_{j \neq i} m_j \frac{(\rho_j - \rho_0)}{\rho_j^2} \nabla_i W_h^{ij} \right] \tag{7}$$

Interpretation

Equation (7) can be interpreted in the following way:

- The first term is a *density gradient descent*, that tends to minimize the difference between current and desired densities.

- The second term is a symmetry term that ensures the action-reaction principle.

The parameter k determines the strengh of the density recovery. It plays the same role than a stiffness parameter in a standard particle system. A large k will simulate a stiff material while a small k models a soft one, that recovers its rest density slowly after a compression or an expansion.

We combine the new pressure/cohesion force $\mathbf{F}_i$ with forces due to viscosity, as was done in the original SPH formalism (section 2.3).

3.2   Choice of a smoothing kernel

The choice of the smoothing kernel W_h is very important: if the particles are considered as sample points, we can compare the kernel with the difference scheme used in a finite-differences method, since it gives a way to approximate values and derivatives of various functions. And if particles are thought of as small matter elements, the kernel is related to the "extent" of a particle in space. In particular, the smoothing length h defining the support of the kernel (see Figure 1) gives the radius of influence of interaction forces created by a particle. Different behaviors can be obtained by tuning h. A small value will create very local interactions so the body will separate more easily into pieces.

We can also note that the kernel's support is related to the computational complexity of the simulation: if particles are well distributed, the mean number m of them in a sphere of radius $2h$ gives the mean number of interactions to compute for each particle.

Previous studies on the SPH formalism [Mon92] have shown that good kernels have a Fourier transform that falls rapidly with wave number. Most researchers use the spline Gaussian kernel:

$$W_h(\mathbf{r}) = \frac{1}{\pi h} \begin{cases} 1 - \frac{3}{2}(\frac{r}{h})^2 + \frac{3}{4}(\frac{r}{h})^3 & \text{if } 0 \leq r \leq h \\ \frac{1}{4}(2 - \frac{r}{h})^3 & \text{if } h \leq r \leq 2h \\ 0 & \text{if } r > 2h \end{cases}$$

This kernel, depicted in Figure 1, mimics the Gaussian bell curve and has a compact support, which implies both a finite radius of influence, and simpler computation. However, difficulties arise when the spline kernel is used for evaluating interaction forces between particles. Forces are more and more attenuated when two particles get closer to each other, since ∇W_h, given in Figure 1, is a factor in the expression of forces. So the spline kernel gives rise to clustering. However, since astrophysicists typically combine pressure forces with gravitational forces, this artifact is turned into feature in their applications.

For our application, we cannot use a kernel that will induce clustering between particles. This would be the opposite of our wish for constant density and regular sampling. Thus, we propose another normalized kernel, depicted in Figure 2:

$$W_h(\mathbf{r}) = \frac{15}{\pi(4h)^3} \begin{cases} (2 - \frac{r}{h})^3 & \text{if } 0 \leq r \leq 2h \\ 0 & \text{if } r > 2h \end{cases}$$

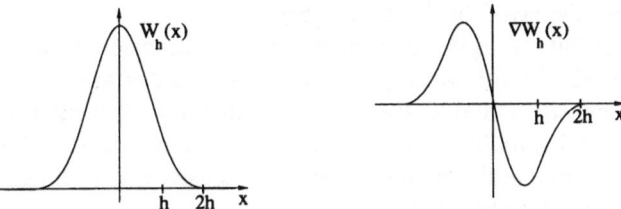

Figure 1: The spline kernel and its first derivative in one dimension.

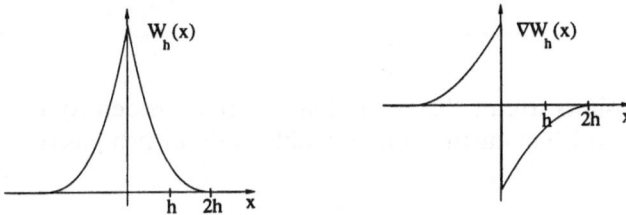

Figure 2: Our alternative kernel and its derivative; clustering is avoided.

This kernel keeps the advantages mentioned above while being better designed to handle nearby particles. As a result, the attraction/repulsion force

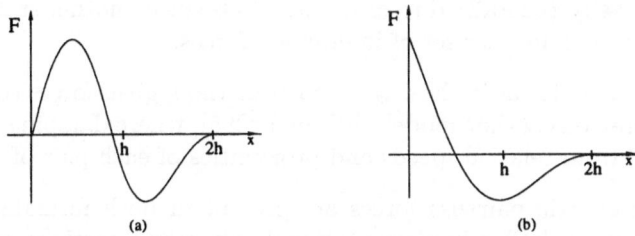

Figure 3: Comparison of pressure/cohesion forces between two particles:
(a) with the spline kernel   (b) with the new kernel.

generated by equation (7) between a pair of particles looks satisfactory since it is very similar to the usual Lennard-Jones attraction/repulsion force, as shown in Figure 3.

3.3   Results

Testing the model in 2D is interesting since it enables to observe the evolution of the mass density in space and time. Density values, that can be computed everywhere, are displayed in shades of grey.

Figure 4 exhibits snapshots from a simple animation where 80 smoothed particles are used. In this example, parameters values are: $k = 10, c = 2$. h is constrained by ρ_0 so that there are approximately 10 particles in the radius of influence of each particle. Other experiments have proven the relevancy of physical parameters c and k which represent viscosity and stiffness, respectively. We also obtain good stability results.

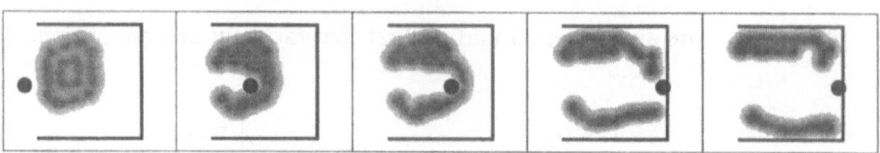

Figure 4: Snapshots from a 2D animation, where mass density is represented in grey-levels: a rigid tool cutting a deformable body in two pieces.

Discussion

We can point out some parallels and differences between smoothed and standard particle systems:

- Cohesion/pressure forces depicted in Figure 3 are very similar to Lennard-Jones forces, with short range repulsion and long range attraction. However, in contrast with Lennard-Jones forces, which result from microscopic observations, we have derived forces from a global equation. Our method could be easily generalized to other materials since another state equation would generate another set of interaction forces.

- Viscosity, modeled as in the original SPH method, gives forces that are very close to previous ad-hoc models [MP89, DG95], where damping forces were computed from relative speeds and proximities of each pair of particles.

- While symmetric pairwise forces are present in both formalisms (which results in very similar implementations), smoothed particles ensure both stability and accuracy since they belong to Monte Carlo approaches.

In conclusion, smoothed particles are algorithmically close to previous models, but are based on a more soundly motivated mathematical basis. Important benefits of this new formalism are detailed in the next sections. Among others, it naturally defines a surface around a deformable body, and gives stability criteria that help efficiency.

4   Associating a surface to smoothed particles

Since our final goal is to create animations for Computer Graphics purposes, we have to provide a continuous representation for our discretized model of matter.

Particle systems have often been coated with implicit functions [MP89, Ton91], which seems to be the easiest way to model objects with unfixed topology. But if the implicit function is chosen arbitrarily, large undesired volume variations can be produced, and their suppression requires more computation [DG95]. This problem should not occur with a coherent definition of the surface, as particle systems are supposed to keep their volume nearly constant. Fortunately, a specific benefit of smoothed particles is to give a natural way of defining a surface.

4.1 Level Sets of Mass Density

As we already consider an object as a set of smeared-out masses, we can easily define where it lies. The density ρ actually is a continuous function that indicates where and how mass is distributed in space. Isovalues of density define implicit surfaces which are coherent with the model we use for simulation. The choice of an adequate isovalue should lead to volume preservation at no extra cost.

4.2 Coherent choice of Iso-Density

We have to find an appropriate iso-contour value which should be coherent with the underlying physical model. If the particles separate into two groups that no longer interact, the isosurface should exhibit two connected components. On the other hand, a single surface should be generated by a set of interacting particles.

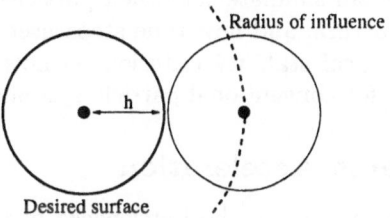

Figure 5: Two particles at their maximum interaction range.

Figure 5 shows that if two particles are a distant of $2h$ apart, no more interaction force occurs. Then, the surface should be located at a distance h from each boundary particle. In the specific case of two particles, the isovalue should be $2 \cdot W_h(h)$. Even if this choice is not compelling for several particles, we made our first experiments with that iso-value of density to display the surface. An example of animation using this technique is shown on Figure 6.

First tests with surface visualization in 2D show that the choice of our isovalue appears relatively good (see figure 7): the surface area undergoes variations of maximum ten percent. But it actually seems that the contour both preserving its surface area (i.e., its volume in 3D) better, and resulting in smooth and realistic shapes remains to be found. The relevant isosurface should surely be based on both W_h and ρ_0.

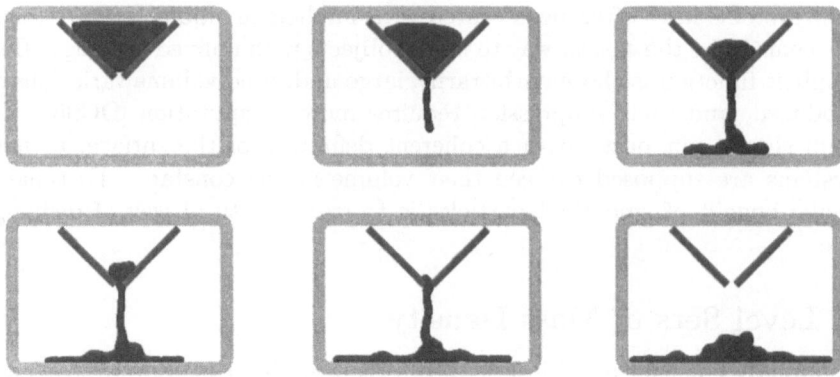

Figure 6: Snapshots from a sequence with a surface coating the particles: a quasi-liquid material (80 particles) falling under gravity.

5   Implementation issues

A basic implementation of smoothed particles would run in $O(n^2)$ with fixed time steps. This is not satisfactory since particle system simulations can require a large number of particles. Moreover, previous approaches were limited by the choice of a very short time step to avoid divergences or oscillations. This section explains how we can simulate smoothed particles in linear time thanks to an adequate data structure, and how time steps used for integration can be adapted according to a local stability criterion—a notion easier to define for smoothed particles than for conventional particle systems.

5.1   Neighbor search Acceleration

As in any N-body problem, one of the bottlenecks of the computation is the amount of time needed to perform force evaluation. In our case, forces are applied only to nearby particles, so a nearest neighbor search must be performed first to identify interacting neighbors. This search will also be used to find particles contributing to the implicit surface at a given point. So a lazy evaluation in $O(n^2)$ is not satisfactory.

As the interaction distance of each particle stays constant, the optimal data structure to perform nearest neighbor searching is a grid of voxels [MP89] of size $2h$. With such a structure, and since our particles are assumed to stay well distributed, the evaluation of forces on particles becomes $O(n)$. Creating the grid of voxels and finding particles lying in each voxel takes $O(n)$ operations too. So the whole simulation results in a linear total complexity, enabling a large number of particles.

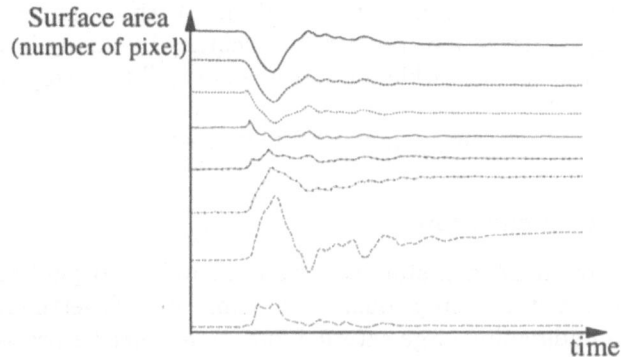

Figure 7: Volume variations for different iso-densities during the animation of Fig. 4.

5.2 Locally adaptive integration

Choosing a time step that both avoids divergence and ensures efficiency is the most important practical problem of conventional particle systems. Moreover, using a same integration time step for all the particles of a scene is not optimal since we are always tightly constrained by the shortest time scale occurring. Fortunately, local stability criteria have been naturally found for smoothed particles that in turn greatly reduce the computation. We actually perform adapted integration time steps for each particle both to reduce computation in stable areas and to automatically avoid divergence.

Time Stepping

In finite differencing methods, a stability criterion that often occurs is the Courant-Friedrichs-Lewy criterion, called here *Courant condition* [PTVF92]. It can be written as: $v\delta t/\delta x \leq 1$ where δt is the time step used for integration, v a velocity, and δx is the grid size. It intuitively means that if a phenomenon propagates with a maximum velocity v, it must not be integrated with a too large time step, or some grid points will be leaped. These leaps will result in a lack of information in these points and will give rise to instability during integration.

Translated into smoothed particles, the Courant condition requires that each particle i must not be passed by, giving a modified condition such as: $\delta t_i \leq h/c$, where h the smoothing length, and c the sound speed in the object, which is the maximum velocity of a deformation wave inside the material. The use of viscosity (see section 2.3) changes the criterion a little [HK92], giving a required time step satisfying:

$$\delta t_i \leq \delta t_i^{Courant} = \alpha \frac{h}{c + 0.6(c + 2 \cdot \max_j \mu_{ij})} \tag{8}$$

where α is the Courant number (approx. 0.3). To this criterion one can add others. In our implementation, we increase accuracy by taking into account the current speed of the particle, which results in an overall time step chosen so that:

$$\delta t_i = \min(\delta t_i^{Courant}, \alpha\frac{h}{v_i}).$$

Adaptive Time Integration

Now that we have defined a stability criterion, we could perform integration with a global adapted time step equal to $\delta t = \min_i \delta t_i$. Nevertheless, only a few particles (those undergoing large external forces) may need a precise integration while the others are quite stable. The solution is then to use individual particle time steps [HK92].

Assume a user-defined simulation rate Δt. To facilitate synchronization of integration, we only use power of two subdivisions of Δt. It means that the effective time step is chosen by finding the smallest positive n_i satisfying $\Delta t/2^{n_i} \leq \delta t_i$. The particle positions are then advanced at every smallest time step, while force evaluations are performed at each individual time step. This method permits forces to be evaluated only when needed, offering substantial gains in performance though guaranteeing stability.

The integration scheme we use is a standard "leapfrog" integrator, which is accurate to second-order:

$$\mathbf{r}_i^{n+1/2} = \mathbf{r}_i^{n-1/2} + \mathbf{v}_i^n \delta t \tag{9}$$

$$\mathbf{v}_i^{n+1} = \mathbf{v}_i^n + \mathbf{a}_i^{n+1/2} \delta t \tag{10}$$

where the indices in superscripts denote at which time step the quantities are computed. Since we use velocity through viscosity to estimate acceleration, second-order accuracy is preserved if we use a predicted estimate $\tilde{\mathbf{v}}_i^{n+1/2}$ obtained from:

$$\tilde{\mathbf{v}}_i^{n+1/2} = \mathbf{v}_i^n + \frac{\delta t}{2}\mathbf{a}_i^{n-1/2}.$$

This estimate is then used to compute the time-centered acceleration $\mathbf{a}_i^{n+1/2}$, from which the new velocity $\mathbf{v}_i^{n+1}$ will be computed from equation (10).

The change of time step during integration can also induce a loss of second order accuracy if no care is taken. That is why, at each change of a particle's own time step, the particle positions must be corrected using:

$$\mathbf{r}_i = \mathbf{r}_{i,old} + \frac{(\delta t_{new}^2 - \delta t_{old}^2)}{8}\mathbf{a}_i.$$

The resulting integration algorithm performs adaptive and individual integrations of our smoothed particles. Note that this algorithm can be used as soon as a stability criterion is known. Its advantage is that the time step is no longer a user-defined parameter but is totally managed by physical and numerical stability criterions.

6 Conclusion

We have defined a new type of particle system. Instead of considering particles as point masses discretizing an object, we prefer to define smoothed particles as samples of mass smeared out in space. While modeling the object in a smoother way, the method also provides equations of motion similar to conventional particles (symmetric central forces between pairs) and offers many new opportunities. Time integration for instance can be handled in a powerful way since each particle is integrated at individual time steps. The choice of the current time step is selected according to different criteria to ensure stability. Others advantages of this technique include an implicit representation coherent with the physical model as derived from the spatial density, efficient complexity, and intuitive parameters provided for the user to choose the kind of viscous material he wants to animate. The Monte-Carlo interpretation also ensures that stability increases with particles number.

All these advantages make this method a coherent and robust way to use particle systems. But a lot of avenues are yet to be explored: varying the smoothing length will provide a spatially adaptive system, which can in turn add efficiency since integration steps are proportional to this length. We can think for instance of creating "large" particles inside objects, and "smaller" particles in the periphery, reproducing the derm-epiderm approach of [LJR+91]. Thermal conduction [Ton91] can also be taken into account with this paradigm.

Animations can be found at:
        `http://w3imagis.imag.fr/~Mathieu.Desbrun/smoothed.html`

7 Aknowledgements

The authors would like to thank Eugene Fiume for pointing us to SPH and for early discussions, Andy Hanson for his continuous help, and François Faure and Rémi Cozot for a full re-reading of the paper.

References

[DG95]   Mathieu Desbrun and Marie-Paule Gascuel. Animating soft substances with implicit surfaces. *Computer Graphics*, pages 287–290, August 1995. Proceedings of SIGGRAPH'95 (Los Angeles, CA).

[Gas93]   Marie-Paule Gascuel. An implicit formulation for precise contact modeling between flexible solids. *Computer Graphics*, pages 313–320, August 1993. Proceedings of SIGGRAPH'93 (Anaheim, CA).

[GLG95]   M.N. Gamito, P.F. Lopes, and M.R. Gomes. Two-dimensionnal simulation of gaseous phenomena using vortex particles. In *6th Eurographics Workshop on Animation and Simulation*, Maastricht, Netherlands, September 1995.

[GMTT89] Jean-Paul Gourret, Nadia Magnenat Thalmann, and Daniel Thalmann. Simulation of object and human skin deformations in a grasping task. *Computer Graphics*, 23(3):21–29, July 1989. Proceedings of SIGGRAPH'89 (Boston, MA, July 1989).

[HK92] Lars Hernquist and Neal Katz. Treesph: A unification of sph with the hierarchical tree method. *App. J. Supp.*, 70:419, 1992.

[LHVD95] A. Luciani, A. Habibi, A. Vapillon, and Y. Duroc. A physical model of turbulent fluids. In *6th Eurographics Workshop on Animation and Simulation*, Maastricht, Netherlands, September 1995.

[LJR⁺91] Annie Luciani, Stéphane Jimenez, Olivier Raoult, Claude Cadoz, and Jean-Loup Florens. A unified view of multitude behaviour, flexibility, plasticity, and fractures: balls, bubbles and agglomerates. In *IFIP WG 5.10 Working Conference*, Tokyo, Japan, April 1991.

[LP95] Jean-Christophe Lombardo and Claude Puech. Oriented particles: A tool for shape memory objects modelling. In *Graphics Interface'95*, Quebec, Canada, May 1995.

[Mon92] J. J. Monaghan. Smoothed particle hydrodynamics. *Annu. Rev. Astron. Astrophys.*, 30:543, 1992.

[MP89] Gavin Miller and Andrew Pearce. Globular dynamics: A connected particle system for animating viscous fluids. *SIGGRAPH '89 Courses 30 notes*, pages 305–309, August 89.

[PTVF92] William Press, Saul Teukolsky, William Vetterling, and Brian Flannery. *Numerical Recipes in C, second edition*. Cambridge University Press, New York, USA, 1992.

[PW89] Alex Pentland and John Williams. Good vibrations: Modal dynamics for graphics and animation. *Computer Graphics*, 23(3):215–222, July 1989. Proceedings of SIGGRAPH'89 (Boston, MA, July 1989).

[Ree83] W. T. Reeves. Particle systems—a technique for modeling a class of fuzzy objects. *Computer Graphics*, 17(3):359–376, 1983.

[Ton91] David Tonnesen. Modeling liquids and solids using thermal particles. In *Graphics Interface'91*, pages 255–262, Calgary, AL, June 1991.

[TPBF87] Demetri Terzopoulos, John Platt, Alan Barr, and Kurt Fleischer. Elastically deformable models. *Computer Graphics*, 21(4):205–214, July 1987. Proceedings of SIGGRAPH'87 (Anaheim, California).

[TPF89] Demetri Terzopoulos, John Platt, and Kurt Fleisher. Heating and melting deformable models (from goop to glop). In *Graphics Interface'89*, pages 219–226, London, Ontario, June 1989.

A   Mathematical bases

Suppose we have a field f defined over all space. We can calculate a mean value within a spatial interval with:

$$< f(\mathbf{r}) > = \int_{space} f(\mathbf{r}') \, W_h(\mathbf{r} - \mathbf{r}') dr' \qquad (11)$$

where $W_h(\mathbf{r})$ is a smoothing kernel, and h the smoothing length specifying the extent of the averaging volume. $W_h(\mathbf{r})$ is peaked about $\mathbf{r} = 0$ so that it tends to the Dirac delta function as $h \to 0$, keeping its integral normalized to 1. Expanding the integrand of (11) as a power series in h gives, if $W_h(\mathbf{r})$ is an even function:

$$< f(\mathbf{r}) > = f(\mathbf{r}) + O(h^2)$$

Suppose now that our kernel W_h has a finite support. Then we can approximate any derivative of f easily. For instance, we have by definition in 1D:

$$< \frac{\partial f}{\partial x}(r) > = \int_{-\infty}^{+\infty} \frac{\partial f}{\partial x}(r') \, W_h(r - r') dr'.$$

Integrating by parts, this yields:

$$\int_{-\infty}^{+\infty} \frac{\partial f}{\partial x}(r') \, W_h(r-r') dr' = [f(r') \, W_h(r - r')]_{r=-\infty}^{r=+\infty} - \int_{-\infty}^{+\infty} f(r') \cdot (-1) \cdot \frac{\partial W_h}{\partial x}(r-r') dr',$$

so that we can write:

$$< \frac{\partial f}{\partial x}(r) > = \int_{-\infty}^{+\infty} f(r') \, \frac{\partial W_h}{\partial x}(r - r') dr'. \qquad (12)$$

It proves that there is no need to know analytical derivatives to calculate their mean values.

B   Pressure forces

A natural way to write the pressure gradient in SPH formalism is:

$$\nabla P(\mathbf{r}) = \sum_j m_j \frac{P_j}{\rho_j} \nabla W_h(\mathbf{r} - \mathbf{r}_j).$$

We can use it in the equation of motion when pressure is exerted on a small volume dV of mass m:

$$m\,\mathbf{a} = \rho \, dV \, \mathbf{a} = \mathbf{F} = -\nabla P \, dV,$$

where $\mathbf{a}$ is the acceleration and $\mathbf{F}$ the pressure force on dV. But a quick observation shows that the action-reaction principle would then not be enforced since $m_i \nabla P_i / \rho_i$ is not equal to $m_j \nabla P_j / \rho_j$ for $i \neq j$. To symmetrize the pressure forces, we can use the simple derivation rule $\nabla P/\rho = \nabla (P/\rho) + P\nabla\rho/\rho^2$ to write:

$$\frac{\nabla P_i}{\rho_i} = \sum_{j\neq i} m_j \frac{P_j}{\rho_j^2} \nabla_i W_h^{ij} + \frac{P_i}{\rho_i^2} \sum_{j\neq i} m_j \nabla_i W_h^{ij}$$

where the notation $\nabla_i W_h^{ij}$ denotes the gradient of $W_h(\mathbf{r}_i - \mathbf{r}_j)$ taken with respect to the coordinates of particle i. The equation of motion for a particle is then:

$$\mathbf{a}_i = \frac{\mathbf{F}_i}{m_i} = -\sum_{j\neq i} m_j \left(\frac{P_i}{\rho_i^2} + \frac{P_j}{\rho_j^2} \right) \nabla_i W_h^{ij}.$$

3

Human Motion Capture and Simulation

A Real Time Anatomical Converter
For Human Motion Capture

Tom Molet, Ronan Boulic, Daniel Thalmann

LIG - Computer Graphics Lab, Swiss Federal Institute of Technology
Lausanne, CH-1015 Switzerland.
E-mail : {molet, boulic, thalmann}@lig.di.epfl.ch

Abstract. There are many possible ways of identifying the posture of a human character from a set of known positions. These methods differ in subtle but important ways. We propose an alternative method to the jacobian-based Inverse Kinematics, one which allows for simple calibration, allows for sensors slippage, and can take advantage of knowledge of the type of motion being performed. This approach gives real-time conversion of magnetic sensors measurements into human anatomical rotations. Our converter is used in a wide range of applications from real time applications to animation design. It provides a useful complement to the traditional keyframe editing software.
Animation : http://ligwww.epfl.ch/ ~molet/EGCAS96.html

1   Introduction

Naive motion capture consists in directly building the position and orientation of independent solids in a global frame according to the sensors attached on the body segments. If each body segment carries a sensor, the resulting set of solids first appears as a connected body even if there is no explicit representation of the body's topological structure. However, for a variety of reasons this method produces abnormal relative translation between adjacent segments, giving the impression that the body is an unnatural and unrealistic collection of independent elements. The possible source for the mismatch between the virtual model and the performer postures are :

- calibration error
- slip of the sensors with respect to underlying bones
- electronic noise
- simplified revolute joints of graphical model

In this paper we consider only a 3D hierarchical representation of the human skeleton where internal joints are only rotations also called anatomical rotations. The main problem becomes the conversion of magnetic sensor data into the rotation parameters of the 3D hierarchy. These rotations traditionally result from the sequential combination of joint angles (i.e. an Euler sequence). However, our methodology is independent of a particular choice of rotation representation. In the following presentation we consider the human motion implicitly described in terms of anatomical rotations.

Applications using motion capture can be classified in two categories : animation design and real-time motion generation (usually driven by user interaction). For animation design, postures or motion sequences can be obtained with motion capture in order to constitute libraries of postures and/or sequences. They can later be reused and combined with standard editing tools. The resulting motion is computed with more or less sophisticated interpolation or optimization techniques. The generation of human movements for real-time applications is either based on the combination of pre-recorded sequences or on live performance. This last method allows to avoid the recording stage.

We propose a very efficient method to capture human motion after a simple calibration. The sensor data are converted into the anatomical rotations of a body hierarchical representation. Such a choice facilitates motion reuse for other human models with the same proportions. After a review of related techniques we describe our human anatomical converter based on the magnetic sensor technology (see section 5 for an overview of this technology). Finally, we present various examples and applications.

2   Background

Design of human motion is a complex task and an active research area [7]. There has been a large amount of literature describing attempts to achieve creation of life like animation (see [18] for a review). Traditional keyframe design is time consuming and this has motivated the development of many algorithms providing higher level control parameters to the animator [5] [8] [13] [25]. Motion reusability has been greatly enhanced by the recent motion warping tools described in [25].

For real-time motion generation, on-the-fly mixing of pre-recorded motions can be used to animate autonomous agents [3] [20] or the user's virtual personae (its so-called *avatar*) [12]. The first class of application needs a large database of recorded motions to cover a wide spectrum of behaviors for the autonomous agents. Limitations may come from the transitions between sequences which can potentially induce self collisions even when the individual motions are collision-free [3]. In the context of a military simulator where a soldier model can adopt about eight basic postures and four locomotion modes, the system recognizes the current posture of the participant with two sensors while the location is specified via a resistive pad sensor. From this information, the system determines which sequence is played back by the corresponding avatar [12].

In a complementary approach, the whole body movement of the avatar is more directly controlled by the participant from the capture of four magnetic sensors [2]. The joints values are computed with Jacobian-Based Inverse Kinematics (in short, noted JBIK) by considering the sensors, attached to two hands, the head and the chest, as end-effectors. The major problem of this technique is that JBIK can not guarantee that the performer and the articulated figure postures remain in a given neighborhood [15]. While position and orientation of the end-effectors can be enforced, there is no constraint on the position/orientation of other body segments because the articulated chain is redundant (i.e. there is an infinity of posture solutions for a desired end-effector situation). As a result the posture may become unrealistic. This appears to be a significant drawback for producing realistic motion since JBIK alone is not suited for that purpose.

More sensors are necessary to effectively reflect the participant's posture and motion. According to [14], seven sensors are the minimal realistic solution for the whole body tracking when using JBIK control. [22] proposes a ten sensors solution to track the whole body movements with closed form solution for the arms and legs. This technique improves the conversion rate compared to the iterative nature of the JBIK solution. However, it relies on some special placement and orientation of the sensors. For example, the z-axis of the sensor strapped to the user's upper arm is supposed to lies along the length of the limb and the y-axis should be perpendicular and pointing away from the center of the limb. This lack of sensor's calibration decreases both the accuracy and the user-friendliness of the system. Moreover, this closed form solution requires that the twisting of upper arms and thighs are captured using the orientations of the sensors attached to the upper arms and thighs. We show in section 4.2 that the local thickness of these segments prevents the correct measurement of the segment twisting.

Biomechanical analysis of human motion describes another approaches for capturing anatomical rotations. One can find such analysis based on optical marker location for the shoulder [17] or the knee [19]. However, their aim is to achieve the highest precision for a local analysis, so the calibration procedures can require very specialized anatomical knowledge [9].

In the next section, we propose a method converting sensor data in anatomical rotations for the whole human body organized as a 3D hierarchy. The system retain the natural dynamics of human movements while not sacrificing efficiency, flexibility and user-friendliness.

3 Human Motion Analysis

This section first describes the hierarchy representing the virtual human skeleton and its calibration. In a second part, we present the sensors calibration and the data conversion.

3.1 Skeleton Calibration
We briefly describe here the 3D hierarchy used to represent the avatar corresponding to the real performer. Our humanoid hierarchy maintains a topological tree information

Fig. 1. Sensor attachment.

which retains all the major degrees of freedom of the human body [6]. Only the spine region is simplified to eight vertebrae in order to facilitate its control.

A humanoid instance is characterized by geometrical information including low level attributes (e.g. segment's length, orientation and mass) as well as high level parameters, for example the character's stature and weight [16]. Our model comprises a total of thirty two joints corresponding to seventy four Degree of Freedom (in short, noted DOF) including a general position-orientation joint (six DOF) henceforth referred as the *global joint*. Each of the hand hierarchies, which are optional, adds thirty DOF (twenty joints).

Conversion process
- skeleton calibration,
- sensors calibration,
- interactive or recorded conversion(s).
or
- load a calibrated-skeleton file,
- sensors calibration,
- interactive or recorded conversion(s).

In our system, the virtual human model used to derive anatomical rotations has to match the animator segment sizes. The computed rotations of the performer stature can be assigned to different statures for animating various models. However, for realistic animation, the variation of statures of model character and modeled character should be small. For example, a tall performer walk mapped on a little character shows a walking speed greater than what would be induced by the smaller legs, thus producing a "sliding" effect.

The virtual skeleton calibration is made once per performer. First, we scale an average human model to the total height of the performer. Second, we eventually adjust some segments statistically showing a low correlation with the total height [16]. For that purpose we simply make hand measurements based on anatomical landmarks. The error of those measurements are estimated to be within two centimeters per segment. In applications where flexibility is more important than accuracy, such as demonstrators dedicated to a wide public, only the first stage is automatically completed. The total height can be estimated from the head sensor measurement in the initial standing posture (Fig. 1).

3.2   Conversion

The basic steps of our conversion program are described in this section. In a first stage, we need to construct the relation between the sensor attached to one performer segment (Fig. 1) and the corresponding proximal joint of the virtual model (Fig. 2).

This step, called "sensors calibration", has to be performed every time the sensor attachments are modified. Once this is done, the performer can switch between the interactive animation control and the animation recording module, which convert the data from the hardware in anatomical rotations. The converter and some refinements for specific joints are described after the "sensors calibration" section.

Sensors calibration. The calibration assumes that the virtual skeleton reasonably matches the performer skeleton as mentioned in the previous section. Sensors are attached on the performer body using the following simple rules :

- one sensor drives one joint and thus has to be fixed on the associated distal segment
- avoid segment regions where muscles and fat abound to attach the sensors (for example, avoid the middle of the upper arm limb and prefer its extremity where less muscle displacement occurs)

Then, we need to establish the orientation of the sensor's coordinate system with respect to the joint coordinate system. In our system, only one sensor requires a position calibration : the *spine sensor* used to track the global position of the participant. All the other sensors need only an orientation calibration. This is an important feature making our approach more robust to local perturbation due to muscles and skin deformations during the movement [19][21].

The initialization algorithm constructs automatically the rigid transformation matrix between the sensor's frame and the final frame system of the virtual joint. While performing this operation, the performer has to be in a predefined posture and orientation, e.g. the default model posture (see Fig. 2) or a customized calibration posture. In the first stage of this calibration, the global position of the virtual skeleton is set using the data taken from the spine sensor attached to the base of the performer's spine.

Sensor	Joint Name	DOF
1	*global joint* (+ lumbar vertebrae)	6 4 + 2 (*)
2, 3	right and left hip	3 each
4, 5	right and left knee	2 each
6, 7	right and left ankle	1 each
8	lumbar vertebrae 2	3
9	thoracic vertebrae	3
10, 11	right and left shoulder	3 each
12, 13	right and left elbow	2 each
14	cervical vertebrae	3

(* : In stand up mode)

Table 1. Sensor-joint correspondence.

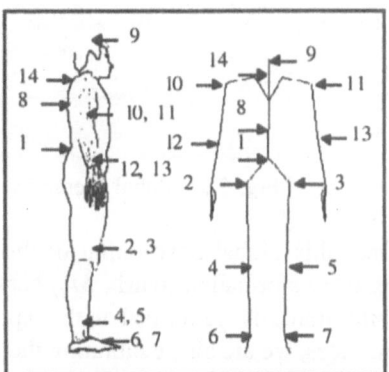

Fig. 2. Sensor attachment positions (left image) and corresponding model joint locations (right image).

Assuming the performer adopts the calibration posture orientation, for example standing up with the frontal body axis oriented as the 'y' axis of the emitter, the global orientation of the virtual actor remains unchanged by this first operation. With this assumption, we are able to attach the sensor on the actor's column base without taking care of the sensor's orientation (as no default or special orientation is assumed). This sensor orientation will be associated to the initial model orientation by the next initialization step.

Sensors calibration process

0. the performer adopts the calibration posture and global orientation,
1. virtual skeleton translation according to the spine sensor (global positioning),
2. construction of the local transformation for each sensor-joint pair

---

The global position *TV* of the virtual skeleton is computed using the following formula :

$$TV = JW + WE + ES + Offset \tag{1}$$

with the following 3D translation vectors :
- TV   the desired translation vector,
- JW   from joint final frame to the world frame,
- WE   from world frame to emitter reference frame (equipment frame),
- ES   from emitter reference frame to sensor's frame (returned by the hardware),
- Offset   from the external spine skin location to the global joint center of rotation, see Fig. 3.b (from skeleton calibration measurements).

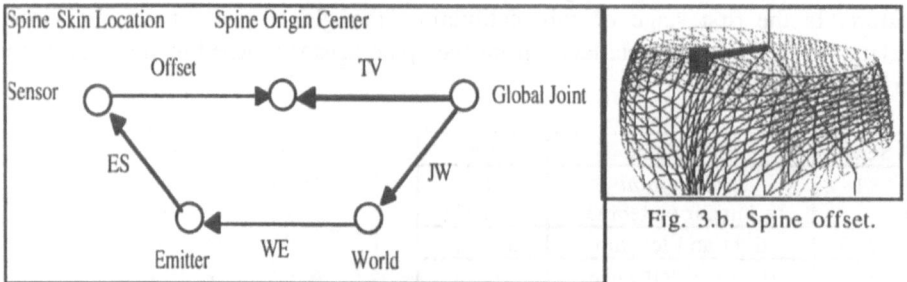

Fig. 3.b. Spine offset.

Fig. 3.a. Global hierarchy translation.

Once this global positioning of the hierarchy has been made, the evaluation of the rigid transformation matrix M_{SJ} between each sensor frame and the associated virtual joint frame is performed with expression (2). By computing rigid transformation matrices, we are also calibrating the sensor's position even if it is not required by the conversion algorithm. Such a sensors calibration can be useful for other methods like JBIK. This operation also defines the spine sensor orientation.

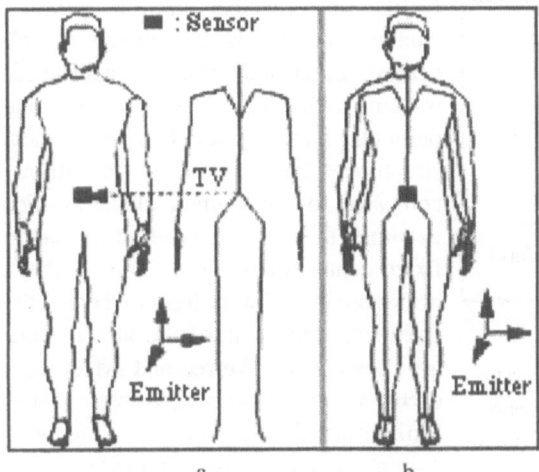

Fig. 4. Translation Vector *TV* of the skeleton in the virtual scene to match the participant position according to the emitter location in the scene. Left image shows the construction of *TV* before translating the virtual skeleton (a). Right image shows the results of the this first calibration stage (b). The orientation of the model remains unchanged.

The position of a sensor is not used to compute the anatomical rotations, but only its orientation. The position could be used to animate more sophisticated joint model with translation components. However this interest is limited regarding human joints translation range compared to the sensor accuracy.

$$M_{SJ} = M_{SE} \cdot M_{EW} \cdot M_{WJ} \qquad (2)$$

with the following rigid transformation matrices (line matrix) :

- M_{SJ} from the sensor frame to the joint final frame,
- M_{SE} from sensor frame to emitter reference frame (returned by the hardware),
- M_{EW} from emitter reference frame to world frame,
- M_{WJ} from world frame to the joint final frame.

The M_{EW} matrix is a simple vertical translation constructed using measurements of the emitter reference frame position in the lab. It ensures the position correspondence between the virtual floor and the lab floor. For Augmented Reality systems more sophisticated emitter calibration is required [24] because virtual objects have to be drawn over real images.

The motivation behind our choice of constructing the rigid transformation matrix between the sensor frame and the virtual joint final frame directly instead of measuring the real location of the performer joint, is the complexity and effort in the methods used to evaluate this location. It requires an additional sensor to perform such a calibration and this degrades the user-friendliness of the system. Moreover, with our technique we are able to perform again the sensor's calibration at any time (e.g. in case a sensor moves) whereas the time needed to re-calibrate by any other procedure discourages users.

86

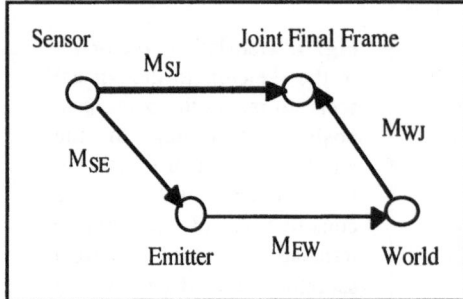

Fig. 5. M_{SJ} matrix construction. This transformation is computed for each sensor just after the virtual skeleton has been moved by the first calibration stage.

Unlike the medical motion analysis studies, our aim is to animate a well defined articulated structure instead of tracking the real motion of one particular human joint. Our hierarchical structure has some limitations, compared to the human skeleton. For example the virtual knee joint has a fixed center of rotation and a direct orthogonal XYZ axis frame whereas the three rotational axis of the human knee are shown to be skewed and offset from each other [19]. However these limitations do not hamper a realistic animation and are also assumed by other animation techniques.

Our method is more robust to muscles and fat movements than other procedure using the position of the sensor because they are more sensitive to position calibration errors. Moreover experience shows that assuming a required orientation for sensors gives bad results. This is due to the sensitiveness of rotations when setting the sensors on segments with deformable surface (skin, muscles). With our calibration, the performer is free to place the sensors with any orientation on his/her body segments. However the sensor attachment remains a difficult question and may have an influence on the results. The best results are achieved with sensors attached at the segment's distal end where there is minimal muscle and fat thickness. Performers are no more required to perform special gesture during the sensor calibration process, and no measurements need to be taken by hand and entered in a calibration file or interface.

Anatomical rotations conversion. Except for the spine sensor for which we fully use the six DOF to track the global position and orientation of the virtual model, we only use the orientation information (three DOF) out of the six DOF available from each sensor. This improves the performance in the sense that less information has to be transferred from the sensor hardware to the host computer. The communication can slow down the system and has to be optimized (in interactive mode) to obtain real-time conversion rates. For example, better results were achieved by transmitting only quaternions (four double per sensor) and reconstructing the rotational matrix instead of transmitting the whole matrix (nine double per sensor).

In order to compute the joint angles associated with one sensor, we have to compute the joint rotation matrix R_J which (in our hierarchy) will be decomposed into angles using an Euler sequence method. This matrix is evaluated using the formula (see Fig. 6) :

$$R_J = R_{JW} \cdot R_{WE} \cdot R_{ES} \cdot R_{SJ} \tag{3}$$

with the following rotation matrices (line matrix) :

- R_J new desired matrix of the joint to be converted in anatomical angles,
- R_{JW} from the joint initial frame to the world frame,
- R_{WE} from the world frame to the emitter reference frame,
- R_{ES} from the emitter reference frame to the sensor frame (inverse of transformation matrix returned by the hardware),
- R_{SJ} rotation part of the (M_{SJ}) calibration matrix computed at initialization stage.

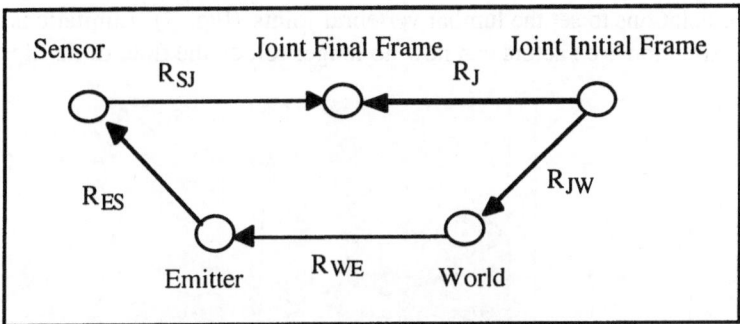

Fig. 6. Joint rotation matrix construction.

Notice that as we consider a hierarchical structure, the matrix from one joint initial frame to the world frame R_J changes when some parent joint in the hierarchy is updated according to sensor input and the computation is performed in parent-to-child order.

At this point, we have to mention that in our human model the number of DOFs varies from joint to joint and consequently not all joints are suitable for three angles decomposition technique. For rotation joints, it varies from one to three whereas for spine sensor six DOFs are considered. Within this set of joints two kind of Euler sequence are found in our hierarchy, namely ZXY and ZYX. We have constructed different Euler-like decomposition functions dedicated to each Euler sequence and our joint's DOF modeling. These computations are model dependent and all the details can be found in [10].

The next section discusses the improvements carried out by studying specific characteristics of some sensor - human joint relations.

4   Improvements on Specific Human Joints

4.1   Spine sensor and vertebral joints

When movements to record are known to be enacted while the performer stand on his/her feet, one can assume that the body global orientation will be mainly modified

88

by the rotation along the vertical axis (turning). In such a context the sensor's tilt and roll rotations (along lateral and frontal axis) are due to spine movements rather than changes in the body orientation. Experience shows that in a great number of recording situations a transfer of the tilt and roll rotations to vertebral joints increases the captured realism. Doing so, we solve the question of the spine sensor orientation interpretation.

Our algorithm has a special command mode, where this transfer is performed by restricting the global position and orientation as a four DOF joint and using the two remaining orientations to set the lumbar vertebral joints (Fig. 7). Limitations of this spine-bend extraction are : actors can now no longer roll on the floor or do flips.

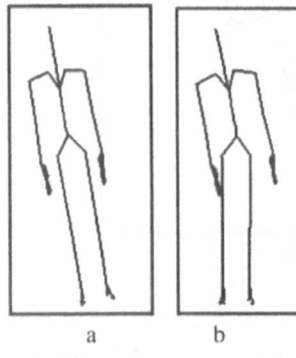
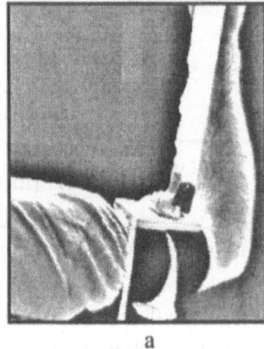

Fig. 7. Using the roll orientation (a) to set the global skeleton orientation. (b) transferred to the vertebral joint assuming a stand up posture.

Fig. 8. Comparison of arm and sensor orientation before (a) and after (b) a 90 Degree shoulder twisting rotation.

4.2 Shoulder and hip twisting component

The sensor attached to the upper arm (resp. the thigh segment) to control the shoulder joint (resp. the hip joint) suffers from the local thickness of the human muscles. The flexion and abduction rotations (e.g. axis S2 and S3 perpendicular to the segment in Fig. 9) are well handled by the sensors but the twisting component (S3 rotation along the segment) is often measured as only half of the real bone rotation (Fig. 8). This can induce significant divergence between the performer posture and the model posture for the dependent parts of the hierarchy (i.e. arms and hands, resp. shanks and feet).

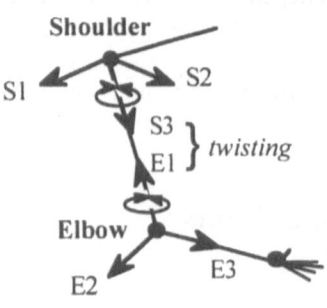

Fig. 9. Arm twisting rotation.

Let us examine our solution for the shoulder twisting (the same principle is applied for the thigh twisting). For such a problem we decompose the anatomical rotation matrices at the shoulder and at the elbow into Euler angles sequences [10]. For the shoulder joint, the anatomical rotation matrix is converted into an Euler sequence ending with the twisting rotation along the arm axis (S_3 in Fig. 9). The value of the twisting S_3 is to be ignored because it is only partially measured from the arm sensor as can be seen on Fig. 8. We can recover this information by considering that the elbow virtually has three degrees of freedom $\{E_1, E_2, E_3\}$ as shown on Fig. 9. This approach is pertinent as the orientation of the forearm sensor associated to the elbow joint is very sensitive to the shoulder twisting. So, the elbow anatomical rotation matrix is interpreted as an Euler sequence beginning with the arm twisting rotation (E_1 in Fig. 9) and followed by the two standard elbow rotations. Finally, the value of the twisting E_1 is used in the shoulder joint in order to get a realistic orientation of the object representing the arm. Figure 12 (see Appendix) compares this technique to the naive method.

5   System Architecture

The hardware includes a set of sixteen magnetic sensors and one extended range transmitter (Flock of Birds™ from Ascension Technology) with integrated filters (FIR notch filter and adaptive IIR lowpass filter). The data transfer between the host computer and the sensor's units is performed through the use of an Annex Communications Server over the ethernet. Thus applications can run on any workstation of the network. In addition, we can have hand motion tracking with the Virtual Technologies Cyberglove™ which is directly connected to the host computer via one serial port connection. The operating range for sensor's measurements is 8 feet around the emitter. The static position accuracy is 0.1" RMS, 0.5° for angular accuracy, averaged over the translation range with a position resolution of 0.03" at 12" and 0.1° RMS at 12" for angular resolution [1]. This accuracy depends on the distance to the base emitter.

The sensor management has been implemented as a two levels library module. The first low level library integrates a sensor data structure in our general purpose 3D hierarchy [4]. This way, we can apply the motion capture to any kind of tree structured hierarchy. The second level library is dedicated to human motion capture, it provides higher level commands and the calibration procedure. Each sensor has been assigned to a particular joint once and for all. So a performer only has to wear each sensor on the segment distal to its associated joint. Then the calibration stage automatically adjusts the location of the corresponding virtual sensor in the virtual model's hierarchy. Motion capture can begin. The algorithm can run either in *interactive* mode or in *motion recording* mode:

- In interactive mode we display each captured posture. The Performer™ multi-processing mode on Onyx™ allows distribution of the display and the conversion to different processors. We can achieve an average conversion rate of 13 Hz with twelve active sensors. This rate decreases to 8 Hz with a single Onyx™ processor

(R4400-200 MHz) and standard SGI Graphic Library display. We have designed an optional live filter to efficiently prevent glitches producing erroneous postures. However, this introduces a three frame lag between the participant and the model posture.

- For motion recording, the display can be switched off (or reduced) in order to speed up the recording rate. We are able to reach the 100 Hz sampling of the hardware by buffering the raw data . The post-processing of a 5 seconds sequence at 100 Hz (thus 500 postures) requires around 9 seconds including file storage. This oversampling is useful for the recording of motion with high dynamics encountered in various sports. The animator can later reduce the sampling with standard tools wherever necessary .

6   Examples

Currently the motion capture system directly drives thirty four DOF with twelve magnetic sensors as shown on Figure 2. In addition, one digital glove controls twenty five DOFs for fingers and two DOFs for the wrist. Figure 10 (see also Appendix) compares some performed and converted postures from soccer motion.

Fig. 10. Performed and converted postures of a soccer motion.

In addition, the motion can be recorded as keyframes and played back with additional information as the spatial trajectories of the joints (Fig. 11). This information helps to analyze the motion for incremental improvements of a desired recording (especially for sport motions).

Figure 11 shows postures from a racket game motion involving significant twisting of the arm. Such conversion cannot be guaranteed when converting with JBIK and fewer sensors.

Fig. 11. Initial and final converted postures together with joint spatial trajectories over the whole motion.

7 Applications

Three kinds of application have been developed based on our anatomical converter :

- The first type needs a real time motion generator to interactively animate the performer representation in the virtual world (its so-called avatar). A clear illustration is given by a teleconferencing application where multiple participants from distant sites can share, move and act within the same 3D environment [23]. It is easy to integrate motion capture and immersion display device as the head tracking sensor can both animate the neck joint (thus moving the model's head) and set the viewing parameters for the head mounted display.

- The second type of applications indirectly use the converter, they rather have important requirement of motion sequence. The converter gives the ability to easily record keyframe sequences of whole or a part of the body. The design time is greatly reduced compared to pure keyframe design even if a second stage of motion refinement is to be planned after the capture [7]. The constitution of pre-recorded motion database allows easier conception of behavioral animation motors [12]. In our case, we chose to restrict recordings of separate body parts (e.g. right arm, left leg) as basic motion elément. The algorithm selects which sequence(s) pilot the autonomous actor in response to environmental and behavioral events [3].

- The third kind of application is the fusion of the two previous classes. For example, a collaborative application can combine a synthetic actor controlled by the participant while other actors are autonomous agents controlled by internal motors. In one application the autonomous agent is able to recognize in real-time the current action of the participant and to react with a repertoire of actions based on a pre-defined set of keyframe sequences and other animation techniques [11].

8   Conclusion

We have presented an efficient technique for human motion capture which is fully compatible with current virtual actors tools using keyframe to describe animation (or posture). The underlying concept can be easily applied to animate any other kind of hierarchical structure (i.e. non human like) with proper initialization. The proposed calibration is highly user-friendly while still capturing the motion realism (some commercial systems suffer from the lack of simple and/or reliable initialization procedure). We can overcome the perturbation introduced by soft tissue and muscle displacement for critical DOF such as the arm and the thigh twisting.

While a wide range of gestures can be performed live or recorded, the main limitation to movement comes from the hardware requirement : magnetic sensors are sensitive to any kind of metallic object in the neighborhood and are connected to the electronic parts by cables that sometimes hamper movement performance. The most important requirement is to ensure a high sampling rate, if possible higher than the standard display rate.

Future investigations will explore a more complete sensor configuration consisting of two gloves and thirteen or fourteen magnetic sensors depending on the desired accuracy of the spine motion capture. A complementary research direction is the refinement of captured motion in order to ensure goal-oriented cartesian constraints.

9   Acknowledgments

We wish to thank our colleagues Jianhua Shen for the human deformations, Serge Rezzonico for sensor's mastery, and Srikanth Bandi, Zhiyong Huang, Luc Emering for many fruitful discussions on related topics. The research was supported by the Swiss National Science Research Foundation and the Federal Office for Education and Science.

10   References

[1] Ascension (1994) "The Flock of Birds Installation and Operation Guide". Ascension Technology Corporation POB 527 Burlington, Vermont 05402 (802) 860-6440.

[2] Badler N., Hollick M.J., Granieri J.P. (1993) "Real-Time Control of a Virtual Human Using Minimal Sensors", a Forum short paper in Presence, 2(1), pp 82-86, MIT.

[3] Bécheiraz P., Thalmann D. (1996) "A Model of Nonverbal Communication and Interpersonal Relationship Between Virtual Actors" Proc. of Computer Animation 96, Geneva.

[4] Boulic R., Renault O. (1991) "3D Hierarchies For Animation". New Trends in Animation and Visualization. Wiley Professional Computing, New York, pp 59-76.

[5] Boulic R., Huang Z., Magnenat-Thalmann N., Thalmann D. (1994) "Goal-Oriented Design and Correction of Articulated Figure Motion with the TRACK System", Journal of Computer. & Graphics, 18(4), pp 443-452.

[6] Boulic R., Capin T., Huang Z., Kalra P., Lintermann B., Magnenat-Thalmann N., Moccozet L., Molet T., Pandzic I., Saar K., Schmitt A., Shen j., Thalmann D. (1995) "A system for the Parallel Integrated Motion of Multiple Deformable Human Characters with Collision Detection" , Computer Graphics Forum special issue of EUROGRAPHICS'95 Proceedings, 14(3), Maastricht, pp C-337-348.

[7] Boulic R., Huang Z., Thalmann D. (1995) "A Comparison of Design Strategies for 3D Human Motions", Workshop on Human Comfort and Security, Brussels, September 1995, to appear with Springer Verlag.

[8] Bruderlin A., Williams L. (1995) "Motion Signal Processing", Computer Graphics Proceedings, Annual Conference Series, 1995, pp 97-104.

[9] Cappozzo A. (1991) "Three-Dimensional Analysis of Human Walking : Experimental Methods and Associated Artifacts", Human Movement Science 10 (1991) pp 589-602, North-Holland.

[10] Craig J.J. (1989) "Introduction to Robotics, Mechanics, and Control", 2nd edition, Addison Wesley, Readings, Mass. , 1989

[11] Emering L., Boulic R., Balcisoy S., Thalmann D. (1997) "Real-Time Human Action Recognition for Behavioral Interactions with Virtual Agents", submitted to the first ACM Conference on Autonomous Agents 1997.

[12] Granieri J., Crabtree J., Badler N. (1995) "Production And Playback Of Human Figure Motion For 3D Virtual Environments". In proceedings VRAIS'95, IEEE, pp 127-135.

[13] Guo S., Robergé J., Grace T. (1993) "Controlling Movement Using Parametric Frame Space Interpolation". In proceedings of Computer Animation '93, pp 216-227.

[14] Hirose M., Deffaux G., Nakagaki Y. (1995) "A Study on Data Input of Natural Human Motion for Virtual Reality System", ICAT/VRST'95, ACM-SIGCHI, pp 245-251, November 1995.

[15] Klein C.A., Huang C.H. (1983) "Review Of Pseudoinverse Control For Use With Kinematically Redundant Manipulators", IEEE Transactions on Systems, Man, and Cybernetics, SMC-13(2), pp 245-250, March/April.

[16] Kroemer K.H.E., Kroemer H.J., Kroemer-Elbert K.E. (1990) "Engineering Physiology, Bases of Human Factors/ Ergonomics", 2nd edition, Van Nostrand Reinhold Publisher, New-York, London, ISBN 0-442-00354-4

[17] Karlsson D., Lundberg A. (1994) "In Vivo Measurement Of The Shoulder Rhythm Using External Fixation Markers". Proceedings of the Third International Symposium on 3-D Analysis of Human Movement 94, pp 69-72.

[18] Maiocchi R. (1996) "3D Character Animation Using Motion Capture", In Advanced Interactive Animation, Thalmann&Magnenat-Thalmann (eds.), Prentice-Hall, to appear in Summer 1996.

[19] Pennock G.R., Clark K.J. (1990) "An Anatomy-Based Coordinate System for the Description of the Kinematic Displacements in the Human Knee", Journal of Biomechanics, 23(12), pp 1209-1218.

[20] Perlin K. (1995) "Real Time Responsive Animation With Personality", IEEE Visualization and Computer Graphics, 1(1), pp 5-15.

[21] Rab G.T. (1991) "Flexible Marker Set for Human Gait Analysis", Technical Note, Journal of Electromyography and Kinesiology, 1(2), pp 139-145, Raven Press Ltd, New-York.

[22] Semwal S. K., Hightower R., Standfield S. (1996) "Closed Form and Geometric Algorithms for Real-Time Control of an Avatar", Proceedings of VRAIS'96, IEEE , pp 177-184.

[23] Thalmann D., Capin T., Magnenat Thalmann N., Pandzic I. (1995) "Participant, User-Guided and Autonomous Actors in the Virtual Life Network VLNET", Proc. of International Conference on Artificial Reality and Tele-Existence '95, Conference on Virtual Reality Software and Technology '95 ICAT/VRST'95, Japan.

[24] Whitaker R. T., Crampton C., Breen D.E., Tuceryan M., Rose E. (1995) "Object Calibration For Augmented Reality". Computer Graphics Forum special issue of EUROGRAPHICS '95 Proceedings, *14(3), Maastricht, pp C-15-27.*

[25] Witkin A., Popovic Z. (1995) "Motion Warping", Computer Graphics Proceedings, Annual Conference Series, 1995, pp 105-108.

Editors' Note: see Appendix, p. 218f. for colored figures of this paper

A High-Level Control Mechanism for Human Locomotion Based on Parametric Frame Space Interpolation

Shang Guo
Department of Computer Science and Information Systems
Marist College, 290 North Road
Poughkeepsie, NY 12601, U.S.A.

James Robergé
Department of Computer Science
Illinois Institute of Technology
Chicago, IL 60616, U.S.A.

Abstract This paper describes a locomotion control technique for articulated figures in which new movements are interactively generated from a set of reference movements. Reference movements based on walking and running gait patterns are used to form a locomotion framework. An animator interactively specifies an envisioned movement as an interpolation between these reference movements by drawing a path within the locomotion framework and by traversing the path to produce a temporal mapping (or by applying a predefined temporal mapping). The result is a high-level locomotion control mechanism that supports real-time creation of new movements from an existing movement base.

Keywords: animation, interpolation, motion control, interpolation, parametric frame space

1 Introduction

One of the significant challenges in computer animation is the development of motion control mechanisms that are both concise and artistically expressive. Early efforts in motion control were based on the keyframing techniques used in traditional hand animation. These parametric keyframing techniques gave an animator considerable control over movement. Unfortunately, this control was obtained at the price of a laborious animation process that entailed specifying every facet of a movement at the most minute level of detail — both when the movement was initially created and each time that it was modified.

Subsequent efforts in motion control attempted to simplify the animation process by providing animators with higher-level control techniques in which movement is specified in terms of inputs to motion models — kinematic/dynamic systems, often with rule-based (or task-oriented) control structures [1, 4, 10, 13, 15]. In these models, motion control is expressed through the application of a set of constraints to a system, with different constraint sets yielding different solutions (movements).

The movements produced by these models appear quite fluid and natural. However, applying these models requires considerable computation [11], as the model must be evaluated anew as refinements are made to a movement. Equally important, significant expertise is required in order for an animator to use dynamic and goal-oriented constraints to produce a desired movement. This is particularly true when the envisioned movement includes stylized motions that are deliberately unnatural in appearance (e.g., dance movements) or physically impossible (e.g., cartoon movements). Having produced a movement that is not quite what was envisioned, an animator is faced with the challenge of modifying the model's constraints so that the movement more exactly conforms to her/his mental image. The costly process of generating a movement must then be repeated.

Because of the difficulty and cost of creating movements from the ground up, researchers have begun to explore the development of animation techniques that construct new movements from existing movements — either captured movements (motion clips) or movements produced by the locomotion models outlined above. These efforts differ in how the existing movements are blended (combined) and how the blending process is expressed by an animator [2, 6, 7, 14].

In this paper, we present a locomotion model for articulated figures that is based on parametric frame space interpolation [6, 7]. In this model, an animator defines a range of movements as a delimited two- or three-dimensional space (a parametric frame space), where a set of reference movements is used to delimit the frame space. New movements are constructed by interpolating between these reference movements. A movement's spatial elements (e.g., joint and limb positions) are specified by drawing a curve within the frame space. Traversing this curve specifies the movement's temporal elements.

The resulting locomotion control technique allows animators to specify the desired movements in measurable terms interactively, for instance, cycle specification, selection of gait pattern, or velocity requirements, and provides animators with separate control over the figure's orientation and the rhythm of the movement. The movements delimiting the frame space can be existing movements — captured or generated — or movements that isolate specific movement styles/patterns [12].

2 Parametric frame space interpolation

If we denote the total number of degrees of freedom (DOF) in an articulated figure by m, then the relative position of the figure's joints and limbs at a given moment in time can be expressed as a point P^m in an m-dimensional space

$$P^m = (a_1, a_2, ..., a_m)$$

Using the notational framework above, keyframe animation can be described as a process that begins with a sequence of points (keyframes) in m-dimensional space, $K_1^m, K_2^m, ..., K_n^m$. Taking these points as interpolated points, a position curve in m-dimensional space representing the positional component of a continuous movement can be constructed using an m-dimensional interpolation function $F(s)$, where s is the arc-length parameter. Each of the points on this curve defines a posture through which the movement must pass.

The position curve represented by the m-dimensional interpolation function F(s) can be mapped to a horizontal line segment through a parameter conversion, and vice versa (Fig.1). Let us consider the conversion from a horizontal line segment to a position curve $s = s(x)$.

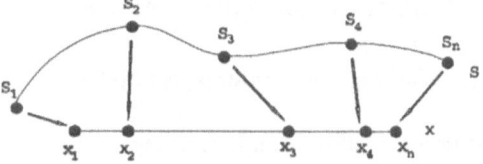

Fig. 1. Parameter conversion.

If we let the conversion be a polynomial function $s = s(x) = b_{n-1}x^{n-1} + ... + b_0$, $b_i (i = 0,1,...n-1)$ can be solved using a set of conditions $s_i = s(x_i)$ $(i = 1,2,...,n)$, where s_i is the distance from the beginning of the curve to the ith m-dimensional point K_i^m on the curve. Through the conversion, each point x on the horizontal line segment uniquely corresponds to a point on the curve in m-dimensional space. Since this conversion $s = s(x)$ is a C^∞ function, $\hat{F}(x) = F(s(x))$ preserves the continuity of the derivatives of the function F(s). For ease of discussion, let us name $\hat{F}(x)$ as F(x) again. The resulting horizontal line segment associated with F(x) is referred to as a 1-D frame space (Fig.2).

A 1-D frame space forms the parameterized positional component of a movement and is called a reference movement. The spatial interpolation function for this 1-D

Fig. 2. 1-D frame space.

space, F, is referred to as a reference interpolation function. The points x_1, x_2, ..., x_n are used as time references and paired with time moments to form a temporal component of the movement. Since this horizontal line segment is a continuum, it contains an infinite number of points and each one represents a position. Applying a temporal mapping $x = x(t)$ with a time series $\{t_i\}$ to the infinite set of positions yields a complete (reference) movement sequence $\{F(x(t_i))\}$.

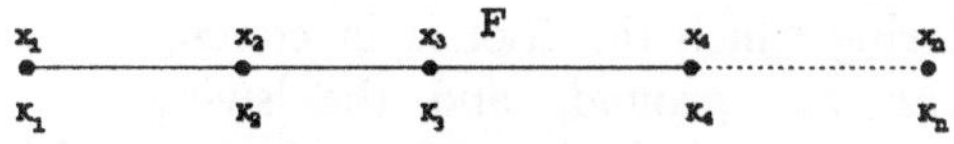

We can use these 1-D frame spaces to build higher-dimensional frame spaces and use these higher-dimensional frame spaces to generate and modify movement sequences. In general, for a point $P = (x_1,x_2,...,x_n)$ in an n-D frame space delimited by k reference movements (k 1-D frame spaces), F(P) is a linear combination (or a weighted sum) of $F_i(x_1)$ $(i = 1,2,...,k)$, where $F_1,...,F_k$ are reference interpolation functions associated with the 1-D frame spaces, x_1 is the coordinate of the 1-D frame spaces and the set of coefficients of the linear combination is determined by $x_2,...x_n$. This F, defined by the x_1 coordinate correspondence, is a mapping formula from P in a frame space to P^m, (F(P)), in m-dimensional space. Using F, any curve P(s) in a frame space can be mapped to a curve in m-dimensional space, where s is the arc-length parameter in the frame space. By applying a temporal mapping $s = s(t)$ with a time series $\{t_i\}$, a sequence of positions can be generated [6, 7].

3 A human locomotion model

3.1 Walking and running gait cycles

Human walking and running are processes of locomotion in which the cyclic pattern of movements is executed repeatedly. During the walking or running process, the support of the body is borne first on one leg and then the other [5, 8]. As the torso passes over the supporting leg, the other leg is swung forward in preparation for its next support phase.

The cycle (stride) in walking is usually divided into the stance phase, during which the foot is in contact with the ground, and the swing

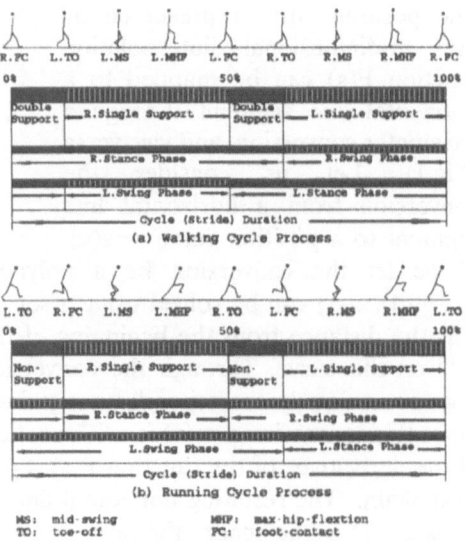

Fig. 3. Cycle process for walking and running.

phase, where the leg is brought forward before repeating the stance phase. This cycle is further divided into phases defined by specific events: mid-swing, max-hip-flexion, foot-contact, and toe-off [8] (Fig. 3a). The stance phase begins and ends with a period during which both feet are in contact with the ground and body support is transferred from one foot to the other. This phase is usually termed the "double support" phase. If we assume that the gait is symmetrical, then the two double support periods in each cycle will appear to the same.

As a person walks faster, these periods of double support become smaller and smaller fractions of the walking cycle until eventually, as a person starts to run, they disappear altogether and are replaced by brief periods when neither foot is on the ground. These periods are referred to as "non-support" phases [1, 8, 15]. These phases occur because the left toe-off occurs before the right foot-contact and the right toe-off occurs before the left foot-contact (Fig. 3b).

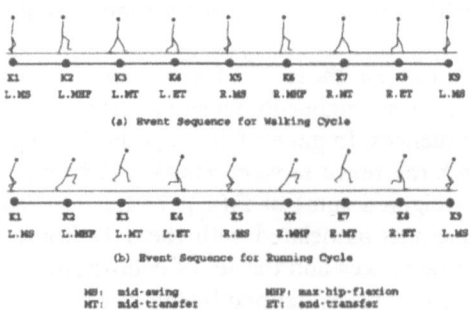

Fig. 4. A general event sequence for walking and running.

As we observed in Fig. 3, during the time that support of the body is transferred, there are three phases in both walking and running. In walking they are single support, followed by double support, and then single support again. In running, on the other hand, the middle period of transfer is a non-support phase.

For the purpose of blending these two different processes of locomotion and deriving a general event sequence for both walking and running cycles, we create a new event called mid-transfer to replace both the event toe-off in running, and the event foot-contact in walking; then we rename both the event toe-off in walking and the event foot-contact in running as the event end-transfer. This change will assist us in building the event correspondence between these two different locomotion gait patterns. In addition, we have reordered the events so that mid-swing becomes the first and last events in the cycle. This rearrangement will allow us to more easily blend one gait cycle with another, perhaps different, gait cycle (Fig. 4).

3.2 A frame space for a locomotion movement cycle

The 3-D frame space expressing the human walking/running gaits described above can be formed by using as delimiters the 1-D frame spaces that correspond to the following four gait patterns:
- Short-step walking (SW)
- Long-step walking (LW)
- Short-step running with maximum jump height (SRH)
- Long-step running with maximum jump height (LRH)

The keyframes in each of these 1-D frame spaces correspond to the events in each movement cycle (Fig. 5). The defining motions in each of the 1-D frame spaces differ in the length and height of the strides and in the body orientation during the strides.

This 3-D frame space can be embedded within the 3-D space determined by the length (L), height (H) and cycle (C) axes (Fig. 6), where the coordinate components in this frame space are interpreted as follows:

l: Stride length variable $(0 \leq l \leq 1)$
h: Stride height variable (jumping) $(0 \leq h \leq 1)$
c: Cycle variable $(0 \leq c \leq 1)$

The values $l=0$ and $l=1$ specify respectively the minimum and maximum stride length. The values $h=0$ and $h=1$ specify respectively the minimum jumping height and the maximum jumping height.

The four 1-D frame spaces already mentioned define this 3-D space and represent the four reference motions listed above:

SW: $l=0$, $h=0$, $0 \leq c \leq 1$,
LW: $l=1$, $h=0$, $0 \leq c \leq 1$,
SRH: $l=0$, $h=1$, $0 \leq c \leq 1$,

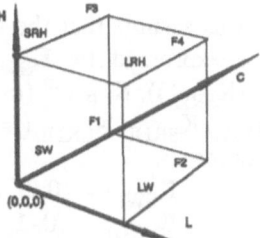

Fig. 6. A frame space for the human locomotion cycle.

LRH:　$l=1$, $h=1$, $0 \leq c \leq 1$.

Their reference interpolation functions are F_1, F_2, F_3, and F_4, respectively. (Note: c is the coordinate of 1-D frame space.)

An arbitrary point $P=(l,h,c)$ in this frame space represents the figure's position at a particular instant during a movement. If $h=0$, the gait is referred to as walking and the length of the stride is determined by l. If $0 < h \leq 1$, the gait is called running. When the figure is running, the parabolic trajectory of the body in the air can be calculated from coordinates h and l.

The gait pattern may vary from step to step during a cycle. The stride (two steps) length cannot be calculated as simply twice the step-length. A step length in a particular cycle is determined by its gait pattern. When $h>0$, the step length is the sum of three parts: the forward distance from the rear foot to the center of the body at the max-

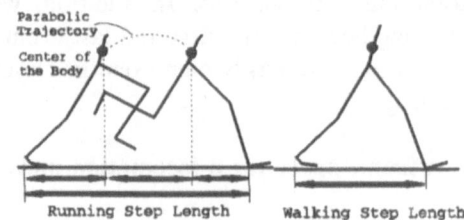

Fig. 7. (a) Running step length
(b) Walking step length.

hip-flexion event (before jumping), the forward displacement of the center of the body in the air, and the forward distance from the center of the body to the front foot at the end-transfer event (after jumping). If the h coordinate is zero, which indicates walking, the step length is the distance from the rear foot to the front foot at event mid-transfer (Fig. 7).

3.3 Event arrangement and event correspondence

A movement results from the combination of the frame space position curve and time mapping. To handle the cursor moving rate easily, the events would ideally be arranged at the points in a 1-D frame space as close as possible to the percentage of time taken in a normal locomotion cycle duration. In that case, moving the cursor at a certain uniform speed along the curve will yield a more natural locomotion sequence that matches the timing in the cycle.

Let us assume that the keyframes (events) in the four reference movement cycles are expressed by K_{SWi}^{m} (or $F_1(K_{SWi})$), K_{LWi}^{m} (or $F_2(K_{LWi})$), K_{SRHi}^{m} (or $F_3(K_{SRHi})$), K_{LRHi}^{m} (or $F_4(K_{LRHi})$) $(i=1,2,...,9)$, and are arranged at points K_{SWi}, K_{LWi}, K_{SRHi}, K_{LRHi} $(i=1,2,...,9)$ in the frame space, where:

$$K_{SWi} = (0, 0, c_{SWi}),$$
$$K_{SRHi} = (0, 1, c_{SRHi}),$$
$$K_{LWi} = (1, 0, c_{LWi}),$$
$$K_{LRHi} = (1, 1, c_{LRHi}), (i=1,2,...9).$$

Using experimental data, the c coordinates of points K_{SWi}, K_{LWi}, K_{SRHi}, K_{LRHi} ($i = 1, 2, ..., 9$) are defined as follows:

i	1	2	3	4	5	6	7	8	9
	L.MS	L.MHF	L.MT	L.ET	R.MS	R.MHF	R.MT	R.ET	L.MS
c_{SWi}:	(0.0,	0.1025,	0.2307,	0.3589,	0.5,	0.6025,	0.7307,	0.8589,	1.0)
c_{LWi}:	(0.0,	0.1333,	0.2333,	0.3333,	0.5,	0.6333,	0.7333,	0.8333,	1.0)
c_{SRHi}:	(0.0,	0.1875,	0.3438,	0.4063,	0.5,	0.6875,	0.8438,	0.9063,	1.0)
c_{LRHi}:	(0.0,	0.1429,	0.25,	0.3571,	0.5,	0.6429,	0.75,	0.8511,	1.0)

As shown in the table above, the same event in each reference movement may not have the same c coordinate in the frame space. If we are blending two or more reference movement cycles using the c coordinate correspondence, the blend will be a curious dance of uncoordinated movements in which the feet no longer strike the ground at regular intervals; indeed, they are no longer assured of striking the ground at all. For this reason, we will establish an event correspondence instead of the c coordinate correspondence to generate convincing movements. This can be done as follows: for every four events K_{SWi}^{m}, K_{LWi}^{m}, K_{SRHi}^{m}, K_{LRHi}^{m}, construct an event surface $S_i(K_{SWi} \rightarrow K_{LWi} \rightarrow K_{LRHi} \rightarrow K_{SRHi} \rightarrow K_{SWi})$. This event surface may not be planar, except for mid-swing event surfaces ($i = 1, 5, 9$). The nine event surfaces divide the space cube into eight sub-spaces SSP_i ($i = 1, 2, ..., 8$), each one being delimited by two event surfaces S_i, S_{i+1}, and by the other edge surfaces ($l = 0$, $l = 1$, $h = 0$, $h = 1$) of the frame space. Any two sub-spaces are disjoint ($SSP_i \cap SSP_j = \emptyset$, $i \neq j$), except for shared edge surfaces.

We then build the relative coordinate system for each sub-space [3]. The figure's position represented by a point P in a sub-space can be determined using relative coordinate calculations. There are two cases to consider: 1. P is on an event surface; 2. P is in a sub-space, but not on any of the event surfaces. In the first case, the position represented by the point is a linear combination of four events which form the event surface; in the second one, the position represented by the point is a linear combination of eight events which delimit the sub-space.

For an arbitrary point $P = (l, h, c)$ in a frame space, we want to know in which sub-space this point is located or on which event surface it lies. This can be done by first constructing a straight line $P_0 = (l, h, 0) \rightarrow P_1 = (l, h, 1)$ passing through P and parallel to axis C, and then getting an intersecting point (l, h, c_j) with each event surface S_j, where $c_j = (1-l) \cdot ((1-h) \cdot c_{SWj} + c_{SRHj}) + l \cdot ((1-h) \cdot c_{LWj} + c_{LRHj})$, $j = 1, 2, ... 9$ (Fig. 8). After determining the location of P, we can derive a new mapping formula, F(P) or P^m, based on event correspondence.

If P is on one of the event surfaces, that is, $c = c_j$, then the mapping is defined as follows:
$$P^m = F(P) = a_1 \cdot F_1(K_{SWi}) + a_2 \cdot F_2(K_{LWi}) + a_3 \cdot F_3(K_{SRHi}) + a_4 \cdot F_4(K_{LRHi})$$
where:

$a_1 = (1-l) \cdot (1-h)$

$a_2 = l \cdot (1-h)$

$a_3 = (1-l) \cdot h$

$$a_4 = 1 \cdot h$$

If P is in a sub-space, that is, $c_i < c < c_{i+1}$, then the mapping is

$$
\begin{aligned}
P^m = F(P) &= a_1 \cdot F_1(K_{SWi}) + a_2 \cdot F_2(K_{LWi}) \\
&+ a_3 \cdot F_3(K_{SRHi}) + a_4 \cdot F_4(K_{LRHi}) \\
&+ b_1 \cdot F_1(K_{SWi+1}) + b_2 \cdot F_2(K_{LWi+1}) \\
&+ b_3 \cdot F_3(K_{SRHi+1}) + b_4 \cdot F_4(K_{LRHi+1})
\end{aligned}
$$

where:

$$
\begin{aligned}
a_1 &= ((c_{i+1}-c)/(c_{i+1}-c_i)) \cdot (1-l) \cdot (1-h) \\
a_2 &= ((c_{i+1}-c)/(c_{i+1}-c_i)) \cdot l \cdot (1-h) \\
a_3 &= ((c_{i+1}-c)/(c_{i+1}-c_i)) \cdot (1-l) \cdot h \\
a_4 &= ((c_{i+1}-c)/(c_{i+1}-c_i)) \cdot l \cdot h \\
b_1 &= ((c-c_i)/(c_{i+1}-c_i)) \cdot (1-l) \cdot (1-h) \\
b_2 &= ((c-c_i)/(c_{i+1}-c_i)) \cdot l \cdot (1-h) \\
b_3 &= ((c-c_i)/(c_{i+1}-c_i)) \cdot (1-l) \cdot h \\
b_4 &= ((c-c_i)/(c_{i+1}-c_i)) \cdot l \cdot h
\end{aligned}
$$

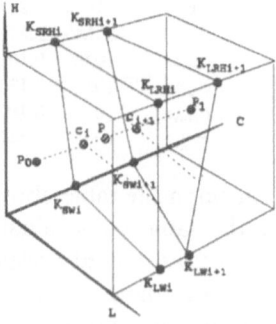

Fig. 8. The location of point P in the frame space.

3.4 Specifying and controlling movements in the extended frame space

Using the above described cycle frame space as a unit, we can construct a frame space of infinite length (an infinite number of cycles) by concatenating cycle frame spaces (Fig. 9). This construction never increases the animator's burden,

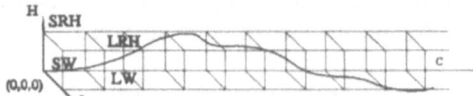

Fig. 9. A position curve defined in the frame space.

because the number of keyframes inputed is fixed, that is, the keyframes for one cycle. The resulting frame space, in turn, allows us to produce a wide range of human locomotion movements between walking and running by specifying a continuous position curve in the frame space.

For a given position curve, the rhythm of a movement can be determined and manipulated by the speed of a cursor moving along the curve, since the speed decides the density of sample points picked from the curve. This control method in a regular 3-D frame space is not as easy to handle as it is in 2-D frame space using a mouse (2-D input device) in real-time. The scheme of controlling a movement in 3-D locomotion frame space is quite different than in other regular 3-D frame spaces, since a position curve defined in the locomotion frame space is strictly increasing with regard to the variable c and a locomotion movement control is usually expressed in terms of cycles. A linear time mapping does not necessarily generate a linear cycle rate, and vice versa, unless the position curve is linearly related to axis C. For this reason, the user can only control the speed of the cursor moving along axis C to yield the corresponding time mapping on the curve.

A cycle has two dimensions: the time period from beginning to end and the stride length, the distance the body moves during the cycle. Changes in speed can be made by adjusting either the stride length or the step frequency [8]. Let us examine some features of position curves, time mappings and movement sequences generated by changing these parameters.

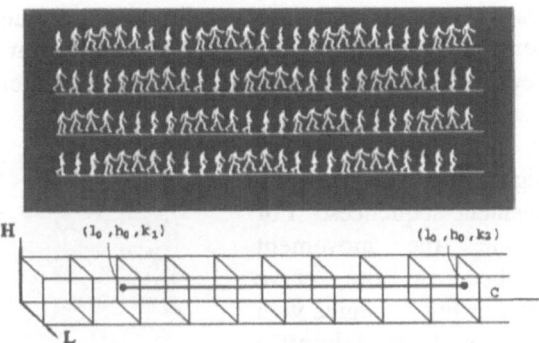

Fig. 10. A rhythmic position curve defined in the frame space.

If a position curve is an arbitrary straight line parallel to axis C ($l = l_0$, $h = h_0$, $k_1 < = c < = k_2$) as shown in Fig. 10, this position curve represents a rhythmic movement which never changes the gait pattern and which keeps cycles identical. This curve is known as a rhythmic gait position curve. Using a time mapping generated from a constant cycle rate ($dc/dt = k$, where k is a positive constant), the position curve associated with the time mapping will result in a rhythmic movement.

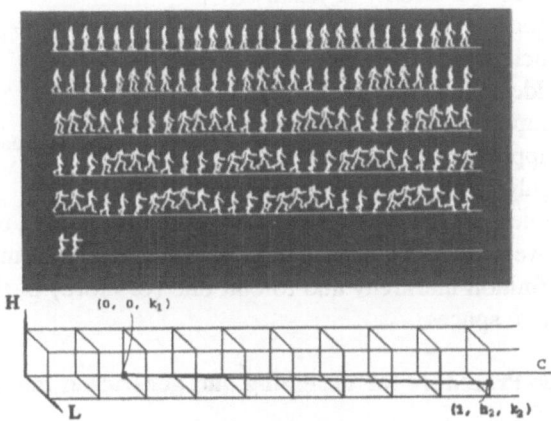

Fig. 11. A position curve defined in a frame space for an acceleration movement.

If a position curve is a straight line beginning at a smaller stride length l_1 ($= 0$) and ending at a larger stride length l_2 ($= 1$) shown in Fig. 11, an acceleration process may be produced using either the constant cycle rate ($dc/dt = k$, $k > 0$) or an accelerated cycle rate ($d^2c/dt^2 > 0$). As the movement progresses, the stride length becomes longer and longer. As a result, the figure will appear to move faster, as well as farther, with each step.

Using this technique, it is easy and intuitive to use a position curve to express the usual sequence of human locomotion, which consists of three distinct phases: development, rhythmic and decay [8] (Fig. 12).

104

These two dimensions, time and distance, are fundamental parameters that largely determine the patterns of motion of a particular gait. Within the range of usual speeds, normal human motion represents changes in both dimensions.

The animator can readily design and create the movement sequences. For example, the movement described by the curve shown in Fig. 9 begins with short, low strides (almost a shuffle); continues with short, higher strides (in the style of a drum major); progresses to long, high strides (a Monty Python-esque "silly walk"); and concludes with long, low strides (a brisk walk). By composing a proper time mapping with the curve, a highly stylized movement sequence can be produced.

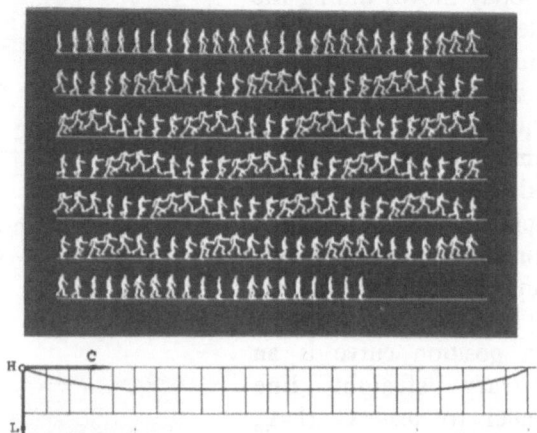

Fig. 12. The usual sequence of human locomotion.

An animator wishing to modify a facet of the resulting movement at the lowest level of detail is free to move down within the movement definition hierarchy and to edit one (or more) of the positions that define the 1-D frame spaces.

3.5 Procedure for designing and generating movement sequences

Step 1. Build an extended frame space.

Step 2. The structural description of movement can be given in clearly defined and measurable terms, for instance, cycle specification, selection of gait pattern, or velocity requirements. These specifications can then be interpreted as a set of points in the frame space (Fig. 13):

$$(l_{k,1}, h_{k,1}, c_{k,1}), (l_{k,2}, h_{k,2}, c_{k,2}), \dots, (l_{k,n}, h_{k,n}, c_{k,n}).$$

Step 3. Using these points as the interpolated points, a position curve, $P\_C(l,h,c)$, is generated by using a cubic B-spline as an interpolation function. Some adjustments may be needed to confine it within the space. As a result, this position curve passes through all the key points (Fig. 13).

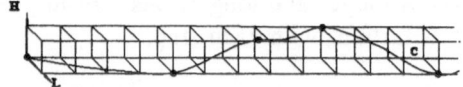

Fig. 13. A position curve passing through all key points converted from the movement specifications.

Step 4. Now we need to assign a time mapping on the curve. Let us rename the beginning of the position curve $(l_{k,1}, h_{k,1}, c_{k,1})$ as (l_1, h_1, c_1), which is the first sample point. There are two ways to determine a next sample point (l_2, h_2, c_2) on the curve.

The first approach lets the user control the time mapping: he simply moves the mouse along the C axis to generate the timing. The rate dc/dt (cycles/sec) at which the mouse moves, associated with the time series $\{t_i\}$, generates $\{c_i\}$, $i = 2, 3, ...$ For each c_i, a corresponding (l_i, h_i) is found on the curve. The resulting points $\{(l_i, h_i, c_i)\}$, $i = 1, 2, ...$, are the required sample points. This method is useful when the user wants to generate more artistic or exaggerated results.

The second approach assigns a timing automatically according to rules adopted in the normal human locomotion process. For example, from experimental data on walking [8, 9], step_frequency (steps/sec) is expressed as:

$$\text{step\_frequency} = \text{step\_length}/(\text{body\_height}*0.004*60).$$

From display_frequency (frames/sec) and step_frequency, we get the increment of c, Δc_1, at c_1,

$$\Delta c_1 = \text{step\_frequency}/(2*\text{display\_frequency})$$
$$= \text{step\_length}/(\text{body\_height}*0.48*\text{display\_frequency}).$$

Thus, $c_2 = c_1 + \Delta c_1$. Similarly, from c_2, get Δc_2, then c_3... For each c_i, (l_i, h_i) is found. Repeat this process until the end of curve.

For each sample point (l_i, h_i, c_i), a frame is calculated and displayed on the screen.

Step 5. View the frame sequence and make desired changes (go back to Step 4 if necessary).

Step 6. Render the figure in each frame.

Figures 14, 15 and 16 show results created by this system which has been developed from the human locomotion model.

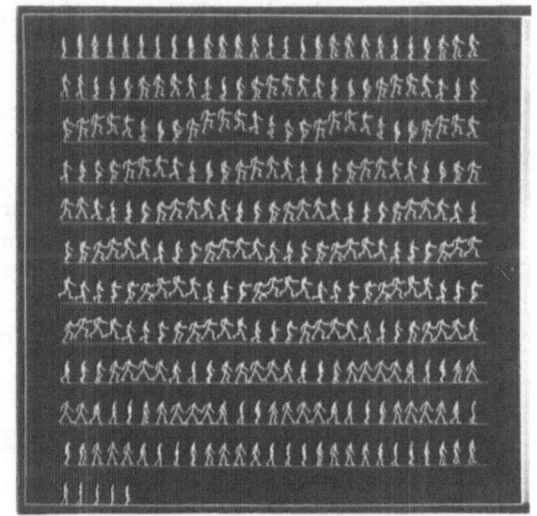

Fig. 14. A locomotion movement sequence with 20 cycles combining a variety of gait patterns.

4 Conclusions and future work

We have presented a high level control mechanism for human locomotion based on parametric frame space interpolation. The main contribution of this mechanism is to provide a means of specifying and controlling locomotion (the natural or the artistically stylized appearance) at a higher level of abstraction than conventional systems support. In our system, the animator is provided with a convenient user interface and powerful tools for interactively editing, designing and modifying high-quality movement sequences.

This locomotion model has significant potential applications. We envision extending this model to integrate dynamics techniques and use motion-captured data rather than keyframing to construct 1-D frame spaces for the purpose of producing more realistic, natural and coordinated human movements in the future.

Acknowledgments

Thanks to Helen Hayes for her support and encouragement. This work was supported by the Marist College Summer Research Grant and the SERF Grant.

References

1. Bruderlin, A. and Calvert, T. "Goal-Directed, Dynamic Animation of Human Walking," Computer Graphics, Vol. 23, No. 3, pp. 233-242, 1989.

2. Bruderlin, A. and Williams, L., "Motion Signal Processing," ACM SIGGRAPH '95, pp. 97-104, 1995.

3. Burtnyk, A. and Wein, M., "Interactive Skeleton Techniques for Enhancing Motion Dynamica in Key Frame Animation," Tutorial: Computer Graphics, Beatty, J. and Booth, K.(eds.), IEEE Computer Society, pp. 516-521, 1982.

4. Cohen, M. "Interactive Spacetime Control for Animation," ACM SIGGRAPH '92, pp. 293-303, 1992.

5. Dagg, A., Running, walking and Jumping, The science of Locomotion," Wykeham Publications Ltd. 1977.

6. Guo, S. An Approach to Computer Keyframe Animation Incorporating Motion Control: Parametric Keyframe Space Interpolation, Ph. D. Thesis, Illinois Institute of Technology, 1992.

7. Guo, S., Robergé, J., and Grace, T. "Controlling Movement Using Parametric Frame Space Interpolation," Models and Techniques in Computer Animation, Magnenat-Thalmann N., Thalmann D.(eds.), Springer-Verlag, pp. 216-227, 1993.

8. Inman, V., Ralston, H., and Todd, F. Human Walking, Williams & Wilkins, Baltimore, 1981.

9. Loizidou, S. and Clapworth, G., "Legged Locomotion Using HIDDS," Models and Techniques in Computer Animation, Magnenat-Thalmann N., Thalmann D. (eds.), Springer-Verlag, pp. 257-269, 1993.

10. Phillips, C., Zhao, J. and Badler, N. "Interactive Real-time Articulated Figure Manipulation Using Multiple Kinematic Constraints," ACM SIGGRAPH '90, pp. 245-250, 1990.

11. Thalmann, D., "Motion Control: From Keyframe to Task-Level Animation," State of the Art in Computer Animation, Magnenat-Thalmann D.(eds.), Springer-Verlag, pp.3-17, 1989

12. Unuma, M., Anjyo, K., and Takeuchi, R., "Fourier Principles for Emotion-based Human Figure Animation," ACM SIGGRAPH '95, pp. 91-96, 1995.

13. Witkin, A. and Kass, M. "Spacetime Constraints," ACM SIGGRAPH '88, pp. 159-168, 1988.

14. Witkin, A. and Popovic, Z., "Motion Warping," ACM SIGGRAPH '95, pp. 105-108, 1995.

15. Zeltzer, D. "Motor Control Techniques of Figure Animation," IEEE Computer Graphics and Applications, Vol. 2, No. 9, pp. 53-59, 1982.

Editors' Note: see Appendix, p. 220 for colored figures of this paper

Simulating Human Movements Using Optimal Control

Xinmin Zhao, Deepak Tolani, Bond-Jay Ting, and Norman I. Badler
xzhao@graphics.cis.upenn.edu, tolani@graphics.cis.upenn.edu,
ting@graphics.cis.upenn.edu, badler@central.cis.upenn.edu

Abstract

This paper presents an optimization based technique for solving optimal control problems. Unlike the spacetime constraint approach which discretizes both the state and control variables, our method transforms the optimal control problem into an optimization task that depends only upon the control variables. Using a spline to represent the control trajectory, we derive an efficient, analytic technique for computing the gradient of the objective function in terms of the spline control points. Our approach has the advantage of reducing the number of unknowns and ensuring consistency between the state and control variables. We demonstrate the viability of our algorithm by using it to simulate a human figure performing a high jump.

Animations: http://www.cis.upenn.edu/~ting/optimalcontrol.html

1 Motivation

Physics-based simulation has gained popularity in computer animation as a technique for generating realistic looking motions. In a physics-based approach, the motion of an object is computed automatically as a function of its physical properties and the external forces acting on it. If the forces acting on an object are completely specified throughout the course of the simulation, the object's position and velocity can be computed by integrating the equations of motion over time. Mathematically, this is known as an initial value problem since the starting state is completely known and the next and subsequent states can be computed from results obtained during the previous time step. This approach is feasible for simple or passive systems, but it suffers from lack of control as it is virtually impossible for the user to guess the forces required to drive an object through a desired path.

Alternatively, a more flexible and intuitive scheme is to allow the animator to specify the position and velocity of the object at key points in time and a set of constraints that must be satisfied throughout the simulation. Since there will generally be an infinite number of feasible solutions for the force trajectory, an additional optimization criteria, such as minimization of work or energy, must be used to select the "best" solution.

Witkin and Kass were among the first to treat physics-based animations in this fashion [13]. They called their approach spacetime constraints to emphasize the fact that the unknowns of the system are solved at all time steps simultaneously instead of sequentially as in the initial value case. Cohen added further refinements to spacetime constraints by introducing the concept of windows that divide the problem into more manageable subproblems, and an interactive user interface that allows the animator to assist the optimizer [4] [7].

The spacetime constraint approach can be viewed as a type of optimal control problem. Explicit uses of optimal control in computer animation include the work of Brotman and Netravali [1] who used a minimum external control energy criteria to perform motion interpolation between frames. Kearney et. al [6] used a cascaded-gain controller to approximate optimal control solutions for throwing and striking motions.

In this paper we introduce an alternative technique to spacetime constraints for converting optimal control problems into constrained optimization problems. Given the gradient of the objective function, the converted optimization problem can be solved using a standard nonlinear programming solver. The major focus of the paper is to present an efficient, analytic method for computing the gradient.

2 Approach

2.1 Problem formulation and solution

Consider a dynamic system governed by the following equation

$$\dot{\mathbf{y}}(t) = \mathbf{f}(t, \mathbf{y}(t), \mathbf{u}(t)).$$

where $\mathbf{y}(t)$ is a $n \times 1$ state vector that describes the system at time t, $\mathbf{u}(t)$ is a $m \times 1$ control vector of control inputs. Assume the initial state of the system $\mathbf{y}(t_0) = \mathbf{y}_0$ is given. The optimal control problem is to find a control trajectory $\mathbf{u}^*(t)$ that minimizes the scalar function

$$J(\mathbf{y}, \mathbf{u}) = l(t_f, \mathbf{y}(t_f)) + \int_{t_o}^{t_f} \eta(t, \mathbf{y}, \mathbf{u})dt \tag{1}$$

subject to the constraints

$$\begin{aligned} \phi(t, \mathbf{y}, \mathbf{u}) &= 0 \\ \psi(t, \mathbf{y}, \mathbf{u}) &\leq 0. \end{aligned}$$

For the purposes of our analysis, it is convenient to transform equation (1) into Mayer form

$$J(\mathbf{y}_{t_f}, t_f) = \sigma(\mathbf{y}_{t_f}, t_f)$$

where $\mathbf{y}_{t_f}$ denotes $\mathbf{y}(t_f)$. The transformation is achieved by augmenting $\mathbf{y}$ with another state variable y_{n+1} defined by

$$\dot{y}_{n+1}(t) = \eta(t, \mathbf{y}, \mathbf{u}), \quad y_{n+1}(t_0) = 0$$

and

$$\sigma(\mathbf{y}_{t_f}, t_f) = l(t_f, \mathbf{y}_{t_f}) + y_{n+1}(t_f).$$

We now present a numerical scheme for solving $\mathbf{u}^*(t)$. Our approach is similar to the "control parameterization" method [5] in that the state variables are eliminated and the problem is cast into a form that involves only the control variables. In this approach, $\mathbf{u}(t)$ is approximated with a m-dimensional polynomial spline

$$\mathbf{u}(t) \approx \bar{\mathbf{u}}(t) = \Sigma_{i=0}^{N} B_i(t)\mathbf{u}_i$$

where $\mathbf{u}_0, \mathbf{u}_1, ...\mathbf{u}_N$ are the control points and $B_0(t), ..., B_N(t)$ are the basis functions. In principle, any set of basis functions can be used. However to keep the analysis simple, we use uniform linear hat functions defined by

$$B_i(t) = \left\{ \begin{array}{ll} (t - t_{i-1})/h & t_{i-1} \leq t < t_i \\ (t_{i+1} - t)/h & t_i \leq t < t_{i+1} \\ 0 & otherwise \end{array} \right.$$

where $h = \frac{t_f - t_0}{N}, t_i = t_o + ih$. Note that the i-th control point $\mathbf{u}_i$ affects the spline only in the interval $[t_{i-1}, t_{i+1})$.

Using our spline approximation for $\mathbf{u}(t)$, we can approximate $\mathbf{y}(t)$ and J as a function of the control points $\mathbf{u}_i$

$$\mathbf{y}(t) \approx \bar{\mathbf{y}}(t, \mathbf{y}_0, \mathbf{u}_0, \mathbf{u}_1, ...\mathbf{u}_N) = \int_{t_o}^{t} \mathbf{f}(x, \mathbf{y}(x), \mathbf{u}(x, \mathbf{u}_0, \mathbf{u}_1, ...\mathbf{u}_N))\, dx + \mathbf{y}_o$$
$$J(\mathbf{y}(t_f)) \approx \bar{J}(\mathbf{y}(t, \mathbf{y}_0, \mathbf{u}_0, \mathbf{u}_1, ...\mathbf{u}_N)).$$

In the discussion that follows $\mathbf{u}$, $\mathbf{y}$, and J are used to denote the spline-based approximations $\bar{\mathbf{u}}, \bar{\mathbf{y}}$, and $\bar{J}$ rather than the original functions.

In order to minimize J as a function of the control points, it is necessary to find the gradient of J with respect to $\mathbf{u}_i$. In the derivation that follows we will assume a piecewise linear basis for $\mathbf{u}$. Derivations for higher order splines can be obtained in a similar fashion.

Applying the chain rule gives

$$\left(\frac{\partial J}{\partial \mathbf{u}_i}\right) = \left(\frac{\partial \mathbf{y}_{t_f}}{\partial \mathbf{u}_i}\right)^T \left(\frac{\partial J}{\partial \mathbf{y}_{t_f}}\right). \tag{2}$$

$\frac{\partial J}{\partial \mathbf{y}_{t_f}}$ is determined by symbolic differentiation. In order to derive a formula for $\frac{\partial \mathbf{y}_{t_f}}{\partial \mathbf{u}_i}$ we apply the chain rule repeatedly

$$
\begin{aligned}
\frac{\partial \mathbf{y}_{t_f}}{\partial \mathbf{u}_i} &= \left(\frac{\partial \mathbf{y}_{t_f}}{\partial \mathbf{y}_{i+1}}\right)\left(\frac{\partial \mathbf{y}_{i+1}}{\partial \mathbf{u}_i}\right) \\
&= \left(\frac{\partial \mathbf{y}_N}{\partial \mathbf{y}_{i+1}}\right)\left(\frac{\partial \mathbf{y}_{i+1}}{\partial \mathbf{u}_i}\right) \\
&= \left(\frac{\partial \mathbf{y}_N}{\partial \mathbf{y}_{N-1}}\right)\left(\frac{\partial \mathbf{y}_{N-1}}{\partial \mathbf{y}_{N-2}}\right)\cdots\left(\frac{\partial \mathbf{y}_{i+2}}{\partial \mathbf{y}_{i+1}}\right)\left(\frac{\partial \mathbf{y}_{i+1}}{\partial \mathbf{u}_i}\right).
\end{aligned}
\tag{3}
$$

To evaluate (3) we need expressions for $\frac{\partial \mathbf{y}_{k+1}}{\partial \mathbf{y}_k}$ and $\frac{\partial \mathbf{y}_{k+1}}{\partial \mathbf{u}_k}$. In order to derive these expressions we make use of the fact that we can view $\mathbf{y}(t)$ as a function of $\mathbf{y}_i \equiv \mathbf{y}(t_i)$

$$
\mathbf{y}(t) = \mathbf{y}_i + \int_{t_i}^{t} \mathbf{f}(x, \mathbf{y}(x), \mathbf{u}(x))dx \qquad t > t_i.
\tag{4}
$$

Setting $t = t_{i+1}$ and taking the partial with respect to $\mathbf{y}_i$ leads to

$$
\frac{\partial \mathbf{y}_{i+1}}{\partial \mathbf{y}_i} = \left.\frac{\partial \mathbf{y}}{\partial \mathbf{y}_i}\right|_{t=t_{i+1}} = \mathbf{I}_{n\times n} + \int_{t_i}^{t_{i+1}}\left(\frac{\partial \mathbf{f}}{\partial \mathbf{y}}\right)\left(\frac{\partial \mathbf{y}}{\partial \mathbf{y}_i}\right)dx.
\tag{5}
$$

Similarly, taking the partial of (4) with respect to $\mathbf{u}_i$ leads to

$$
\begin{aligned}
\frac{\partial \mathbf{y}_{i+1}}{\partial \mathbf{u}_i} &= \left.\frac{\partial \mathbf{y}_i}{\partial \mathbf{u}_i}\right|_{t_i} + \int_{t_i}^{t_{i+1}}\left[\left(\frac{\partial \mathbf{f}}{\partial \mathbf{y}}\right)\left(\frac{\partial \mathbf{y}}{\partial \mathbf{u}_i}\right) + \left(\frac{\partial \mathbf{f}}{\partial \mathbf{u}}\right)\left(\frac{\partial \mathbf{u}}{\partial \mathbf{u}_i}\right)\right]dx \\
\left.\frac{\partial \mathbf{y}_i}{\partial \mathbf{u}_i}\right|_{t_i} &= \underbrace{\left.\frac{\partial \mathbf{y}_{i-1}}{\partial \mathbf{u}_i}\right|_{t_{i-1}}}_{0} + \int_{t_{i-1}}^{t_i}\left[\left(\frac{\partial \mathbf{f}}{\partial \mathbf{y}}\right)\left(\frac{\partial \mathbf{y}}{\partial \mathbf{u}_i}\right) + \left(\frac{\partial \mathbf{f}}{\partial \mathbf{u}}\right)\left(\frac{\partial \mathbf{u}}{\partial \mathbf{u}_i}\right)\right]dx.
\end{aligned}
\tag{6}
$$

The matrices $\frac{\partial \mathbf{f}}{\partial \mathbf{y}}$ and $\frac{\partial \mathbf{f}}{\partial \mathbf{u}}$ are determined by symbolic differentiation. The value of $\frac{\partial \mathbf{u}}{\partial \mathbf{u}_i}$ depends on the type of spline used to approximate $\mathbf{u}(t)$. For the piecewise linear spline described previously, $\frac{\partial \mathbf{u}}{\partial \mathbf{u}_i}$ is given by

$$
\begin{aligned}
\mathbf{u}(t) &= \mathbf{u}_i + (\mathbf{u}_{i+1} - \mathbf{u}_i)\left(\frac{t - t_i}{h}\right); t \in [t_i, t_{i+1}) \\
\frac{\partial \mathbf{u}}{\partial \mathbf{u}_i} &= \begin{cases} \frac{t-t_{i-1}}{h} & t \in [t_{i-1}, t_i) \\ 1 - \frac{t-t_i}{h} & t \in [t_i, t_{i+1}) \\ 0 & otherwise \end{cases}
\end{aligned}
$$

Note that equations (4),(5) and (6) represent the integral analogies of initial value problems and they must be evaluated using an ODE solver. The results are then substituted into equations (3) and (2) to obtain $\frac{\partial J}{\partial \mathbf{u}_i}$.

2.2 Analytic versus Finite difference gradients

In the previous section, we derived an analytical formula for the Jacobian matrix $\frac{\partial \mathbf{y}_{t_f}}{\partial \mathbf{u}_i}$. Alternatively, we could compute $\frac{\partial \mathbf{y}_{t_f}}{\partial \mathbf{u}_i}$ using a finite difference formula

$$\frac{\partial \mathbf{y}_{t_f}}{\partial \mathbf{u}_i} \approx \frac{\mathbf{y}_{t_f}(..., \mathbf{u}_i + \delta \mathbf{u}_i, ...) - \mathbf{y}_{t_f}(..., \mathbf{u}_i - \delta \mathbf{u}_i, ...)}{2\delta \mathbf{u}_i}$$

which would eliminate the need for the tedious derivations given in equations (2), (3), (4), (5) and (6). Moreover the finite difference method only requires integrating $\mathbf{y}$ whereas the analytic formula requires integrating $\mathbf{y}, \frac{\partial \mathbf{f}}{\partial \mathbf{y}} \frac{\partial \mathbf{y}}{\partial \mathbf{y}_i}$, and $\frac{\partial \mathbf{f}}{\partial \mathbf{y}} \frac{\partial \mathbf{y}}{\partial \mathbf{u}_i}$.

However, the analytic formula is more accurate than the finite difference approximation. An adaptive step integrator, like the one used in our implementation ($bsstep$ [11]), allows the user to specify any desired level of precision. On the other hand, the accuracy of a finite difference approximation depends on selecting a suitable magnitude for $\delta \mathbf{u}_i$ based on the precision of $\mathbf{y}_{t_f}$. Since $\mathbf{y}_{t_f}$ is computed by integration, at best only an upper-bound on the global error can be obtained which makes it difficult to reliably select a good value for $\delta \mathbf{u}_i$.

Another advantage of the analytic formula is that it can be considerably less expensive to compute. The finite difference approximation requires evaluating $\mathbf{y}_{t_f}$ by integrating over the interval $[t_0, t_f]$ for $2N * m$ sets of control points. If we count an integration over the interval $[t_0, t_f]$ as a single operation, the total cost of computing the Jacobian with the finite difference method is $O(N*n*m)$. Of course in a clever implementation, one can take advantage of the fact that

$$\int_{t_0}^{t_f} \mathbf{f}(..., \mathbf{u}_{i+1} + \delta \mathbf{u}_{i+1}, ...)dt = \int_{t_0}^{t_i} \mathbf{f}(..., \mathbf{u}_i, ...)dt + \int_{t_{i+1}}^{t_f} \mathbf{f}(..., \mathbf{u}_{i+1} + \delta \mathbf{u}_{i+1}, ...)dt$$

to effectively reduce the amount of computation by a factor of two, but the order of the time complexity remains unchanged.

The analytic formula requires evaluating $\mathbf{y}_{t_f}$ once at a cost of $O(n)$ integrations, and the computation of $\left(\frac{\partial \mathbf{y}_N}{\partial \mathbf{y}_{N-1}}\right), ..., \left(\frac{\partial \mathbf{y}_2}{\partial \mathbf{y}_1}\right)$ and $\left(\frac{\partial \mathbf{y}_2}{\partial \mathbf{u}_1}\right), ..., \left(\frac{\partial \mathbf{y}_N}{\partial \mathbf{u}_{N-1}}\right)$. To compute $\left(\frac{\partial \mathbf{y}_N}{\partial \mathbf{y}_{N-1}}\right), ..., \left(\frac{\partial \mathbf{y}_2}{\partial \mathbf{y}_1}\right)$ we evaluate equation (4) N times. Note that each of these integrals is only over the range $[t_i, t_{i+1}]$. Therefore, irrespective of the size of N the total interval of the sum of these integrations is $[t_0, t_f]$ and the cost of this step is only $O(n*n)$. Similarly, $\left(\frac{\partial \mathbf{y}_2}{\partial \mathbf{u}_1}\right), ..., \left(\frac{\partial \mathbf{y}_N}{\partial \mathbf{u}_{N-1}}\right)$ can be computed by evaluating equation (5) N times at a cost of $O(n * m)$. Thus, the total time complexity for the analytic scheme is $O(n * (m + n))$ and is independent of N.

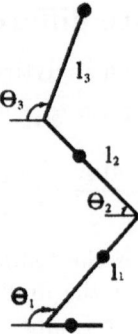

Figure 1: Dynamics Model of the Human Body

3   Implementation

In summary, by approximating the control function as a piecewise spline of $N+1$ control points $(\mathbf{u}_0, ..., \mathbf{u}_N)$, the optimal control problem

$$\min \quad J(\mathbf{y}, \mathbf{u}) = l(t_f, \mathbf{y}(t_f)) + \int_{t_o}^{t_f} m(t, \mathbf{y}, \mathbf{u})dt$$

$$\phi(t, \mathbf{y}, \mathbf{u}) = 0$$
$$\psi(t, \mathbf{y}, \mathbf{u}) \leq 0$$

can be rewritten as a multi-variable optimization problem of the form

$$\min J(\mathbf{u}_0, ..., \mathbf{u}_N)$$
$$\phi(\mathbf{u}_0, ..., \mathbf{u}_N) = 0$$
$$\psi(\mathbf{u}_0, ..., \mathbf{u}_N) \leq 0.$$

The analytic gradient $\frac{\partial J}{\partial \mathbf{u}_i}$ is given by equations (2), (3), (4), (5) and (6), and the optimization problem can be solved using any constrained nonlinear programming package. Note that state constraints can be handled by converting them into constraints on the control input. In our particular implementation we used $LBFGSB$ ([2]). To integrate the terms required to compute the gradient we used the $bsstep$ subroutine from "Numerical Recipes in C" [11].

4   Example

We have used an implementation of our algorithm to simulate a human figure performing a high jump. Figure 1 depicts a simplified version of a model of the human body used in [8]. It is a planar model consisting of four links representing the foot, the lower and upper legs, and the torso. There are three degrees of freedom θ_1, θ_2, and θ_3 denoting the ankle, knee and hip joints respectively. The corresponding joint torques are identified as τ_1, τ_2 , and τ_3. The dynamics of the system are defined by

$$\mathbf{A}\ddot{\mathbf{q}} = \mathbf{B}\dot{\mathbf{q}}^2 + \mathbf{C} + \mathbf{D}\tau$$
$$\ddot{\mathbf{q}}(t) = \mathbf{A}^{-1}(\mathbf{B}\dot{\mathbf{q}}^2 + \mathbf{C} + \mathbf{D}\tau)$$

where

$$\mathbf{q} = [\theta_1, \theta_2, \theta_3]^T, \quad \dot{\mathbf{q}}^2 = \left[\dot{\theta}_1^2, \dot{\theta}_2^2, \dot{\theta}_3^2\right]^T, \quad \tau = [\tau_1, \tau_2, \tau_3]^T$$

$$c_{ij} = \cos(\theta_i - \theta_j), \quad s_{ij} = \sin(\theta_i - \theta_j)$$

$$c_1 = m_1 lc_1 + (m_2 + m_3 + m_4)l_1, \quad c_2 = m_2 lc_2 + (m_3 + m_4)l_2$$

$$c_3 = m_3 lc_3 + m_4 l_3, \quad c_4 = m_4 lc_4$$

$$a_{11} = I_1 + m_1 lc_1^2 + (m_2 + m_3)l_1^2, \quad a_{22} = I_2 + m_2 lc_2^2 + m_3 l_2^2$$

$$a_{33} = I_3 + m_3 lc_3^2, \quad a_{12} = c_2 l_1, \quad a_{13} = c_3 l_1, \quad a_{23} = c_3 l_2$$

$$\mathbf{A} = \begin{bmatrix} a_{11} & a_{12}c_{21} & a_{13}c_{31} \\ a_{12}c_{21} & a_{22} & a_{23}c_{23} \\ a_{13}c_{31} & a_{23}c_{23} & a_{33} \end{bmatrix}, \quad \mathbf{C} = \begin{bmatrix} -c_1 g \cos(\theta_1) \\ -c_2 g \cos(\theta_2) \\ -c_3 g \cos(\theta_3) \end{bmatrix}$$

$$\mathbf{B} = \begin{bmatrix} 0 & a_{12}s_{21} & -a_{13}s_{13} \\ -a_{12}s_{21} & 0 & -a_{23}s_{23} \\ a_{13}s_{13} & a_{23}s_{23} & 0 \end{bmatrix}, \quad \mathbf{D} = \begin{bmatrix} 1 & -1 & 0 \\ 0 & 1 & -1 \\ 0 & 0 & 1 \end{bmatrix}.$$

The dynamics parameters used in our simulation, taken from [10], are shown below:

Link Mass (kg)	$m_1 = 7.5$	$m_2 = 15.15$	$m_3 = 51.22$
Link Inertia ($kg \cdot m^2$)	$I_1 = .065$	$I_2 = .126$	$I_3 = 6.814$
Link Length (m)	$l_1 = .435$	$l_2 = .400$	$l_3 = .343$
Link Center of Mass (m)	$lc_1 = .274$	$lc_2 = .251$	$lc_3 = .343$
Min Joint Torque ($nt \cdot m$)	$\tau_{min,1} = -200$	$\tau_{min,2} = -300$	$\tau_{min,3} = -300$
Max Joint Torque ($nt \cdot m$)	$\tau_{max,1} = 200$	$\tau_{max,2} = 300$	$\tau_{max,3} = 300$

Assume that the starting posture of the human figure, $\mathbf{q}(t_0)$ and $\dot{\mathbf{q}}(t_0)$, is given. In this example, the goal is to compute the function $\tau(t)$ that maximizes the jump height subject to bounded constraints on the joint torques.

Let $h(t_f)$ and $\dot{h}(t_f)$ represent the vertical position and velocity of the center of mass of the torso link at the take-off time t_f. Assuming that $\dot{h}(t_f) > 0$, the maximum height achieved by the center of mass can be computed as

$$H = h(t_f) + \dot{h}(t_f)^2/(2 * g)$$

where g is the gravity constant and h, $\dot{h}$, $q(t_f)$ and $\dot{q}(t_f)$ are

$$
\begin{aligned}
h(t_f) &= l_1 sin(\theta_1(t_f)) + l_2 sin(\theta_2(t_f)) + lc_3 sin(\theta_3(t_f)) \\
\dot{h}(t_f) &= l_1 cos(\theta_1(t_f))\dot{\theta}_1(t_f) + l_2 cos(\theta_2(t_f))\dot{\theta}_2(t_f) + lc_3 cos(\theta_3(t_f))\dot{\theta}_3(t_f) \\
\dot{q}(t_f) &= \left[\dot{\theta}_1, \dot{\theta}_2, \dot{\theta}_3, \dot{\theta}_4\right]^T = \int_{t_0}^{t_f} \mathbf{A}^{-1}(\mathbf{B}\dot{q}^2 + \mathbf{C} + \mathbf{D}\tau)\, dt \\
q(t_f) &= [\theta_1, \theta_2, \theta_3, \theta_4]^T = \int_{t_0}^{t_f} \dot{q}(t)\, dt.
\end{aligned}
$$

The optimization problem is to maximize

$$
\max_{\tau(t)} \quad H = h(t_f) + \dot{h}(t_f)^2/(2*g)
$$

subject to

$$
\tau_{min} \le \tau(t) \le \tau_{max}
$$

where τ_{min}, τ_{max} are vectors of the maximum and minimum available joint torques as reported by [3]. We utilized the technique described in the previous section to solve for the optimal torque trajectories. The results from our simulation are summarized below:

1. As a starting guess we used a torque curve that produced a jump height of only 16 cm. Our optimization algorithm produced a new torque trajectory, shown in figure 2, that yielded a jumping height of 63cm, which is close to the range of measured jump heights of 49 cm to 60 cm observed in human athletes [8].

2. The computed joint trajectories are similar to the results obtained using a more sophisticated biomechanics model [9] [10].

3. The computed take-off time is 1.0 second which is close to Pandy's measurements of 1.1 to 1.3 seconds in human trials [8].

4. Our algorithm typically takes less than ten minutes to compute the optimal control trajectories on a SGI workstation INDIGO 2.

5 Comparison with traditional approaches

There are a large variety of techniques used to solve optimal control problems, and an exhaustive comparison of our method with other approaches is beyond the scope of this paper. We will restrict ourselves to a comparison with finite difference methods as these seem to be the most popular numerical procedures used in the computer graphics literature.

In finite difference based approaches the dynamics equation and objective function are discretized. Then by replacing derivatives with finite difference approximations, each differential equation is replaced by a set of nonlinear algebraic equations evaluated at N equally spaced control points. For example, if

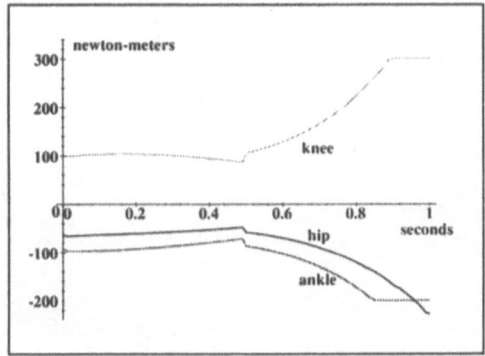

Figure 2: Computed Optimal Torques at the Ankle, Knee and Hip Joints

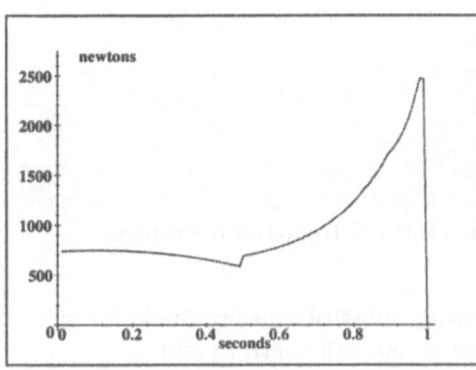

Figure 3: Ground Force

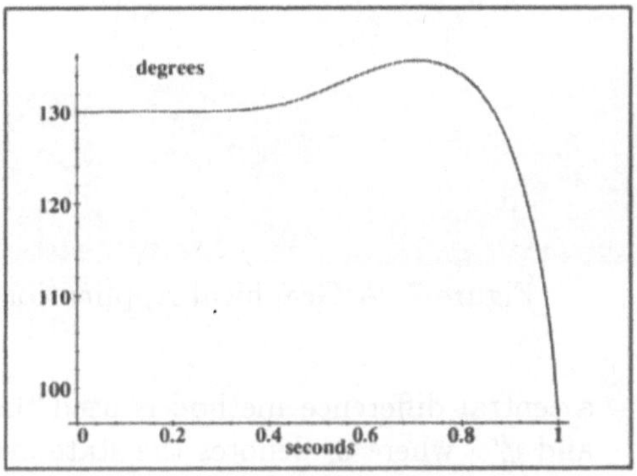

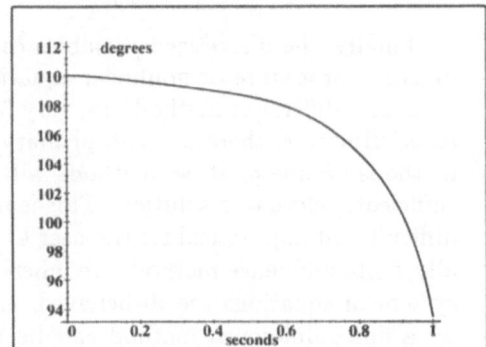

Figure 4: Ankle Joint Displacement

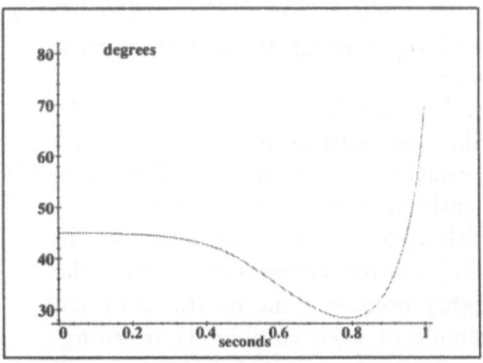

Figure 5: Knee Joint Displacement

Figure 6: Hip Joint Displacement

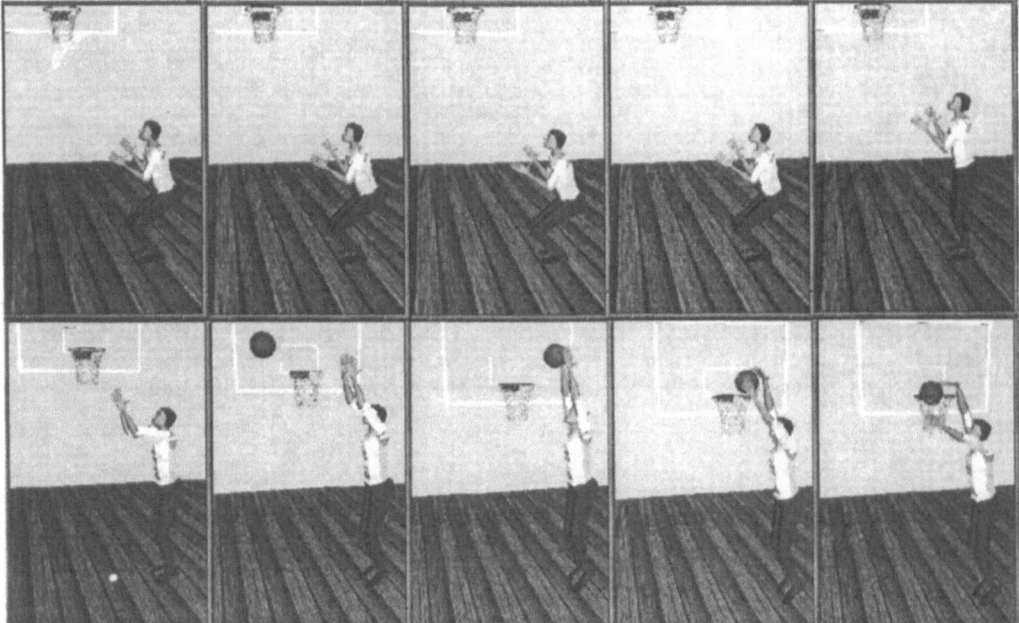

Figure 7: A Graphical Application of the Optimal High Jump Problem

a central difference method is used the following substitutions are made for y_i' and y_i'', where y_i denotes the state evaluated at the i-th control point.

$$y_i' \approx \frac{y_{i+1} - y_{i-1}}{2h}, \quad y_i'' \approx \frac{y_{i+1} - 2y_i + y_{i-1}}{h^2}.$$

Finally, the discretized variables can be solved through the use of an optimization procedure or nonlinear equation solver.

Finite difference methods are very fast and work well on some types of problems. However, there are two primary weaknesses with finite difference based methods. Some of these methods will not converge unless the initial guess is sufficiently close to a solution. This is frequently a serious problem as it is often difficult and impractical for the user to furnish a good starting guess. Additionally, finite difference methods are inherently inaccurate. Consequently, when the system of equations are ill-behaved and highly nonlinear the results obtained by a finite difference method can be unreliable or even completely meaningless. In their comparison of boundary-value methods, Stoer and Bulirsch [12] concluded that even in the case of linear boundary-value problems the finite difference methods are feasible "only if the solution need not be computed very accurately". Our numerical experiments on the jumping simulation corroborate their evaluations. When we used a finite difference method to solve the problem, the procedure diverged wildly even after the objective function and torques were omitted and the only requirement was to satisfy the dynamics equations.

Convergence occurred only when the procedure was given a close to optimal starting approximation, and even in this case more than fifty thousand mesh points were required to obtain better than two digit accuracy for all the state variables.

Our approach requires $N * m$ variables compared to $N * (m + n)$ variables with a traditional finite difference formulation. Moreover, because the state variables are obtained directly from integrating the control inputs, our approach permits more accurate computation of the state and ensures that the dynamics equations are obeyed. By contrast, in a finite difference method the state and control variables are treated as separate variables, and Lagrange multipliers or projection techniques are used to enforce the constraints. Because of errors produced by approximating derivatives with finite differences, inconsistencies between the state and control variables frequently arise, and may be quite large if the dynamics equations are highly nonlinear. Another advantage of using integration occurs when the function is ill-behaved over small regions of time. A smart integrator can automatically adjust the step size to account for this behavior, but in a finite difference scheme this problem is more difficult to handle.

These reasons give some intuitive justification for using our approach on highly nonlinear problems or problems where high accuracy is required. On the other hand, numerical integration is computationally expensive, and it is therefore likely that our method is more time consuming than a well implemented finite difference procedure. Moreover, the reduction in the dimension of the variable space in our approach comes at the expense of making the constraints more complicated and ill-behaved. For example, even linear constraints on the state variables become nonlinear integral constraints on the control variables.

6 Conclusion

We have presented a general algorithm for converting an optimal control problem into a constrained nonlinear optimization problem. By approximating the control trajectory with a spline we can describe the objective function, its gradient, and the constraints as functions of the spline control points. A solution for the optimal control curve can then be obtained through the use of a nonlinear programming subroutine. Because the objective function and its gradient is computed analytically, the method is better suited than the finite difference based algorithms for highly nonlinear problems or problems that require a high degree of accuracy.

Acknowledgment

We would like to thank the reviewers for many comments and suggestions which helped clarify the paper.

References

[1] L. Brotman and A. N. Netravali. Motion interpolation by optimal control. *Computer Graphics*, 22(4):309–315, August 1988.

[2] R. H. Byrd, P. Lu, J. Nocedal, and C. Zhu. A limited memory algorithm for bound constrained optimization. *SIAM J. Scientific Computing*, 16(5), 1995.

[3] Don B. Chaffin and Gunnar B. J. Andersson. *Occupational Biomechanics*. John Wiley and Sons, 1991.

[4] Michael F. Cohen. Interactive spacetime control for animation. In *Computer Graphics (SIGGRAPH '92 Proceedings)*, volume 26, pages 293–302, July 1992.

[5] C. J. Goh and K. L. Teo. Control parameterization: a unified approach to optimal control problems with general constraints. *Automatica*, 24(1):3–18, 1988.

[6] Joseph K. Kearney, Dinkar Bhat, Bevra Prasad, and Samuel Yuan. Efficient generation of whip-like throwing and striking motions. In N. Magnenat Thalmann and D. Thalmann, editors, *Models and Techniques in Computer Animation*, pages 270–284. Springer-Verlag, Tokyo, 1993.

[7] Zicheng Liu, Steven J. Gortler, and Michael F. Cohen. Hierarchical spacetime control. In *Proceedings of SIGGRAPH '94*, pages 35–42. ACM SIGGRAPH, ACM Press, July 1994.

[8] M. G. Pandy, F. C. Anderson, and D. G. Hull. A parameter optimization approach for the optimal control of large-scale musculoskeletal systems. *Journal of Biomechanical Engineering*, 114:450–460, November 1992.

[9] M. G. Pandy and F. E. Zajac. Optimal muscular coordination strategies for jumping. *Journal of Biomechanics*, 24(1):1–10, 1991.

[10] M. G. Pandy, F. E. Zajac, E. Sim, and W. S. Levine. An optimal control model for maximum-height human jumping. *Journal of Biomechanics*, 23(12):1185–1198, 1990.

[11] William H. Press. *Numerical recipes in C: The art of scientific computing*. Cambridge University Press, 1992.

[12] J. Stoer and R. Bulirsch. *Introduction to Numerical Analysis*. Springer-Verlag, New York, 1993.

[13] Andrew Witkin and Michael Kass. Spacetime constraints. In *Computer Graphics (SIGGRAPH '88 Proceedings)*, volume 22, pages 159–168, August 1988.

A Biomechanical Musculoskeletal Model of Human Upper Limb for Dynamic Simulation

W. Maurel[1], D. Thalmann[1], P. Hoffmeyer[2]
P. Beylot[3], P. Gingins[3], P. Kalra[3], N. Magnenat Thalmann[3]

(1) Computer Graphics Laboratory, Swiss Federal Institute of Technology, DI-LIG, EPFL, CH-1015 Lausanne, Switzerland, Email:{maurel,thalmann}@lig.di.epfl.ch
(2) Hopital Cantonal Universitaire - Clinique d'orthopédie, CH-1211 Geneve
(3) MIRALab, C.U.I., University of Geneva, CH-1211 Geneva, Switzerland

Abstract. In this paper, we provide the biomechanical model of human upper limb we have designed and applied to the three-dimensional left human arm reconstructed from the Visible Human imaging Dataset. This model includes the mechanical properties for bones, joints and muscles lines of action. This work has been done as a part of the European Esprit Project CHARM. Its objective is to develop a Comprehensive Human Animation Resource Model allowing the dynamic simulation of complex musculoskeletal systems, including finite element deformation of soft-tissues and muscular contraction. In our approach, simplifications have been done so as to ensure the feasibility of the project while preserving the biomechanical validity of the model.
Animations: http://ligwww.epfl.ch/~maurel/EGCAS96.html

1 Introduction

The European Esprit Project CHARM involving several universities proposes the development of a comprehensive human resource data base, allowing the dynamic simulation of complex musculoskeletal systems, including finite element deformation of soft-tissues and muscular contraction [CHARM 93]. To begin with the development, we have chosen to model the human arm and shoulder, which has been reported to be one of the most complex articulations of the human body [Engin 80]. The reason for this choice lies in the confidence that beginning with the harder is more likely to ensure we can achieve the simpler. We have thus developed a biomechanical model of the human upper limb including biomechanical properties for bones, joints, and muscle lines of action, as required for a proper dynamic analysis [Helm 92]. In the project, this model will serve as a concrete basis for the development of the topological data structure [Kalra 95] and the various tools needed to perform its edition, dynamic analysis, motion control and rendering. To simplify the problem, we have considered the hand as a rigid prolongation of the forearm, approximated the arm segments by rigid cylinders, assumed the articulations as ideal kinematic joints and modeled the muscles according to anatomical criteria only. However, our choices have focused on preserving the biomechanical validity of the model and the easy interpretation of the parameters by practitioners. Our constraints have been to meet the objective of an interactive application as to ensure that the following analysis, especially the finite element modeling, are feasible.

In this paper, we provide first a brief description of the musculoskeletal anatomy of the human upper limb with an analysis of the joint kinematics and muscular synergism. We then present a survey of the major biomechanical models which have been previously developed [Engin 89(a,b), Högfors 91, Helm 94b]. Then we provide a complete description of our model including bone mechanical properties, joint kinematics and muscle topology. As a result of the approach, we have used our topological modeling tool to apply the theoretical model to the 3D left human arm we have reconstructed from the Visible Human (male) Dataset, provided by the U.S. National Library of Medecine [Beylot 96].

2 Human Arm Anatomy

In order to develop a consistent topological data structure, a preliminary modeling of the musculoskeletal structure is necessary. Since biomechanical modeling is intended, it is natural to begin with the observation of the system components and their motion before modeling. In the following section, basic anatomical descriptions of the upper limb are presented to outline various structures involved in its mechanics.

2.1 Skeletal structure

The upper limb is composed of three chained mechanisms, the shoulder girdle, the elbow and the wrist, whose association allows a wide range of combined motion, and confers to the human arm the highest mobility in the human body. Due to the complexity of the hand mechanics, the wrist was not studied and the hand was taken as another rigid segment in the extension of the forearm. Considering bones in pairs, seven joints may be distinguished: the *sterno-clavicular joint*, which articulates the clavicle by its proximal end onto the sternum, the *acromio-clavicular* joint, which articulates the scapula by its acromion onto the distal end of the clavicle, *the scapulo-thoracic* joint, which allows the scapula to glide on the thorax, the *gleno-humeral* joint, which allows the humeral head to rotate in the glenoid fossa of the scapula [Kapandji 80], the *ulno-humeral* and the *humero-radial* joints, which articulate both ulna and radius on the distal end of the humerus, and finally the *ulno-radial* joint where both distal ends of ulna and radius join together [Chao 78].

Assuming translations negligible compared to rotations, all, except the scapulo-thoracic joint, are usually assumed as ball and socket joint, having more or less 3 rotational degrees of freedom (DOF). The scapulo-thoracic joint is a special case since it does not properly involve articular structures between scapula and thorax. However, due to its surrounding muscles, the scapula is usually considered as constrained to glide on the thorax [Dvir 78]. This reduces the number of DOF of the scapulo-thoracic joint to 4. Considering all joints independently, the number of DOF of the upper limb would amount to 22. However, as they are organized in closed chains, the number of DOF of the upper arm reduces to 12 [Högfors 87].

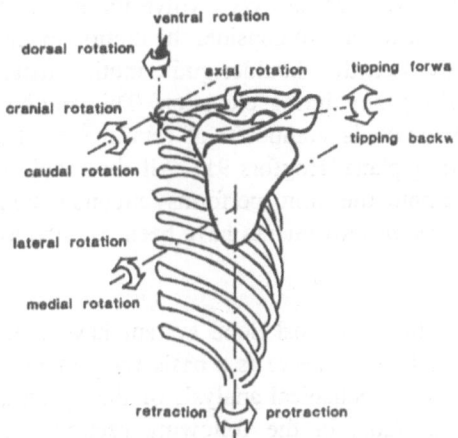

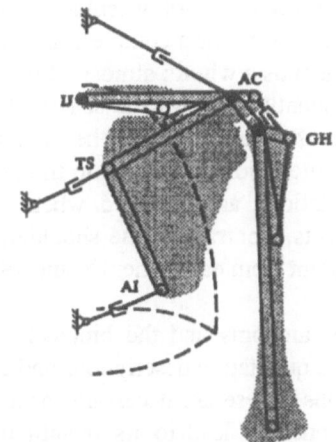

Fig. 1. Shoulder rotations
from [Pronk 91] with permission.

Fig. 2. Finite element shoulder model.
from [Helm 94b] Copyright (1994), with permission
from Elsevier Science Ltd, The Boulevard,
Langford Lane, Kidlington OX5 IGB, UK.

Fig. 1 illustrates the rotations of the shoulder girdle [Pronk 91]. These are usually referred to as ventral/dorsal, cranial/caudal and axial rotations for the *sterno-clavicular* joint (3 DOF), as abduction/adduction, flexion/extension and axial rotation for the *gleno-humeral* joint (3 DOF), as protraction/retraction, tipping forward/backward and medial/lateral rotations for the *scapulo-thoracic* joint (4 DOF), and as flexion/extension and pronation/supination movements for the forearm joints (2 DOF) [Hainaut 76].

2.2 Musculature

To perform these movements, the upper limb is equipped with at least 22 muscles actuators, some of which even divide in several bundles attached onto different bones [Högfors 87]. They can be divided in several groups according to the bones they move and the DOF they control (cf. Fig. 6). Dvir and Berme noticed that most muscles acting on the scapula insert close to its medial border [Dvir 78]. This concerns the *levator scapulae*, the *rhomboids*, the middle and lower parts of the *trapezius*. These muscles make the scapula a strong basis for performing the arm movements. The rotator cuff refers to the group of muscles which covers the humeral head and control some of its rotations. These are the *subscapularis / teres major* as opposed to the *infraspinatus / teres minor* for controlling the axial rotations, and the *supraspinatus / deltoideus* which handle the abduction. The other actuators of the humerus are the *latissimus dorsi* and *pectoralis major*, which cooperate in its adduction, but they oppose each other in flexion/extension and axial rotation [Grant 91]. Two prime antagonist groups of muscles control the flexion/extension movements of the forearm: the *brachialis* and *biceps brachii* for the flexion as opposed to the *anconeus and triceps brachii* for the extension. When the *brachialis* is inactive, the *biceps brachii* also contributes for controlling the supination movement of the forearm, together with the *brachioradialis*, as opposed to the *pronator teres*, which controls the pronation [Chao 78].

As muscles never work in isolation, natural movements always involve the motions of all the bones. For a complete analysis, it is necessary to consider the motion of the mechanism as a whole: almost all investigations on the shoulder girdle motion focus on the quantification of the scapulo-humeral rhythm during elevation. This rhythm describes the way in which the humerus elevation is composed of rotations in the gleno-humeral joint and scapulo-thoracic gliding plane [Hogfors 91]. All the shoulder bone rotations are involved when for example the arm performs circumduction movements. Contrary to the shoulder, the forearm movements have been reported as independent from each other [Youm 79].

Once the anatomy and the biomechanics of the musculoskeletal system have been observed, qualitative descriptions and classifications can serve as a basis for parameter definitions. These are necessary for a theoretical mechanical analysis of the system, which generally lead to its quantitative description. In the following section, we present a brief review of the biomechanical models which have been developed for the human arm.

3 Existing Models

The computer animation of human characters requires more or less the development of idealized underlying mechanical models. They generally take the form of a wireframe hierarchy of one-DOF rotational joints [Huang 94]. Though this approach is generally sufficient for most human joints, like the forearm joints for example, when applied to the shoulder joint, it hardly led to easy (and) realistic animations. An effort to account for the shoulder rhythm was realized by Badler *et al.* [Badler 93] who applied empirical results formulating the clavicular and scapular elevations as functions of the humeral abduction. However, such relationships only apply for a given motion, and therefore are not sufficient to realistically describe the general motion of the shoulder.

In 1980, Engin *et al.* [Engin 80] presented a research program for determining the three-dimensional passive resistive joint properties beyond the shoulder complex sinus [Engin 87, Peindl 87]. This research has provided a shoulder model with quantitative descriptions of the individual joint sinus cones [Engin 89]. Though this is an improved description of the shoulder, the model does not provide information on the simultaneous motions of the shoulder bones, unless optimization analysis is applied.

In 1987, another modeling program was initiated by Högfors *et al.* [Högfors 87] who used optimization techniques to predict the forces in the muscles, modeled as straight or curved strings, as functions of the static arm position and the external loads [Karlsson 92]. They used three-dimensional polynomial hypersurfaces fitting to relate the angular variables of each bone to the global orientation of the arm. Their result is a set of equations expressing the angles of each bone as functions of the arm angles with respect to the thorax [Högfors 91]. Contrary to the previous study, here the complete description of the shoulder kinematics was achieved. Dynamic modeling of the shoulder complex became, therefore, the next challenge.

A complete dynamic shoulder model has been finally suggested by van der Helm *et al.* by means of the finite element method [Helm 94b]. In this approach, the bones were modeled as usual as rigid segments connected by ball and socket joints. The specific scapulo-thoracic joint was modeled as a triangular structure constrained in contact on an ellipsoid (cf. Fig. 2). All muscles and ligaments were taken into account and modeled as straight or curved lines of action between their connections on the bones. A previous analysis had provided a discretization method for the modeling of muscles with large attachment sites [Helm 91]. Geometrical [Helm 92] and mechanical parameters [Veeger 91] were also collected to enable the kinematic and dynamic analysis of the shoulder [Helm 94a]. From this analysis, a definitive human shoulder description has been established by van der Helm *et al.* and validated on the basis of anatomical and practical criteria as well as experimental results [Helm 95].

However, their definitions proved to be inconvenient for our application. First, they have defined coordinate systems for a right shoulder, while we began reconstructing of the left arm of the Visible Human. Second, they have chosen coordinate systems with axes penetrating the bones, which is not appropriate for the visualization purpose of our interactive application using the topological modeler [Beylot 96]. Third, they have described joint rotations with respect to a global coordinate system, instead of the local coordinate system of the proximal bone. They justified this choice arguing that *'no flexion/extension or abduction/adduction axes with respect to the proximal bone have been defined'* [Helm 95]. However, we have felt that the parameters subsequent to their choice don't really represent the relative rotations between two bones, and thus are not proper to describe the joint sinus cones introduced by articular structures. Though we have not currently taken this property into account, we wanted the data structure to allow such extensions in future. For this reason, we defined our joints rotations with respect to the local frame of the proximal bone. Our model however preserves the easy interpretation of the parameters of the model.

4 Our Model

The purpose of our biomechanical modeling approach is more extracting a general mathematical representation of the musculoskeletal structure than providing another analysis of the human shoulder. First, mechanical parameters are required for the bones in order to allow their rigid body dynamics analysis. Second, a convention of rotation composition must be adopted to describe the joint kinematics, and three-dimensional coordinates systems must be defined on the bones in order to describe their relative degrees of freedom. Finally, the mechanical properties and topology of muscles are necessary to model their actions on the bones, which will serve as input to the dynamics and motion control analysis. This section presents how we have modeled bones, joint rotations and muscle forces.

4.1 Bones mechanical properties

The left arm model provided by the reconstruction procedure has been obtained in the form of seven polygonal bones defined in their own local *geometrical frames*. These frames are arbitrarily defined at the reconstruction stage with no specific anatomical criteria. At that stage, neither hierarchy nor structural dependency relationships exist among the bones: each one is referred to the global *reference frame* of the scene by the way of its 4x4 *transfer matrix*. Mechanical dependencies are further introduced with the definitions of the joints mechanics. In our case, all bones have been reconstructed in the same coordinate system (O_0, X_0, Y_0, Z_0) defined in Table 4. Thus, all *geometrical frames* are identical to the global *reference frame*, and every *transfer matrix* is identity. In order to allow the rigid body dynamics analysis, we have made the usual assumption of undeformable bones, and we have assigned to them mechanical properties, i.e. *mass*, *inertial frame* and *inertia matrix*.

Considering their reduced sizes and motions as well as muscular environments, we assume that clavicle and scapula have negligible inertia with respect to their somewhat quasi-static movements. Furthermore, since the inertia properties apply to the segments accounting for their surrounding flesh, not only for the bones, we assume that the inertia of humerus, ulna and radius may be approximated to those of equivalent homogeneous cylinders. With these assumptions, the centers of mass, the *inertial frames* and *inertia matrix* of the segments have been approximated to those of the corresponding cylinders. Data from Veeger *et al.* [Veeger 91] for segments mechanical modeling are provided in Table 1. Inertial frames are defined in Table 4. Since for cylinders the transverse axes are indifferent, we choose them arbitrarily.

4.2 Joint rotations

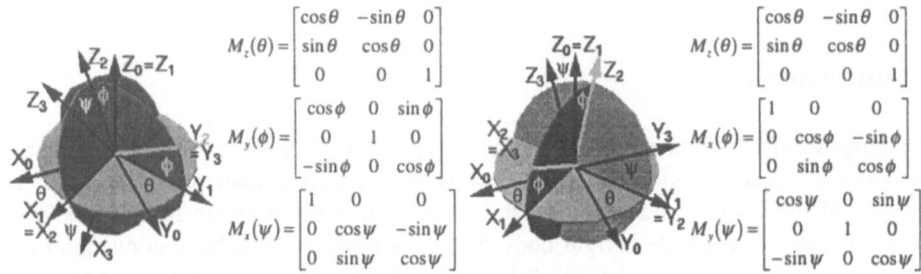

Fig. 3. Rotations for the left arm. **Fig. 4.** Rotations for the right arm.

To model a joint, it is first necessary to define the respective *joint frame* of each bone in a pair to enable the parametric description of its state. Such description is then fully achieved with a transfer matrix relating its *relative frame* to its *reference frame*. Various compositions exist to describe the three-dimensional orientation of a frame with respect to another. In our model, we have chosen successive local rotations with respect to the reference frame of the joint: the rotation matrix changing the global frame (X_0, Y_0, Z_0) into the local frame (X_3, Y_3, Z_3) of the joint is given by:

$$M(\theta, \varphi, \psi) = M(\theta)M(\varphi)M(\psi)$$

and the coordinates in the global frame of any vector V and its image vector V' by the above rotation may then be obtained by the relationship:

$$V' = M(\theta, \varphi, \psi).V$$

Due to the planar symmetry between the left and right sides, it has been necessary to define a different rotation order for each one, in order to respect the convention of "direct coordinate system" and the anatomical rotation order usually considered by practitioners. The intermediate successive rotations around the local axis are shown in Fig. 3. for the *left* arm and in Fig. 4. for the *right* arm.

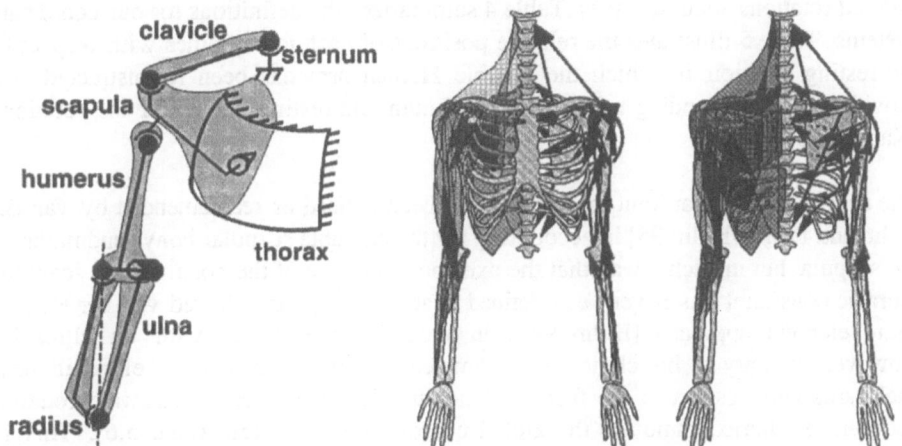

Fig.5. Arm skeleton model.   **Fig.6.** Arm musculature model.

Following our predecessors [Engin 80, Högfors 87, Raikova 92, Helm 94b], we have modeled most of the shoulder joints as ideal ball and socket joints allowing their relative bone to rotate about three orthogonal axis. This concerns the *sterno-clavicular* joint, the *acromio-clavicular* joint and the *gleno-humeral* joint. For each one, the joint center of rotation has been estimated with respect to the joint anatomy, and the joint frames have been adjusted so that one axis lies along the longitudinal axis of the corresponding bone.

Since the forearm movements are independently performed around two rotation axis defined by three joints in pairs (cf. Fig. 5), we have modeled the *ulno-humeral* and *ulno-radial* joints as hinge joints, each allowing only one rotation about the axis going through their respective center and the *humero-radial* joint center. Modeling the *scapulo-thoracic joint* constitutes the main challenge in human shoulder modeling.

Since the shoulder girdle is a closed kinematic chain, the orientation of the scapula is doubly defined with respect to the thorax as well as with respect to the clavicle. As it is usually described with respect to the clavicle, we choose to define the scapular orientation by the *acromio-clavicular* joint rotation, and following van der Helm's finite element model [Helm 94b], we modeled the *scapulo-thoracic* joint as a constraint in contact of the scapula on the thorax approximated by an ellipsoid (cf. Fig. 7). For an easier description, instead of Cartesian coordinates, we used spherical coordinates to define the position of the contact on the ellipsoid.

4.3 Joint frames

Fig. 7. shows the joint frames as we have modeled with the topological modeler on the 3D Visible Human arm model. For most joints, the center has been positioned on the corresponding anatomical joint center. For convenient use of the topological modeling features, we have chosen our coordinate system to be visible in such a way that each one can be deduced from the proximal one simply by few permutations and ordered rotations about the axes. Table 4 summarizes the definitions for our coordinate systems. Table 5 illustrates the relative positions of each joint frames with respect to the resting position in which the Visible Human arm has been reconstructed, and provides the corresponding minimum, maximum and resting values for the rotations [Kapandji 80].

The acromio-clavicular joint local frame has been defined as recommended by van der Helm and Pronk [Helm 95] in accounting for the palpable scapular bony landmarks of the scapula, but in such a way that the axes point outside of the bone. As the scapulo-thoracic constraint has never been defined anatomically, we followed van der Helm's finite element approach [Helm 94b] in modeling the thorax with an ellipsoid. However, contrary to his choice, we estimated the fit better with an ellipsoid bent backwards with respect to the frontal plane, and thus introduced a backward rotation between the thorax frame and the global coordinate system (cf. Table 5.6). This is however no major change on the description of the scapulo-thoracic contact since no specific parameters exist for it. The description of the contact was found to be easier in terms of spherical coordinates than of Cartesian ones.

4.4 Muscle force

Concerning muscle force modeling, there are basically two methods: the straight line approach which connects the origin and insertion of a muscle, as applied by Seireg and Arvikar [Seireg 1989] and the centroid line approach which estimates the muscle curved line of action that is formed by its centroid [Jensen 1975]. The main disadvantage of the latter method is that it is only applicable to one position of the model. An intermediate approach called segment-line approach strikes a balance between accuracy and simplicity [Raikova 92]. In all cases, it is assumed that the line of action is representative of the muscle force at a cross-section and that the muscle exerts no moment around that line.

This approximation is not always valid from anatomical and mechanical points of view [Zuylen 88]. In our model, we have chosen the intermediate segment-line approach to represent the muscles lines of action while preserving the anatomical topological information [Beylot 96].

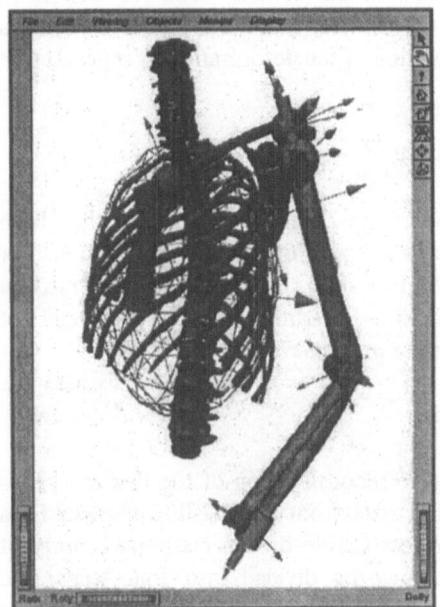 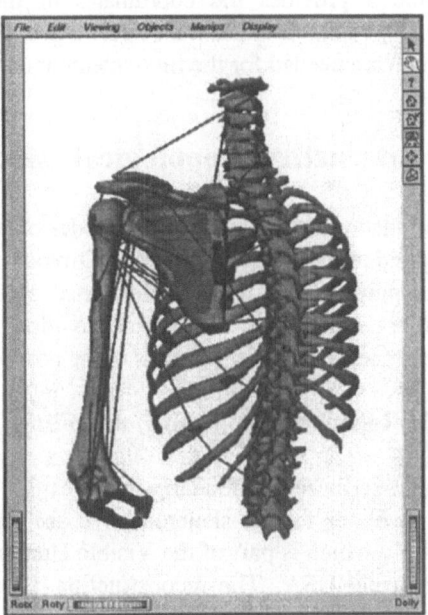

Fig. 7. Joint frames modeling.   **Fig. 8.** Action lines topology.

In practice, some muscles have very broad attachments while some others divide in several bundles attached onto different bones. These may be modeled in dividing the muscles into several lines of action. The choice of the lines must be made on the basis of anatomical as well as mechanical considerations [Högfors 87]. It was observed that small changes in the directions or points of application of the forces can have large effects on the resulting moment vectors. For this purpose, van der Helm *et al.* have developed a method to determine the number of muscle force vectors, capable of representing the mechanical effect of muscles with large attachment sites, accounting for the form and size of the attachments as well as for the distribution of the fibers in the muscle [Helm 91]. However, their results implied to model most of the shoulder muscles with no less than 6 force vectors, which seems to us far too complex for our application, for the time being. As the CHARM project plans the simulation of human motion with realistic finite element muscle deformations, we decided to start with a reduced model, in applying muscle subdivisions based on anatomical considerations only, such as those suggested by Wood's [Wood 89].

Thus, we have assigned to the muscles mass and strength parameters, while their lines of action have been characterized by their activation parameter, their physiological cross-sectional area (PCSA) and the coordinates of their attachments.

The topology is needed to compute the direction of the muscle force, which changes with the motion of the bones. The PCSA is a parameter useful for estimating the maximal force that the muscle or the bundle can bear [Helm 91]. Fig. 8 shows the muscular topology as we interactively with the topological modeler [Beylot 96]. Table 3 provides the coordinates of the attachments of the lines of action in (O_0,X_0,Y_0,Z_0). Besides this, Table 2 provides the muscles mass and PCSA parameters which are needed for the finite element computation of the deformation [Veeger 91].

5 Interactive Topological Modeling

The theoretical biomechanical model of human upper limb presented here has been applied to the modeling of the 3D reconstructed left arm of the Visible Human. For this purpose, we have implemented a topological data structure, and developed an elaborate modeling tool, in order to allow its interactive editing with the parameters of the model [Beylot 96]. Details of the procedure are presented hereafter.

5.1 Reconstruction and modeling tools

The first phase of modeling involves 3D surface reconstruction of the desired organs (e.g., bones for the skeleton). We use imaging data from the Visible Human Data (VHD) which is part of the Visible Human Project started by the National Library of Medicine, USA. The reconstruction process may be divided into four steps: the preprocessing consisting of image filtering and resolution reduction, labeling using snakes for semi-automatic delineation of each organ of interest in the cross-sectional images, 3D reconstruction to join the cross-sectional contours, and postprocessing including matching of reconstruction from different sources (CT, MRI...) [Beylot 96].

In a second phase, we have designed an object-oriented data structure where each anatomical element is represented by a class which encompasses its physical, geometrical and mechanical attributes. This data structure contains models for bones, joints, ligaments, skin, and muscle lines of action. The 3D interactive topological modeler has then been developed to allow the editing of the data base with structural, topological and mechanical information. The modeler provides extensive 3D visualization and direct interaction and manipulation. The users can specify the kinematic parameters (angular limits) of the joints, the dynamic parameters like inertia matrix of the bones, and the lines of action and force generating parameters of the muscles. In the following section, we illustrate the editing of the joints frames as defined in §.4. The editing of the muscle topology is not developed since it just involves the selection of the successive attachments sites of the action lines. Their Cartesian coordinates are provided in (O_0,X_0,Y_0,Z_0) in Table 4.

5.2 Joint topological modeling

First we have approximately placed the bone coordinate systems as defined by van der Helm [Helm 95], after adjustment for the left arm, as a basis to build our frames. A feature of the topological modeler allows the rigorous alignment of any frame on any other one and the rigorous relative permutations between its axes. Thus from one frame, it is possible to obtain any configuration of its axis around the height octants. We have then created each joint by the successive selection of the reference bone and the relative bone, and placed its center on the corresponding anatomical joint center. Then we have adjusted successively the joint frames for the *sterno-clavicular*, *acromio-clavicular* and *gleno-humeral* joints: for each one, the joint reference and local frames have been defined respectively on the basis of the local frame of the previous joint and on the basis of those we call van der Helm's frames. While the frame orientations are being defined, the angular parameters of the model are automatically extracted from the rotation matrix and saved in the data base. Thus, the complete 'rest' state of the Visible Human is directly available. In annex are summarized the definitions for bones (Table 1), muscles (Table 2&3), coordinate systems and hierarchical transfer matrix (Table 4), and joint parameters minimal, maximal, and current values (Table 5).

6 Conclusion

The computer simulation of human complex joints requires the development of elaborate biomechanical models underlying the geometrical objects representing the anatomical components. In this paper, we have provided the complete model of human upper limb that we have applied to the 3D left human arm, reconstructed from the Visible Human imaging Dataset. This analysis is necessary to allow the development of the data structures, topological modeling tools and dynamic simulation procedures on concrete basis. In our approach, we have achieved a balance between accuracy and simplicity for preserving the biomechanical validity, as well as the the feasibility of the project. However, the model and data structure have been designed to allow further improvements, such as a finer discretization of the muscles or the replacement of the current kinematic joints by dynamic joints, which is of interest for joint dislocation simulation. The next step is the motion control of the upper limb.

Acknowledgments. We are grateful to the other partners of the CHARM project: Ecole des Mines de Nantes (EMN), University de las Islas Baleares (UIB), University of Karlsruhe (UK) and Technical University of Lisbon (IST) for the instructive collaboration we have. We would also like to thank Dr. J Fasel for his medical advice in anatomy and physiology.

References

[Badler 93]   N.I. Badler, C.B. Phillips, B.L. Webber, (1993), *Simulating Humans,* Oxford University Press.

[Beylot 96]   P. Beylot, P. Gingins, P. Kalra, N. Magnenat Thalmann, W. Maurel, D. Thalman, J. Fasel, (1996), "3D interactive topological modeling using visible human dataset", accepted at Eurographics'96

132

[Chao 78]   E.Y. Chao, B.F. Morrey, (1978), "Three-dimensional rotation of the elbow", *J. Biomechanics*, 11, 57-73

[CHARM 93]   CHARM, (1993), Esprit Project 9036, Part I : "Technical Annex"

[Dvir 78]   Z. Dvir, N. Berme, (1978), "The shoulder complex in elevation of the arm: a mechanism approach", *J. Biomechanics*, 11, 219-225.

[Engin 80]   A.E. Engin, (1980) "On the biomechanics of the shoulder complex", *J. Biomechanics*, 13, 575-590

[Engin 87]   A.E. Engin, R.D. Peindl, (1987) "On the biomechanics of human shoulder complex - I. Kinematics for determination of the shoulder complex sinus", *J. Biomechanics*, 20, 2, 103-117

[Engin 89a]   A.E. Engin, S.T. Tumer, (1989) "Three-dimensional kinematic modeling of the human shoulder complex - I. Physical model and determination of joint sinus cones", *J. biomech. Engng.*, 111, 107-112

[Engin 89b]   A.E. Engin, S.T. Tumer, (1989) "Three-dimensional kinematic modeling of the human shoulder complex - II. Mathematical modeling and solution via optimization" - *J. biomech. Engng.*, 111, 113-121

[Grant 91]   *Grant's Atlas of Anatomy* - Ninft Edition - ed. Anne M.R. Agnus - Baltimore: Williams & Wilkins

[Hainaut 76]   K. Hainaut, (1976), "Introduction à la biomécanique", Paris: Maloine

[Helm 91]   F.C.T. Van der Helm, R. Veenbaas, (1991), "Modeling the mechanical effect of muscles with large attachment sites: Application to the shoulder mechanism", *J. Biomechanics*, 27, 1151-1163

[Helm 92]   F.C.T. Van der Helm, H.E.J. Veeger, G.M. Pronk, L.V.H. Van der Woude, R.H. Rozendal, (1992), "Geometry parameters for musculoskeletal modelling of the shoulder system", *J. Biomechanics*, 25, 2, pp. 129-144, 1992

[Helm 94a]   F.C.T. Van der Helm, (1994), "Analysis of the kinematic and dynamic behavior of the shoulder mechanism", *J. Biomechanics*, 27, 527-550

[Helm 94b]   F.C.T. Van der Helm, (1994), "A finite element musculoskeletal model of the shoulder mechanism", *J. Biomechanics*, 27, 551-569

[Helm 95]   F.C.T. van der Helm, G.M. Pronk, (1995) "Three-dimensional recording and description of motions of the shoulder mechanism", *J. biomech. Engng.* 117, 27-40

[Högfors 87]   C. Högfors, G. Sigholm, P. Herberts, (1987) "Biomechanical model of the human shoulder - I. Elements" - *J. Biomechanics*, 20, 157-166

[Högfors 91]   C. Högfors, B. Peterson, G. Sigholm, P. Herberts, (1991) "Biomechanical model of the human shoulder joint", *J. Biomechanics*, 24, 699-709

[Huang 94]   Z. Huang, N. Magnenat Thalmann, D. Thalmann, (1994) "Interactive human motion control using a closed form of direct and inverse dynamics", *Pacific Graphic Conference Proceedings*, Beijing 94

[Jensen 75]   R.H. Jensen, D. T. Davy, (1975) "An investigation of muscle lines of actions about the hip: a centroid approach vs the straight line approach", *J.Biomechanics*, 8, 103-110

[Kalra 95]   P. Kalra, P. Beylot, P. Gingins, N. Magnenat Thalmann, P. Volino, P. Hoffmeyer, J. Fasel, F. Terrier, (1995) "Topological modeling of human anatomy using medical data", *Proc. Comp. Anim. '95*, Geneva, IEEE Computer Society Press, 172-10

[Kapandji 80]   I.A. Kapandji, (1980) *Physiologie articulaire - Tome 1: Membre supérieur* - Maloine S.A. Editeur

[Karlsson 92]   D. Karlsson, B. Peterson, (1992) "Towards a model for force predictions in the human shoulder", - *J. Biomechanics*, 25, 189-199

[Peindl 87]   R.D. Peindl, A.E. Engin, (1987) "On the biomechanics of human shoulder complex - II. Passive resistive properties beyond the shoulder complex sinus", *J. Biomechanics*, 20, 2, 119-134

[Pronk 91]   G. Pronk, (1991) *The Shoulder Girdle, Analysed and Modelled Kinematically*, Diss., Technische Universiteit Delft

[Raikova 92]   R. Raikova, (1992) "A general approach for modelling and mathematical investigation of the human upper limb", *J. Biomechanics*, 25, 857-867

[Seireg 89]   R.A. Seireg, Arvikar, (1989) *Biomechanical Analysis of the Musculoskeletal Structure for Medicine and Sports*, Himisphere Publishing Corporation.

[Thomson 64]   Arthur Thomson, *A Handbook of Anatomy for Art Students* - Dover Publications Inc.1964 - Oxford University Press 1896.

[Veeger 91]   H.E.J. Veeger, F.C.T. Van der Helm, L.H.V. Van der Woude, G.M. Pronk, R.H. Rozendal, (1991) "Inertia and muscle contraction parameters for musculoskeletal modelling of the shoulder mechanism", *J. Biomechanics*, 24, 7, 615-629

[Wood 89]   J.E. Wood, S. G. Meek, S. C. Jacobsen, (1989) "Quantitation of human shoulder anatomy for prosthetic arm control - I. Surface modelling", *J. Biomechanics*, 22, 3, 273-292.

[Youm 79]   Y. Youm, R.F. Cryer, K. Thambyrajah, A.E. Flatt, B.L. Sprague, (1979) "Biomechanical analysis of forearm pronation-supination and elbow flexion-extension", *J. Biomechanics*, 12, 245-255

[Zuylen 88]   E.J. van Zuylen, A. van Velzen, J.J. Denier van der Gon, (1988) "A biomechanical model for flexion torques of human arm muscles as a function of elbow angle", *J. Biomechanics*, 21, 183-190

Appendix

Cylindrical inertia : $\quad C = \dfrac{mr^2}{2}$

$$I = \begin{bmatrix} A & -F & -E \\ -F & B & -D \\ -E & -D & C \end{bmatrix}$$

$D = E = F = 0$

$A = B = \dfrac{mr^2}{4} + \dfrac{mh^2}{12}$

z: long axis
r: radius
h: height

segment Parameters	humeral	forearm + hand	ulnar	radial
m (kg)	1.81	1.6	0.8	0.8
h (m)	0.25	0.225	0.225	0.225
r (m)	0.05	0.080	0.040	0.040
A (g.m²)	10.6	7.39	3.695	3.695
B (g.m²)	10.6	7.39	3.695	3.695
C (g.m²)	2.2625	0.64	0.64	0.64

Table 1. Segments masses and inertias. from [Veeger 91]

Muscle	Mass (g)	Muscle	Mass (g)
Biceps	114.1	Teres minor	28.3
Triceps	99.7	Infraspin.	109.8
Coracobr.	30.6	Supraspin.	36.2
Levator sc.	37.9	Subscapul.	138.6
Rhomboids	71.4	Deltoideus	314.4
Latissimus	226.1	Pect. major	202.6
Trapezius	185.8	Pect. minor	41.5
Teres major	88.3	Serratus ant	204.8

Table 2. Muscles masses. [Veeger 91].

Lines / PCSA	Coordinates (X, Y, Z)	Bone
Anconeus 2.50	O(601, 285, -588)	Hum.
	I(596, 289, -611)	Ulna
Biceps long	O(487, 246, -291)	Scap.
	G1(499, 215, -297)	Hum.
	G2(506, 213, -317)	Hum.
3.21	G3(518, 227, -355)	Hum.
Biceps short 3.08	O(472, 210, -302)	Scap.
Biceps	I(565, 254, -622)	Radius
Brachialis 8.40	O(552, 257, -467)	Hum.
	I(572, 278, -620)	Ulna
Brachiorad. 4.70	O(585, 279, -532)	Hum.
	I(490, 117, -752)	Radius
Coracobrach. 2.51	O(476, 211, -301)	Scap.
	I(535, 249, -423)	Hum.
Deltoideus anterior	O(468, 231, -272)	Clav.
	G1(493, 217, -319)	Hum.
8.63	G2(526, 229, -376)	Hum.
Deltoideus lateral	O(511, 222, -273)	Scap.
	G1(524, 207, -303)	Hum.
8.63	G2(526, 210, -318)	Hum.
Delt. post. 8.63	O(484, 288, -274)	Scap.
	G(540, 250, -376)	Hum.
Deltoideus	I(547, 241, -405)	Hum.
Infraspinatus	O(449, 315, -355)	Scap.
	G(532, 243, -300)	Hum.
9.51	I(528, 216, -297)	Hum.
Latis. upper 2.83	O(341, 321, -431)	VT07
	G(440, 336, -419)	Scap.
Latis. medial 2.83	O(342, 325, -558)	VT11
	G(420, 326, -484)	R09
Latissimus dorsi lower	O(344, 299, -692)	V3
	G1(440, 310, -590)	R11
	G2(461, 299, -551)	R10
2.83	I(512, 231, -348)	Hum.
Levator 2.82	O(354, 228, -203)	VC3
	I(402, 283, -278)	Scap.
Pect. maj. up. 6.80	O(407, 190, -310)	Clav.
Pect. maj. low 6.80	O(356, 133, -437)	Stern.
	G(416, 145, -413)	R03
Pectoralis major	I(524, 220, -344)	Hum.
Pect. min. 3.74	O(432, 139, -448)	R04
	I(462, 217, -301)	Scap.

Lines / PCSA	Coordinates (X, Y, Z)	Bone
Pronator teres 2.00	O(559, 303, -573)	Hum.
	I(531, 182, -686)	Radius
Rhomb. upper 3.14	O(334, 265, -256)	VC6
	I(402, 311, -288)	Scap.
Rhomb. lower 3.14	O(332, 302, -332)	VT03
	I(419, 335, -363)	Scap.
Serratus ant. upper	O(458, 159, -457)	R05
	G(461, 239, -384)	R04
7.00	I(407, 317, -302)	Scap.
Serratus ant. lower	O(478, 173, -561)	R08
	G(466, 260, -453)	R07
7.00	I(421, 330, -362)	Scap.
Subclavius 2.00	O(399, 207, -326)	R01
	I(458, 234, -278)	Clav.
Subscapularis 13.51	O(445, 312, -341)	Scap.
	I(491, 223, -319)	Hum.
	O(600, 288, -569)	Hum.
Supinator	G1(598, 299, -611)	Ulna
	G2(584, 251, -623)	Radius
3.00	G3(565, 230, -635)	Radius
	I(547, 219, -654)	Radius
Supraspinatus	O(461, 270, -301)	Scap.
	G(504, 233, -284)	Hum.
5.21	I(511, 207, -297)	Hum.
Teres major 10.20	O(469, 310, -391)	Scap.
	I(506, 237, -339)	Hum.
Teres minor 2.92	O(475, 305, -373)	Scap.
	I(535, 235, -311)	Hum.
Trap. upper 5.30	O(330, 248, -185)	VC2
	I(498, 236, -259)	Clav.
Trap. medial 5.30	O(331, 312, -333)	VT03
	I(408, 324, -303)	Scap.
Trapezius lower	O(340, 330, -507)	VT09
	G(427, 334, -363)	Scap.
5.30	I(472, 294, -276)	Scap.
Triceps long 2.30	O(498, 261, -331)	Scap.
Triceps lateral 2.30	O(532, 233, -333)	Hum.
Triceps short 2.30	O(530, 259, -385)	Hum.
Triceps	I(593, 316, -594)	Ulna

(O: origin; I: insertion; G: guide)

Table 3. Muscle PCSA(cm^2) [Veeger 91] and topology (cm) in $(O_0,(X_0,Y_0,Z_0))$.

	Absolute Reference		SC reference frame		GH reference frame
O_0	1st right higher voxel	O_{SC}	center, on sternum	O_{GH}	center, on scapula
X_0	⊥ to FP, forward	X_{SC}	⊥ to FP, forward	Z_{GH}	⊥ to scap. plane, forw.
Y_0	⊥ to SP, forward	Y_{SC}	⊥ to SP, to the left	X_{GH}	from Trigonum Spinae
	ST reference frame		SC local frame		GH local frame
O_T	center of ellipsoid	O_{SC}	center, on clavicle	O_{GH}	center, on humerus
Y_T	⊥ to SP, to the left	Y_C	// to ($O_{SC}O_{AC}$), to O_{AC}	Z_H	⊥ to hfp, forward
Z_T	long axis, upwards	X_C	⊥ to Y_C, in clp, forward	Y_H	long humeral axis, upw.
	AC reference frame		UH reference frame		UR reference frame
O_{AC}	center, on clavicle	O_{UH}	center, on humerus	O_{UR}	center, on ulna
X_{AC}	// to ($O_{SC}O_{AC}$), to O_{AC}	Z_{UH}	// to ($O_{UH}O_{HR}$), outward	Z_{UR}	// to ($O_{HR}O_{UR}$), to hand
Y_{AC}	⊥ to X_{AC}, in clp, backw.	X_{UH}	⊥ to ($O_{GH}O_{UH}O_{HR}$), forw.	Y_{UR}	rest, ⊥ ($O_{HR}O_{UR}O_R$), inw.
	AC local frame		UH local frame		UR local frame
O_{AC}	center, on scapula	O_{UH}	center, on ulna	O_{UR}	center, on radius
Y_S	⊥ to scap. plane backw.	Z_U	// to ($O_{UH}O_{HR}$), outward	Z_R	// to ($O_{HR}O_{UR}$), to hand
X_S	from Trigonum Spinae	X_U	⊥ to ($O_{UH}O_{HR}O_{UR}$), forw.	Y_R	⊥ to ($O_{HR}O_{UR}O_R$), inw.
	Humerus inertial frame		Ulna inertial frame		Radius inertial frame
O_{HI}	center of humerus	O_{UI}	center of ulna	O_{RI}	center of radius
Z_{HI}	⊥ to hfp, forward	Z_{UI}	// to ($O_{UH}O_{HR}$), outward	Z_{RI}	// to ($O_{HR}O_{UR}$), to hand
Y_{HI}	long humeral axis, upw.	X_{UI}	⊥ to ($O_{UH}O_{HR}O_{UR}$), forw.	Y_{RI}	⊥ to ($O_{HR}O_{UR}O_R$), inw.

$(O_T X_T Y_T Z_T)$ in $(O_0 X_0 Y_0 Z_0)$				$(O_{SC} X_{SC} Y_{SC} Z_{SC})$ in $(O_0 X_0 Y_0 Z_0)$				$(O_{AC} X_{AC} Y_{AC} Z_{AC})$ in $(O_{SC} X_C Y_C Z_C)$				$(O_{GH} X_{GH} Y_{GH} Z_{GH})$ in $(O_{AC} X_S Y_S Z_S)$				$(O_{ST} X_S Y_S Z_S)$ in $(O_{AC} X_S Y_S Z_S)$			
0	1	0	337.2	0	1	0	356.1	0	-1	0	0	1	0	0	2.71	1	0	0	-122.26
-0.996	0	0.089	233.3	-1	0	0	180.2	1	0	0	165.4	0	0	-1	-3.41	0	1	0	-17.02
0.089	0	0.996	-483.9	0	0	1	-335.2	0	0	1	0	0	1	0	-42.3	0	0	1	-90.43
0	0	0	1	0	0	0	1	0	0	0	1	0	0	0	1	0	0	0	1

$(O_{UH} X_{UH} Y_{UH} Z_{UH})$ in $(O_{GH} X_H Y_H Z_H)$				$(O_{UR} X_{UR} Y_{UR} Z_{UR})$ in $(O_{UH} X_U Y_U Z_U)$				$(O_{UI} X_{UI} Y_{UI} Z_{UI})$ in $(O_{UH} X_U Y_U Z_U)$			
0	0	1	-4.95	0	1	0	0.195	-0.978	-0.187	-0.0872	-12.26
0	-1	0	-293.6	-0.115	0	0.993	241.8	0.0519	0.185	-0.981	120.3
1	0	0	7.99	0.993	0	0.105	46.13	0.2001	-0.965	-0.172	23.59
0	0	0	1	0	0	0	1	0	0	0	1

$(O_{RI} X_{RI} Y_{RI} Z_{RI})$ in $(O_{UR} X_R Y_R Z_R)$				$(O_{HI} X_{HI} Y_{HI} Z_{HI})$ in $(O_{GH} X_H Y_H Z_H)$					
-.83	-.55	-0.1	13.5	0	1	0	-0.92	⊥ : normal to ...	// : parallel to ...
-.56	0.83	0.03	0.89	0	0	1	-140.6	ST: Scapulo-Thoracic	SC: Sterno-Clavicular
-.08	0.08	-.99	-109	1	0	0	0	FP: Frontal Plane	SP: Sagital Plane
0	0	0	1	0	0	0	1	UH: Ulno-Humeral	UR: Ulno-Radial
								O_{HR}: HR center (Tab 5.4)	HR: Humero-Radial
								O_R: radius end (Tab 5.5)	GH: Gleno-Humeral

clp:clavicular plane scp: scapular plane hfp: humeral front plane AC: Acromio-Clavicular

Table 4. Coordinates systems and matrices for hierarchical modeling.

5.4 Ulno-Humeral joint

angle	θ_U
axis	Z_U
min	-140°
max	+0°
rest	-57°

5.5 Ulno-radial joint

angle	θ_R
axis	Z_R
min	+0°
max	+180°
rest	+100°

5.3 Gleno-Humeral joint

angle	θ_H	φ_H	ψ_H
axis	Z_H	X_H	Y_H
min	-40°	-100°	-90°
max	+100°	+50°	+90°
rest	-13°	+3°	+0°

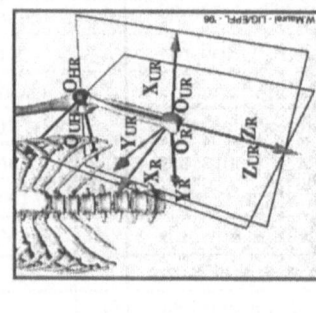

5.2 Acromio-Clavicular joint

angle	θ_S	φ_S	ψ_S
axis	Z_S	X_S	Y_S
min	-68°	-10°	-10°
max	-60°	+0°	+0°
rest	-65°	-7°	-6°

parameter	a	b	c
axis	X_T	Y_T	Z_T
value	+120	+150	+210

angle	θ_ON	φ_ON
min	+120°	+20°
max	+140°	+40°
rest	+130°	+29°

5.1 Sterno-Clavicular joint

angle	θ_C	φ_C	ψ_C
axis	Z_C	X_C	Y_C
min	-5°	+0°	-30°
max	+30°	+40°	+10°
rest	+22°	+24°	+0°

5.6 Scapulo-thoracic joint

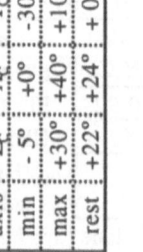

(a, b, c) ellipsoid parameters
$(\theta_{O_{ST}}, \varphi_{O_{ST}})$ spherical coordinates

$$\begin{cases} x_{O_{ST}} = a \cdot \cos \varphi_{O_{ST}} \cos \theta_{\varphi_{ST}} \\ y_{O_{ST}} = b \cdot \cos \varphi_{ST} \sin \theta_{\varphi_{ST}} \\ z_{O_{ST}} = c \cdot \sin \varphi_{O_{ST}} \end{cases}$$

Table 5. Joints Rotations.

Editors' Note: see Appendix, p. 221 f. for colored figures of this paper

4

Plant Development

Interactive Modelling and Animation of Branching Botanical Structures

Bernd Lintermann and Oliver Deussen

Department of Computer Science, University of Karlsruhe
76128 Karlsruhe, Germany
Net: [linter | oliver]@informatik.uni-karlsruhe.de
WWW: http://i31www.informatik.uni-karlsruhe.de/[~linter | ~oliver]

Abstract. We present a method for interactive modelling and animation of natural branching structures such as plants. Objects are created according to a rule based description. Geometric information is encapsulated in the objects and can be edited by methods such as free form deformation and spline techniques. Global and partial constraints allow the modelling of specific plants. The rule system is represented by a structure tree with components of high functionality, that can be edited graphically. Keyframe techniques are applicable and allow to simulate parts of the models with local time. In comparison to other rulebased approaches, complex branching structures can be developed faster and more flexible.

1 Motivation

During modelling of natural objects such as trees, bushes or flowers their enormous structural complexity must be handled as well as the large amount of geometrical data. If, for instance, one wants to create not only a tree but a specific pine with a given shape, many structural and geometric aspects have to be modelled.

Different approaches have been introduced to help creation of branching objects. Among formal techniques the most popular ones are textual edited grammars, known as L-systems [7]. A sequence of letters is derived from a starting word by parallel application of string rewriting rules. In a second step the generated string serves as a command sequence for a turtle graphics interpreter that generates geometric data. Extensions such as context sensitive and parametric grammars as well as stochastic application of rewriting rules are presented in [6]. DL-Systems [5] define additional differential equations to introduce continuity to the so far discrete approach. Other specialized methods reduce the problem and concentrate on the generation of models with a restricted structure such as natural trees ([2, 3, 8]).

We try to combine the modelling power of a rule based system with the proper handling of the geometric information. In contrast to the rule based generation and subsequent graphical interpretation of letters in L-systems, we propose the rule based generation of

140

objects. The rule system consists of components with high functionality that create a hierarchy of objects that holds the geometric data.

The rule system is defined and modified graphically. Components are represented by icons and rules are displayed as intermediate links. Rules are esthablished by moving icons with the mouse upon other icons as shown in Figure 3.

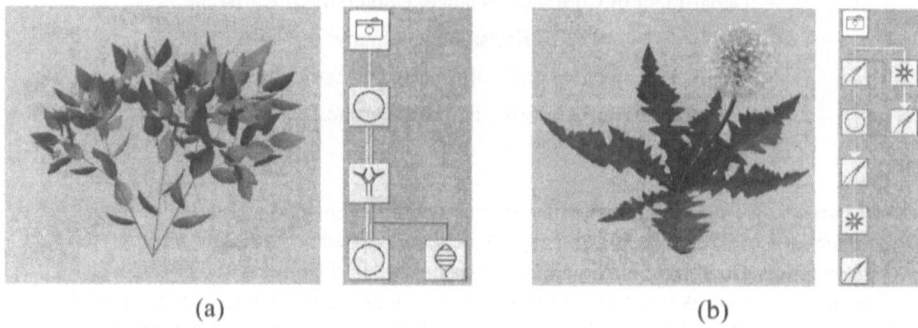

(a)   (b)

Figure 1: Bush and dandelion with corresponding structure trees.

The components encapsulate the geometric description as well as instantiation rules for subsequent components. Each component defines at minimum a transformation towards its predecessor, a geometric primitive and a maximum recursion depth.

The interactive modeller offers a set of predefined component types as seen in (Figure 2(a)). Components are combined to a so called structure tree that describes the model (Figure 3). If one component follows another one in the structure tree, it is created by the predecessor and produces geometric data. By double clicking on a component the corresponding parameters are displayed (Figure 2(b)) and can be changed.

In the structure tree of the bush in Figure 1(a), the camera component is the general root. The component with the tree-like symbol produces a branch and defines the positions of subsequent leaves. The component related to the circular symbol multiplies its successors and creates three branches. The double line indicates a recursion. The leaf component defines the geometry of the natural leaves.

The creation of the dandelion will be discussed in the next section to give a better understanding of the graphical interactive generation. In the following we describe some components and show how they can be used to generate specific plants. The last section deals with animating the models.

2   Modelling a dandelion

Modelling a dandelion gives a good example for the techniques that can be used in combination with the rule based object generation. Figure 4 shows six steps during the modelling process. In (a)-(c) an umbrella is created. The user selects a component that produces the geometry of a hair (a). The geometry is shown if the component is connected to the camera component. In the next step an iterator component (named rosette in this example) is inserted to arrange the hair on a rosette. In (c) the rosette is placed on a small stem.

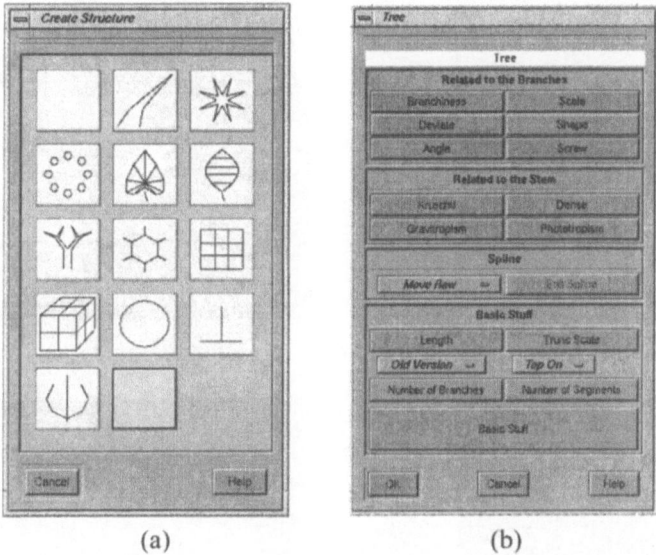

(a)

(b)

Figure 2: (a) Graphical icons of the components that are offered by the system; (b) parameter set of a tree component.

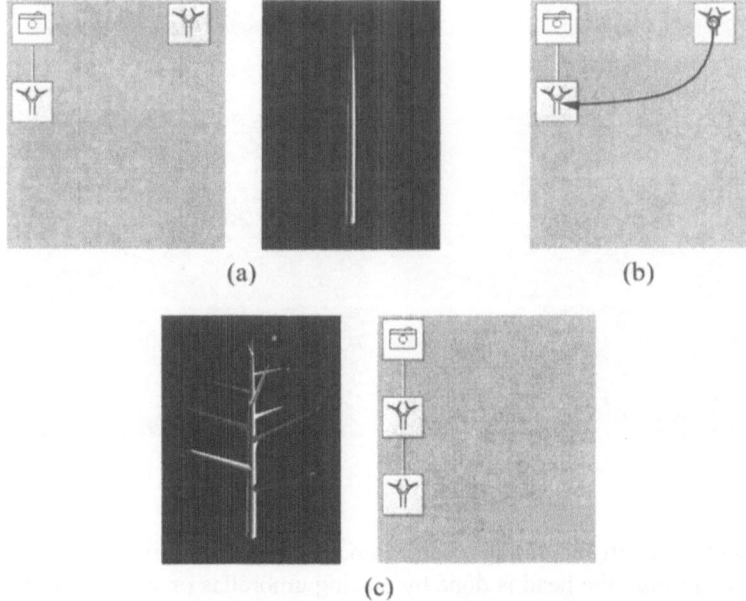

(a)

(b)

(c)

Figure 3: Rules are esthablished graphically: (a) editing window with a simple structure tree and a new created tree component on the right; (b) the tree component is added to the structure tree by moving the icon upon the desired parent icon; (c) resulting structure tree and geometrical result.

142

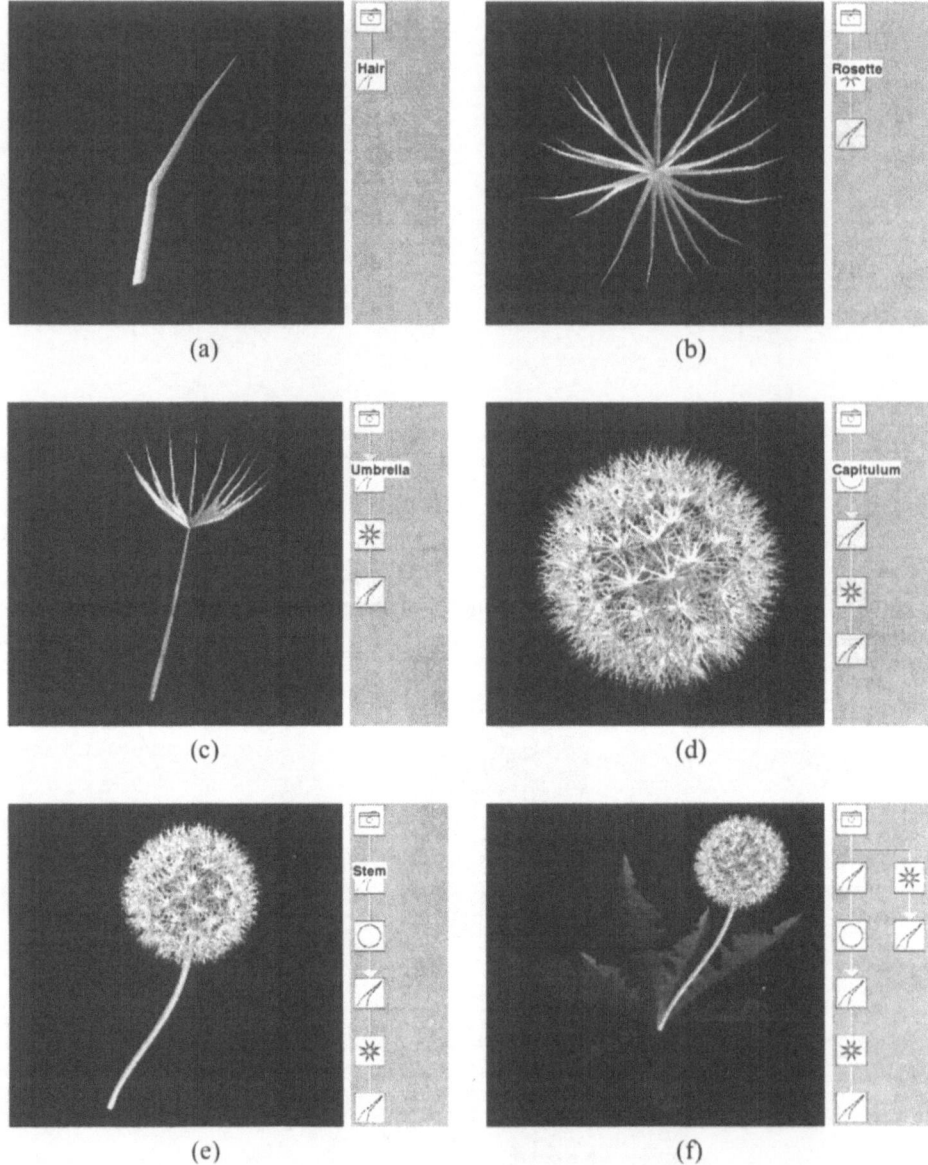

Figure 4: Some steps in generating a dandelion. The umbrellas are modelled by arranging hair on a rosette, the head is done by placing umbrellas on a sphere according to the golden section. Leaves are defined by a sweep component via splines and iterated around the stem by its predecessor.

So far the structure tree consists of three components (excluding the camera). In the next steps the umbrellas are iterated and placed on a sphere according to the golden section (d) and a stem is placed under the head. The stem is defined by a spline to get a smooth curvature. In the last step a leaf is defined by the same component as used for the hair and for the stem. The shape of the leaf is also defined by a spline, axial and lateral curvature increases the natural outline. Six leaves are iterated around the stem.

The generation of the geometric data according to the final structure tree in Figure 4(f) is done as follows: the camera component defines the view and creates the iterator component for the leaves. By this component six leaf components are created by rotating them around the origin. Also created by the camera is the component named stem. This component creates the iterator component (Capitulum) which for its part creates several hundred umbrellas and so on.

The dandelion has about 150k triangles that are created and displayed on a SGI Indigo 2 Extreme with 130 MHz in less than 4 seconds. Creation is done after each changing of a parameter for immediate feedback. It is often useful to reduce the displayed complexity of the model during modelling. This can be done either by reducing the number of generated triangles or by hiding components, which is supported by the system.

3 Components of the system

The modeller offers 14 component types with distinct functionality. All components offer a basic functionality e.g. they can produce point lists that are triangulated in a post-processing step for generating geometric data. These lists can be seen as cross sections of a generated volume (see section 3.2). The position of each point can be edited graphically or displaced at random.

Some components multiply the produced primitives or cross sections algorithmically. By this, the user can edit complex shapes the same way as simple ones. Specialized components encapsulate complex operations or generate special shapes. The components can be classified as follows:

- **generation of complex geometries** (surfaces of revolution, sweep volumes, natural objects (e.g. natural leaves).

- **iteration and arrangement of components** (arrangement of components on curves and splines, fan-like or circular arrangement of components, arrangement according to the golden section for positioning seeds and leaves of a flower, definition of the geometric arrangement of branches).

- **global parameters** (definition of light and gravitation fields, definition of photo- and gravitropism).

- **transformation of subhierarchies** (transformation of successors, deformation of triangle-meshes functionally or by Bézier-hyperpatches).

In the following the components for iteration and arrangement as well as those for trees and for free form deformations are described more detailed.

3.1 Iterator Components

The system gets its power mostly by the iterating components. If one component is created, it runs an associated algorithm. The algorithm can multiply and arrange the successors of the component.

144

An example will clarify this. A special component multiplies its successors and arranges them on a sphere according to the golden section. Different authors supposed the golden section to be a universal principle in nature (c.f. [1]). The golden section component allows to simulate the arrangement of seeds, leaves and umbels of natural flowers.

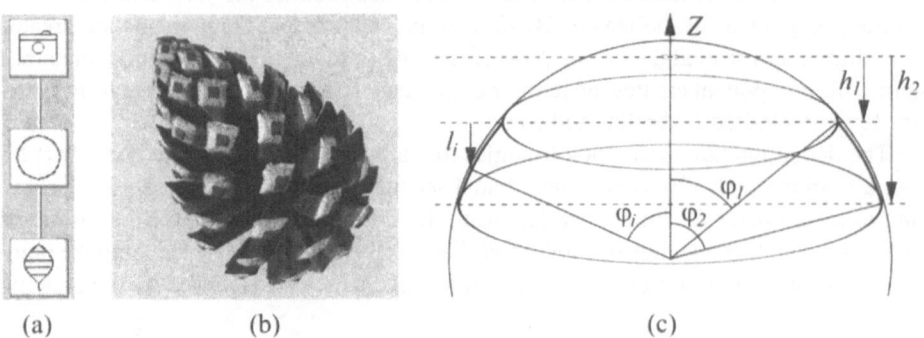

(a) (b) (c)

Figure 5: (a)-(b) Modelling of a cone using an iterating component; (c) some variables used for calculating the sperical golden section.

Figure 5(a) shows the structure tree defining the cone-like model in (b). Parameter variation of the iterating component leads to cones of different shape. The iterating component is represented by the icon with the circular symbol, the geometry of the lamellas are defined by distinct successor components. Parameters of the golden section component are the angles (φ_1, φ_2) defining a circular section on the sphere (see Figure 5(c)), the number of objetcs to be created, the radius of the sphere, an additional vertical translation and a geometric scaling of the created objects.

The mathematical model for arrangements according to the golden section is given for a circular plates and cylinders in [4]. We extend this model to arbitrary spherical sections.

In a first step the distributed objects are supposed to be of unique size. We will extend the method to objects of variable size afterwards. The sphere has a rotation axis $\vec{Z}$. Suppose, N objects are to be placed sucessively around the $\vec{Z}$-axis with accumulating angle $\Phi = 2 * \pi / ((1 + \sqrt{5})/2)$ (the golden section). Each object is then rotated around an axis perpendicular to the $\vec{Z}$-axis by angle φ_i.

We will now derive the formular for computing φ_i during each iteration i. First we compute the height of a spherical section that provides space for i objects. The object i is placed on the outermost edge of this spherical section. On a sphere with the radius R the spherical section $S(\varphi_1, \varphi_2), 0 \leq \varphi_1 < \varphi_2 \leq \pi$ takes an area of

$$A = 2 * \pi * R * h \quad \text{with} \quad h = h_2 - h_1, \quad h_1 = 1 - \cos(\varphi_1), \quad h_2 = 1 - \cos(\varphi_2). \quad (1)$$

To place N objects with an area $A_N = N * A_E$ a sphere with radius

$$R = \frac{A_N}{2 * \pi * h} \quad (2)$$

is needed. For computing φ_i within the i-th iteration, we express the area taken by i

objects $A_i = i * A_E$ as a function of a spherical sections height

$$A_i = 2 * \pi * R * l_i \quad \text{with} \quad l_i = \frac{A_i}{2 * \pi * R} = \frac{A_i * h}{A_N}. \tag{3}$$

Now we compute the angle φ_i by

$$\varphi_i = \text{asin}(h_1 + l_i - 1) = \text{asin}(1 - \cos(\varphi_1) + \frac{A_i * h}{A_N} - 1) \tag{4}$$

$$= \text{asin}(\frac{i}{N} * (\cos(\varphi_1) - \cos(\varphi_2)) - \cos(\varphi_1)). \tag{5}$$

For objects of variable size let a_j be the area of the object j. In this case in equation (4) the variables A_i and A_N are computed by

$$A_N = \sum_{j=1}^{N} a_j \quad \text{and} \quad A_i = \sum_{j=1}^{i} a_j.$$

We assume the area needed by a component to be correlated to its scaling by the iterating component ($a_j \sim Scale(j)^2$).

Figure 6: Some trees: (a) spruce (picea abies); (b) pine (pinus); (c) birch

3.2 Tree Component

Trees usually are built by tree components either in a recursive way as done in the bush of Figure 1 or by cascading them as shown in Figure 3. In Figure 6 two pines and a birch are shown. The structure trees defining the pines (a) and (b) are identical, the characteristic shape was elaborated by modification of the geometric parameters which are encapsulated in the components.

This fact allows the fast design of new trees. If one wants to model another pine than shown in Figure 6(a), the structure tree can be reused, only some geometric parameters have to be changed. The pine in Figure 6(b) was modelled by a trained user in about one hour by reusing the structure tree of part (a). Figure 6(a) was created in two hours.

The tree component distributes branches along a stem according to a density function which is edited graphically. The orientation of single segments (consecutive point lists rsp. cross sections that are triangulated in a post process) is influenced by parameters such as phototropism, gravitropism and "kruschtl" (a helical rotation of the segments around the main axis of the stem as shown in Figure 7(b). Parameterized are also the number of segments, number of forks, fork angles, taper and more.

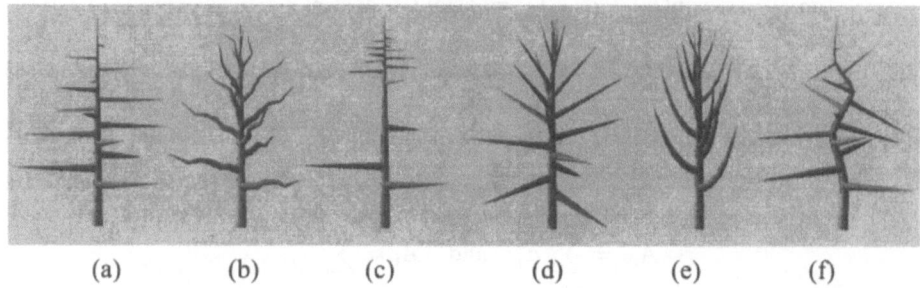

Figure 7: Parameter variations in a tree component: (a) default outline; (b) kruschtl; (c) density; (d) branching angle; (e) phototropism; (f) stem curvature.

Our tree model is similar to a model presented in [8]. Actual parameters at forks delimit the taper, length and the number of subbranches in the next level. The parameter set in each level of branching is defined by a related tree component. Most of the parameters are edited using splines.

In Figure 7 two combined tree components are used to show the effect of some parameters. As can be seen in Figure 6, natural trees are modelled by combining some tree components each defining one level of branching.

Figure 8: Tropisms can be used to model different effects: (a) phototropism of a hemlock (cicuta virosa); (b) gravitropism of a weeping willow; (c) horizontal tropism for simulating the influence of wind.

3.2.1 Tropisms

Tropism parameters of a tree component can be used to model the tendency of plants to grow in special directions. They are realized by postprocessing that re-orients the segments of branches to predefined directions for sunlight and gravity. Figure 8 shows some tropisms. The blossoms of the hemlock are directed towards the sun, the leaves of the weeping willow are directed to the ground. The influence of wind is modelled by a horizontal tropism, circular tropism can be used to model the growth around a stick (see the ivy in Figure 12, see Appendix).

The strength of deviation is delimited by a spline. A special environment component can override the default directions. In this case, three dimensional functions define gravitation and light fields. Influence of the environment, for example the moving sun, wind or partial shadowing, can be simulated by defining corresponding functions.

3.3 Free form deformation

In addition to tropisms, an overall change of the model shape can be achieved by geometric transformation of the generated data. This can be used to fit a model to the users imagination and therefore allows some kind of goal-oriented modelling.

Free form deformation is also done in a postprocessing step. An important feature is that parts of the model can be deformed while other parts are left unchanged.

(a)   (b)   (c)

Figure 9: Applying free form deformation to the stems of a pine (pinus brutia), the leaves stay unchanged.

The free form deformation is done mathematically by mapping the data to the unit cube, deforming the data and finally remapping it. Partial deformation is realized by flags within the components which indicate weather the generated data is to be deformed or not. In Figure 9 (b) and (c) only the branches are deformed, the leaves stay undeformed. Figure 10 shows a simplified pine with the corresponding structure tree. The icons with the box symbol represent the FFD components. The influence range of the deformation component which is connected to the camera is marked with a dashed line.

The deformation can either be defined functionally or by direct manipulation of control points of a Bézier-hyperpatch as shown in Figure 10. The user can capture one or more of the control points and move them parallel to one axial plane. Functional definitions are yet done by editing the function textually, we plan to integrate a voxel-like

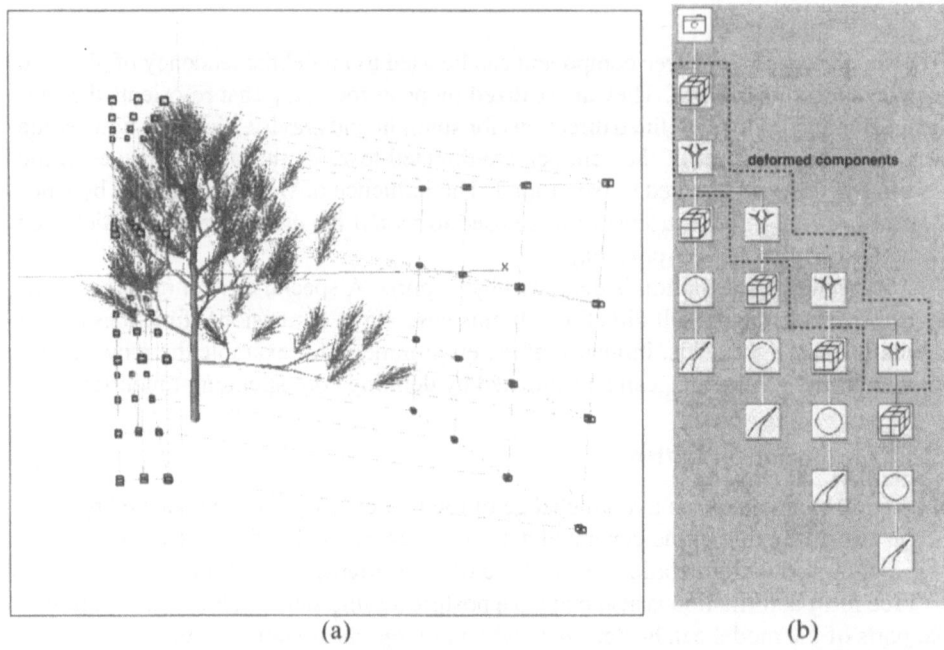

Figure 10: (a) Definition of a free form deformation by a Bézier-hyperpatch in 3-D; (b) corresponding structure tree. Special FFD components are used to switch free form deformation. Only the components in the marked area are deformed.

graphical metapher.

To that point we have shown how to model structural and geometrical properties of real plants by our extended rule based approach. In Figure 12 (see Appendix) some more examples are given which show the flexibility of this approach. In the next section we focus on animation.

4   Animating models

The algorithmical generation of objects has another important advantage over string re-writing systems like L-systems: real keyframing is applicable. While L-Systems were adapted to animation by introducing additional differential equations (c.f. [5]) in our ap-proach nearly every parameter can be animated over time. Keyframing is simply done on the parameter sets of the components within the structure tree. This includes for ex-ample the number of objetcs created by an iterator, the scale of a free form deformation, colors and the outline of a single leaf.

Local time is used to get specific behaviour of parts of a growing plant. If the num-ber of blossoms of a flower increases over time, the growing of every blossom is the same process due to the rule based approach. Local time beginning with the birth of each blossom enables a natural behaviour of the overall growth. Figure 11 shows the process within the growth of a fern. Each twig and each leaf grows according to its local time.

Figure 11: Example frames of an animation with embedded keyframing. The growth of the twigs and leaves starts at different times, each leaf uses its local time for growing.

The twigs are arranged according to the golden section by an iterating component which increases the number of twigs over time.

Any subhierarchy of the structure tree that is iterated and shall grow in respect to a local time is defined in a separate keyframe sequence called entity. Special components serve as interfaces between the main structure tree and those entities. These components administrate a multidimensional dynamic array that holds for any iteration the corresponding local time. The global time is mapped to the local time of the entities in respect to the time of their birth. By a supposed life duration and a user definable mapping function even sequential, cyclic and sinoidal processes can be simulated. Keyframing of the life duration parameter enables also growth of an entity with distinct speeds for different iterations.

If an interface component is created, it locates its iteration number and creates the associated entity with the interpolated parameter set according to the determined local time. In respect to the hierachical structure of keyframe sequences we named this method embedded keyframing.

5 Conclusion and Future Work

We presented a new concept for modelling natural branching objects. The use of objects as elements of the rule system introduces new features into the modelling process. Well-known modelling methods such as spline techniques and free form deformation can be integrated. Objects can be iterated algorithmically. This can not be done in conventional string rewriting systems. Based on this method we built an interactive modeller. The rule system is represented by a structure tree which can be edited graphically.

The object orientated approach allows to apply keyframing techniques to a rule based system, the algorithmical iteration of components introduce simulation of partial growth according to a local time. Future work will focus on global growth constraints as well as deformation and dynamic simulation of model structure and geometry.

The modeling software is available as a shareware, more information can be obtained by looking at http://www.greenworks.de .

References

1. A. Beutelspacher and B. Petri. *Der Goldene Schnitt.* BI Wissenschaftsverlag, Zürich, 1988.
2. P. de Reffye, C. Edelin, J. Francon, M. Jaeger, and C. Puech. Plant models faithful to botanical structure and development. In J. Dill, editor, *Computer Graphics (SIGGRAPH '88 Proceedings)*, volume 22, pages 151–158, August 1988.
3. M. Holton. Strands, gravity and botanical tree imagery. *Computer Graphics Forum*, 13(1):57–67, 1994.
4. R. V. Jean. Mathematical modelling in phyllotaxis: The state of the art. *Mathematical Biosciences*, 64:1–27, 1983.
5. P. Prusinkiewicz, M. S. Hammel, and E. Mjolsness. Animation of plant development. *Computers Graphics Proceedings*, pages 351–360, 1993.

6. P. Prusinkiewicz and A. Lindenmayer. *The Algorithmic Beauty of Plants*. Springer-Verlag, New York, 1990.

7. P. Prusinkiewicz, A. Lindenmayer, and J. Hanan. Developmental models of herbaceous plants for computer imagery purposes. In J. Dill, editor, *Computer Graphics (SIGGRAPH '88 Proceedings)*, volume 22, pages 141–150, August 1988.

8. J. Weber and J. Penn. Creation and rendering of realistic trees. In *Computer Graphics (SIGGRAPH '95 Proceedings)*, pages 119–128, August 1995.

Editors' Note: see Appendix, p. 223f. for colored figures of this paper

An Efficient Estimation of Light in Simulation of Plant Development

Bedřich Beneš

Department of Computer Science, Czech Technical University,
Karlovo nám. 13, Prague, Czech Rep.
e-mail: benes@sgi.felk.cvut.cz

Abstract. During a simulation of plant development evaluation of the amount of light plays a significant role. Most of the previous works take into account only constant amount and constant direction of the light in the scene without respect to local shadows in the tree. In the other works this evaluation strongly depends on the number of objects in the scene.

This paper introduces a new method for evaluation of amount of light for the artificial plants. This technique is based on Z-buffer algorithm and has the ability to evaluate the direction and the amount of light for every leaf in the plant with a significantly decreased time of calculation. Several new aspects of lifetime of the plant elements and of the whole plant are discussed.

1 Introduction

Plenty of papers have been written about the plants in the computer graphics and also many classifications of published methods have been presented. One classification would be done from the view of the aim of the method. Some of the methods are useful for particular reason e.g for modeling of the the phylotaxis [4], for generating plants in real time [10, 22], for the film industry [17]. The others use formal methods and they try to describe some model or method in general regardless to the application which is found subsequently. Some of these methods generate climbing plants in voxel space [5], some use strands topology for description of branching [6], some use string rewriting systems for simulation of plant development [14] or use a combinatorial approach for describing the branching structure [21].

Another possible classification introduced by [19] focuses the generated structure. The model is said to be *topological* or *structural* oriented if the generated structure carries information mostly about the adjacency of the parts [6, 14, 19] or [21]. On the other hand, the model is *geometrically* or *space* oriented if it primary consists of the information about the space occupation [1, 4, 5] or [8].

Another view emphasizes only the final shape of the plant on a desired level of accuracy. The speed of such generation of the model is the strongest requirement in this kind of modeling. This is always in contradiction to the requirement of the quality of the model [10, 22].

The ability of simulation of the plant development [2, 5, 7, 11, 12, 15] is the next way how to classify these methods. In this paper we will point out those methods which take into account ability of interaction with environment. We will discuss several aspect of simulation on level of buds and we will focus in the size of the bud. Then we will introduce a new algorithm for the estimation of light. We will also briefly present a continuous model of simulation.

2   Previous work

In 1968 Lindenmayer introduced a definition of a string rewriting system which he used for simulation of development of multicellular organisms [9]. In 1984 Smith used this formalism for generation of the plants [19] and subsequently named this method *L-system*. The result of this simulation which is "almost" fractal he denoted *graftal*. The theory of *L-systems* has been extensively developed. The last works include continuous simulation of development [11], using differential equations and ability to interact with the environment using so called *query modules* [12, 13]. The query modules are components of the rewriting process and have the form

$$?X(x,y,z); \; X = P, H, U, L \tag{1}$$

where H, U, L are axis and P denotes a position of a local coordinate system of element in 3D space. Parameters x, y, z are attributes of query module. The values of the attributes are set when the process of rewriting asks the query model for them. The independence of structural and geometrical representation which is one of the advantages of *L-systems* is lost here. We must always construct the whole plant when we need to rewrite the string.

Reeves introduces *particle systems* in [16] for purposes of the film industry. He uses particles for the generation of stochastic models of grass and forests two years later [17] and does not concentrate on detail of the individual plant. He also uses special methods for the rendering of such groups of plants where the light is scaled down by exponential function in the forest [17] page 317. Although the light parameters of the scene are simulated they are not used when the plants are generated. The result of this model was again used in movies.

Very impressive results were obtained in voxel space [5]. Greene performs stochastic growth where multiple trials are attempted. Position of a growing element and its orientation are randomly perturbed, fitness function is evaluated and the best position and orientation are used as a result of the new growth direction. For every element the distance from the "center of mass" is evaluated. If the trial which lies the closest distance from the obstacle is used the effect of climbing plants is very easily obtained in this simulation. The amount of light is achieved by 3DDA sampling of the trajectory of the sun. Several rays are cast for every growth element and the coefficient of *sky exposure* is evaluated as a relative number of occluded and free rays. The effect of heliotropism is achieved by constructing the illumination table at each node. Several rays are cast to cover as much from the sky as possible. The black table entries represent obstructed rays and the white unobstructed ones. The low pass filter is then used and the "hot spot" on the sky is found. This place represents the direction of further growth of the growing element.

An alternative method of the light direction estimation is represented in work [7]. Chiba et al. work on the assumption that the amount of the light is constant for every point on the celestial sphere. They introduce a *leaf ball* which is an approximation of a cluster of leaves. This object is translucent with transparency according to the number of leaves in the leaf ball. The light estimation is determined by projection of these balls to the celestial sphere. The estimation is executed by applying the hidden surface algorithm or 3DDA in voxel space. In [7] the brightest direction is defined as a sum of the participating vectors associated with each ray which reaches the celestial sphere.

Holton's philosophy of *strands* comes from the fact that every branch consists of a collection of threads [6]. These threads run indivisible from root to the leaves. To describe the topological structure we need to know only the branching probabilities. About 2000 - 8000 strands are necessary to generate a realistic model. Bézier curves are used as the axis of generalized cylinders when branches are generated. The biggest advantage of this method is its clearness. We do not need very wide experience to describe the model of the plant. Holton also included in his model:

- *gravicentrism* – the tendency of the stem of the plant to grow against gravity,
- *gravimorphism* – the tendency of the branches to grow against or with the gravity,
- *phototropism* – the tendency of branches to grow in direction of the light,
- *orthotropism* – the tendency of the plant to grow vertically upward,
- *plagiotropism* – the tendency to grow in a horizontal direction,
- *planatropism* – the tendency of the plane defined by two branches to be perpendicular to the axis of the parent branch.

Although he mentioned in the case of phototropism that the light should be evaluated for every branch [6] page 61, Holton does not say how to do that.

3   The growth model

In our work we do not concentrate on precise geometry of the plant. We use lines as a branches and simplified leaves consisting of several triangles. This representation is then used as a skeleton of the model introduced by [1], which can be ray traced.

We use the stochastic model according to de Reffye at al. [2]. This model works on the level of *buds* (see figure 1). The bud is a basic growing element which can perform several actions. The action depends on external (environmental) and internal conditions of the plant. A bud can either

156

- die or
- bloom and die or
- sleep for a while or
- become an internode (see figure 2).

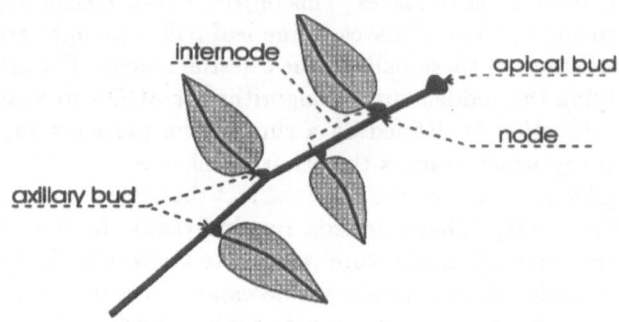

Fig. 1. A branch model according to de Reffye.

One of the problems of plant simulation is the lifetime of the plant. We have extended the model [2] in such a way that every bud has a defined *size*. The size corresponds to the amount of apical meristem allowing a bud to grow. This size consequently corresponds to the lifetime of the bud and controls the length of the branch.

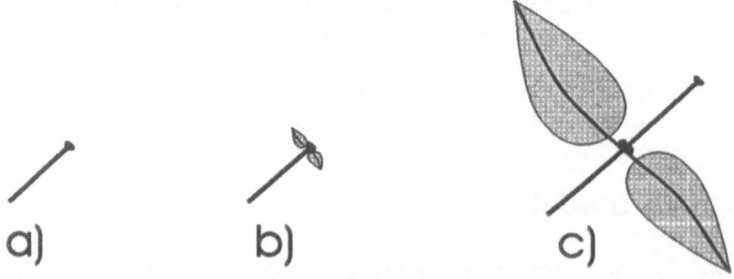

Fig. 2. Apical bud becoming an internode. a) Apex with an apical bud. b) Several leaves and lateral buds appear at their axil. c) The apical bud produces a piece of stem.

Until the bud can grow it produces axil buds with orientation depending on phylotaxis. The size of the generated buds depends on the size of the generating apical buds. The size of the new bud should always be smaller than the size of the apical bud. If the size of new bud is the same or even bigger than the size of apical bud we obtain infinite growth. Denote $a, b \in \mathcal{R}^+ \cup \{0\}$ to be size of the apical and of the axial bud respectively. Having

$$b = \frac{a}{k}; \; k > 1 \tag{2}$$

the length of branches at different orders forms a geometrical succession.

Another phenomenon we can simulate using size of buds are different branching patterns. There are three basic types of branching patterns in nature: *basitonic*, *mesotonic* and *acrotonic* [13] page 19. All of these cases are shown in figure 3.

Assume linear time flow and $t \in \langle 0, 1 \rangle$ to be a lifetime of the bud a. In case of acrotonic growth an axial bud b will have size

$$b = t \, a \tag{3}$$

Changing the size of the axial bud b according to the following formula we obtain the basitonic growth:

$$b = (1 - t) \, a \tag{4}$$

And finally mesotonic growth can be described with:

$$b = \left(\frac{1}{2} - \left| \frac{1}{2} - t \right| \right) \, a \tag{5}$$

Fig. 3. Different branching pattens generated using different sizes of the bud: (from left) mesotonic, basitonic and acrotonic.

3.1 Estimation of the light

Light estimation is a very important part in the simulation of plant development. The buds will die due to lack of light coming to the leaves or become a bloom if the amount of the light is enough. The branch has a tendency to raise leaves and flowers to the light so new growth direction depends on the direction of the highest quantity of the light that is, on the position of a brightest spot as watched from the growth element.

158

Evaluating the amount of the light. We use sampling methods for the light estimation. The sampling direction is opposite to that in the works [5] and [7]. We sample from the sky to the fixed point (e.g the basis) of the plant. One sample consists of moving the camera to the proper point on the hemisphere and having a look at the plant. Using the Z-buffer algorithm we see from this view only those parts of the plant which are affected by the light coming from the direction corresponding to the position of the camera.

The best advantage of this method is independency of the number of samples to the number of objects in the scene. The number of samples is always constant. The quality of the sampling is affected only with the size of the sampling area (see figures 4 and 5).

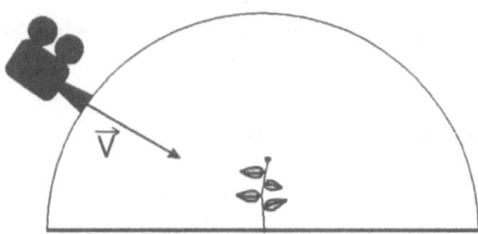

Fig. 4. Sampling of the plant from the hemisphere.

We must ensure in our algorithm that every leaf in the scene is unique. The ordering number in which a leaf was born is assigned to every leaf. During the sampling phase the plant is rendered in such a way that every leaf has assigned a different color according to its ordering number. This is easily achieved with a simple mapping function between RGB space and the ordering number. Only the leaves have different color. Every other elements have the same color as a background, so they may occlude the light.

What is essential for further computation is the area of the leaf which is visible from the sampling direction. This area is computed from the *histogram* of the sampled picture (see figure 5). The histogram is a vector of absolute frequencies of values in the picture. In our case the histogram corresponds to the visible area of the leaves projected to the plane perpendicular to the projection direction (vector v at picture 4).

We need to know a relative number of exposure of every leaf. Denote $e_i \in \langle 0, 1 \rangle$ to be the relative number of exposure of leaf i. Value zero corresponds to absolute hiddenness and value e_i equal to one corresponds to total exposure of the leaf. Denote by h_i a value obtained from the histogram for the leaf i. Because *parallel projection* [3] was used we know that the maximal possible value h_i^{max} obtained for the leaf i might be

$$h_i^{max} = a_i * \frac{res_x * res_y}{ortho_x * ortho_y} \qquad (6)$$

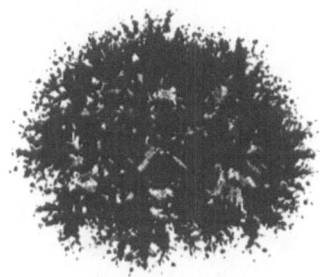

Fig. 5. A snap from the sampling camera with different color for every leaf assigned.

where a_i is the absolute area of the leaf in the space of camera, res_x, res_y are values of the resolution of the sampled snap in pixels and $orho_x, ortho_y$ are values of the camera viewport.

There are several tips on how to evaluate the area of the leaf a_i. A very straightforward way is to approximate the leaf by several triangles and compute the area of every triangle in the following way. Let $t_j; j = 1, \ldots, n$ be a triangular approximation of the leaf. Every triangle t_j consist of points x_j, y_j and z_j. The area s_j of the triangle can be calculated using the vector product:

$$s_j = \frac{|(x_j - y_j) \times (y_j - z_j)|}{2} \tag{7}$$

The area of the leaf i will be:

$$a_i = \sum_{j=1}^{n} s_j. \tag{8}$$

The relative number of exposure can be easily evaluated from equation (6) and the histogram value h_i;

$$e_i = \frac{h_i}{h_i^{max}} \tag{9}$$

The total amount of light coming to the leaf would be increased by the amount of ambient light presented in the crown of the tree. In our simulation we use the value 0.1.

The only problem is with aliasing. If the leaf becomes smaller than one pixel it is invisible on the display. This situation is represented in the histogram with a value of zero and the leaf should be removed. We have stated a so called "preserving time" for every leaf. This means if the area of the leaf is less than some constant we state that it has total exposure.

Suppose an artificial example with one direction of light coming from the top and no ambient light present. Assume the leaf will die due to lack of light if there is less than 5% exposure. Figure 6 shows the shedding due to lack of light.

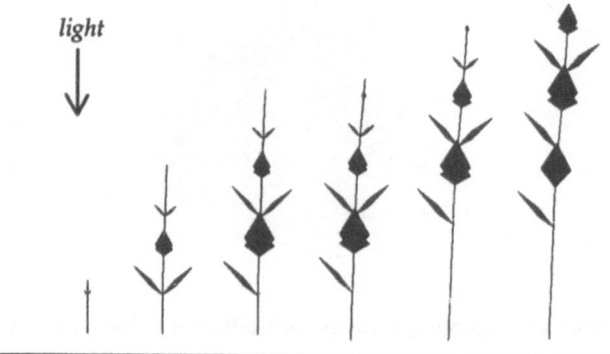

Fig. 6. Process of dying of leaves due to lack of the light.

Evaluating the growth direction. Chiba et al. state [7] on page 6:

> ...the brightest direction vector is defined as *the sum* of the vectors each
> of which has the same direction as each ray which reaches the celestial
> sphere...

This approach leads to wrong results as can be seen in the 2D example in figure 7.
Having one leading shoot and an obscuring plane over it we obtain two brightest

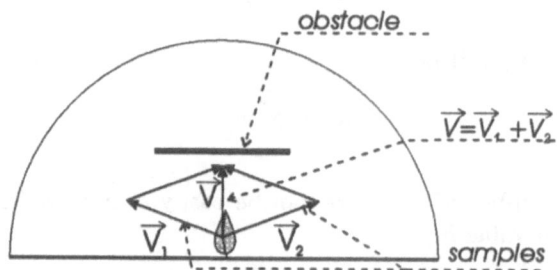

Fig. 7. Estimation of the brightest spot on the sky using sum of the samples leads to
unadequate results.

direction vectors v_1 and v_2. Their sum v is direct to the center of the black space.

In our simulation the direction vector for every sample has an opposite sign
to the potential growth direction (see figure 4). The brightest direction vector is
the vector from the direction which brings the maximal amount of light from all
of these samples. If there is more than one possibility one of them is *randomly*
chosen. In the case of our example from the figure 7 we would choose one of the
vectors v_1 or v_2.

The direction vector of the leaf with maximum exposure nearest to the bud
is used as a new growth direction. We modify this direction in such a way as

in [6], it is: the new direction vector v_{new} is computed as a vector sum of the old one and of one giving the direction of the brightest spot s multiplied by the coefficient of sun seeking k_s:

$$v_{new} = v_{old} + k_s s. \tag{10}$$

Figure 8 demonstrates a change in the shape of the plant under the very strong light source coming from the direction $(1, 1, 0)$.

Fig. 8. Left figure demonstrates plant with phylotaxis $2\pi/3$ and acrotonic growth. On the right is the same plant under the influence of very strong light coming from the direction $(1, 1, 0)$

There are several ways to sample the sky. Greene [5] samples the sun trajectory and Chiba et al. [7] state that the sky has constant exposure at its every point. We must estimate the relative weights of the samples depending on the duration of the simulation. These weights represent the percentage of the maximal possible amount of the light coming from one direction. It is obvious that

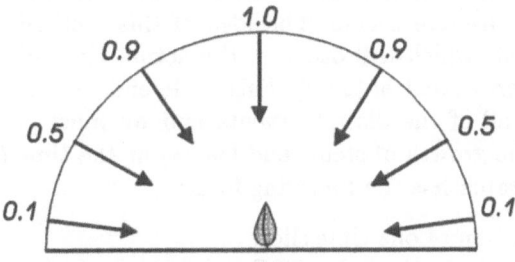

Fig. 9. The relative weights of the samples are smaller in the morning than at noon.

162

for a long period there is no reason why to sample the sun trajectory. But on the other hand, the power of the sun is less in the morning than at noon. We propose a solution as shown in figure 9.

Figure 10 demonstrates the following two approaches. A constant amount of light from every side was used on the right picture. The left picture demonstrates the sample weighting according to figure 9. This result seems to be more realistic.

Fig. 10. Left figure demonstrates plant with exposure weighting, on the second one constant light coming from all of the sides was used

4 Simulation algorithm

We use continuous simulation in our model. Input to the algorithm is a desired number of frames, duration of the simulation and parameters of the plant. We use an algorithm with a discrete time step. This method works on the assumption that in every time slice $\langle t, t + \delta \rangle$ the environment conditions do not change. Events like ramification and death of the bud, the leaf or the branch are inherently discrete. They can occur anytime in the time slice. We use a method called "event planning" for discrete events. The idea of this method is following: we find first discrete event which will occur in the actual time slice. This event is performed and new first event is found. This cycle ends at the end of the time slice. We have done all of the discrete events and we must perform all of the continuous events (the growth of stems and leaves) at the time $t + \delta$.

The algorithm scratch has the following form:

- compute the duration of one time slice:
  $\delta = lengthOfSimulation/numberOfFrames$
- for every time slice $\langle t, t + \delta \rangle$ do
  - estimate the amount of light for every leaf.

- • do every discrete event in $\langle t, t + \delta \rangle$
- • growth continuous elements to time $t + \delta$
- • generate geometry
- • save script for ray tracer
- – increase time by δ

5   A note about artificial life

Smith [19] mentioned the term *database amplification* also cited by [3] and [13]. Database amplification is the possibility of generating complex structures from small data sets. The second study [13] also state that this term is related to *emergence* what is one of the central themes of the study of the artificial life [20]. Emergence is a process in which a collection of interacting units acquires qualitatively new properties [20].

We can look to the plant modeling as described in this paper also from this viewpoint. The buds are the interacting entities. They compete together for the light obtaining a positive fitness value (see also [18]) if the light is reached. The worst are removed from the simulation. The final shape of the plant is the emergent phenomenon.

6   Implementation and results

Silicon Graphics Indigo^2 with Extreme graphics board and R4400/200MHz has been used. We use hardware *Z-buffer* for the light estimation. A generating of a sequence consisting of 200 frames of the plant with the final number of leaves about 3000 and 50 samples per frame takes approximately two hours. The bottleneck of this method is the histogram evaluation. On the other hand even only 10 samples bring valuable results and the difference between 50 and 500 samples is below the level of recognition. A sampling area on 400×400 pixels resolution was used.

7   Conclusion

A new method for estimation of the amount of light and growth direction of the growing elements of the plant has been presented in this paper. This method uses taking snaps of the plant from the celestial hemisphere and evaluating the histogram for calculation of the exposure. The number of samples is independent to the number of objects in the scene. We have also presented the size of the bud as a control mechanism for the generating of the branching pattern of the plant.

8   Acknowledgements

We would like to thank Mr. Jiří Žára, Mr. Pavel Slavík, Mr. Aleš Holeček and Mr. Jan Přikryl for their valuable discussion.

References

1. J. Bloomenthal. Modeling the mighty maple. In *Proceedings of SIGGRAPH '85, in Computer Graphics Proceedings, Annual Conference Series 1985*, volume 19(3), pages 305–311, 1985.

2. P. de Reffye, C. Edelin, J. Fracon, M. Jaeger, and C. Puech. Plants models faithful to botanical structure and developement. In *Proceedings of SIGGRAPH '88, in Computer Graphics, Annual Conference Series 1988*, volume 22(4), pages 151–158, 1988.

3. J. Foley, A. van Dam, and J. Hughes. *Computer Graphics: Principles and practice.* Addison-Wesley, Reading, 1990.

4. D. Fowler, P. Prusinkiewicz, and J. Batjes. A collision-based model of spiral phyllotaxis. *ACM Computer Graphics*, 26:361–368, 1992.

5. N. Greene. Voxel space automata: Modeling with stochastic growth processes in voxel space. In *Proceedings of SIGGRAPH '89, in Computer Graphics Proceedings, Annual Conference Series 1989*, volume 23(4), pages 175–184, 1989.

6. M. Holton. Strands, gravity and botanical tree imagery. *Computer Graphics Forum*, 13(I):57–67, 1994.

7. N. Chiba, S. Okawa, K. Muroaka, and M. Muira. Visual simulation of botanical trees based on virtual heliotropism and dormancy break. *The Journal of Visualization and Computer Animation*, 5:3–15, 1994.

8. Y. Kawaguchi. A morphological study of the form of nature. *ACM Computer Graphics*, 16(3):223–232, 1982.

9. A. Lindenmayer. Mathematical models for cellular interaction in development. *Journal of Theoretical Biology*, Parts I and II(18):280–315, 1968.

10. P. Oppenheimer. Real time design and animation of fractal plants and trees. In *Proceedings of SIGGRAPH '86, in Computer Graphics, Annual Conference Series 1986*, volume 20(4), pages 55–64, 1986.

11. P. Prusinkiewicz, S. Hammel, and E. Mjolsness. Animation of plant development. In *Proceedings of SIGGRAPH '93, in Computer Graphics, Annual Conference Series 1993*, volume I, pages 351–360, 1993.

12. P. Prusinkiewicz, M. James, and R. Měch. Synthetic topiary. In *Proceedings of SIGGRAPH '94, in Computer Graphics, Annual Conference Series 1994*, volume I, pages 351–358, 1993.

13. P. Prusinkiewicz, M. James, R. Měch, and J. Hannan. The artifical life of plants. In *Course Notes of SIGGRAPH '95, in Computer Graphics, Annual Conference Series 1995*, volume I, pages 1–38, 1995.

14. P. Prusinkiewicz and A. Lindenmayer. *The algorithmic beauty of plants.* Springer-Verlag, New York, 1990.

15. P. Prusinkiewicz, A. Lindenmayer, and J. Hanan. Developmental models of herbaceous plants for computer graphics imagery purposes. In *Proceedings of SIGGRAPH '88, in Computer Graphics, Annual Conference Series 1988*, volume 22(4), pages 141–150, 1988.

16. W. Reeves. Particle systems – a technique for modeling a class of fuzzy objects. *ACM Transaction on Graphics*, 2(2):12–22, 1983.

17. W. Reeves and R. Blau. Approximate and probabilistic algorithms for shading and rendering structured particle systems. In *Proceedings of SIGGRAPH '85, in Computer Graphics, Annual Conference Series 1985*, volume 19(3), pages 313–322, 1985.

18. K. Sims. Evolving 3D morphology and behavior by competition. In *Artificial Life IV Proceedings*, volume I, pages 28–39, 1994.

19. A. Smith. Plants, fractals and formal languages. In *Proceedings of SIGGRAPH '84, in Computer Graphics, Annual Conference Series 1984*, volume 18(3), pages 1–10, 1984.

20. C. Taylor. *"Fleshing out" Artificial Life II*, volume II. Addison-Wesley, Redwood City, 1992.

21. X. Viennot, G. Eyrolles, N. Janey, and D. Arques. Combinatorial analysis of ramified patterns and computer imagery trees. In *Proceedings of SIGGRAPH '89, in Computer Graphics, Annual Conference Series 1989*, volume 23(3), pages 31–40, 1989.

22. J. Weber and J. Penn. Creation and rendering of realistic trees. In *Proceedings of SIGGRAPH '95, in Computer Graphics Proceedings, Annual Conference Series 1995*, volume 22(4). ACM SIGGRAPH New York, 1995.

Editors' Note: see Appendix, p. 225 for colored figures of this paper

5

Motion Control and Motion Management

A Planning Algorithm for Dynamic Motions

Pedro S. Huang[1]
Michiel van de Panne[2]

Department of Computer Science
University of Toronto

Abstract

Motions such as flips and jumps are challenging to animate and to perform in real life. The difficulty arises from the dynamic nature of the movements and the precise timing required for their successful execution. This paper presents a decision-tree search algorithm for planning the control for these types of motion. Several types of results are presented, including cartwheels, flips and hops for a two-link gymnastic 'acrobot'. It is also shown that the same search algorithm is effective at a macroscopic scale for planning dynamic motions across rugged terrain.

Animations: `http://www.dgp.utoronto.ca/people/van/ani.html`

1 Introduction

Creating realistic movement for animated objects is a difficult task, one which remains difficult even if a physical simulation is used. Controlling a simulated gymnast involves solving the same problem that the real gymnast faces in executing a sequence of manoevres. Of particular interest to us are unstable, dynamic motions which must typically rely on careful timing and accumulated momentum in order to be successful. These dynamic motions also make for visually-compelling animations, in part because of the recognition of the difficulty of performing these motions.

In this paper we show that classical techniques borrowed from early work in Artificial Intelligence (AI) can do well at solving difficult control problems. In particular, the decision-tree search algorithm we exploit is well suited to taking advantage of the many constraints that arise in control problems. The algorithm also has some very undesirable characteristics, notably its exponential complexity with respect to the dimensionality and discretization of the control space. The goal here, however, is to further understand the control of motions which are difficult because of their dynamic nature and natural instability.

---

[1] Author's present address: Rhythm & Hues Studios, `huang@rhythm.com`.
[2] `van@dgp.utoronto.ca`

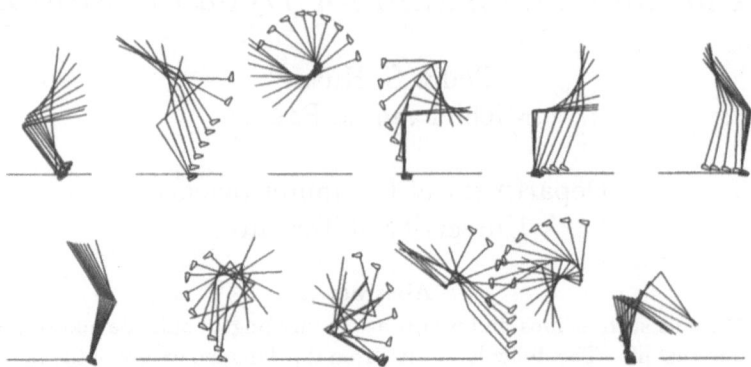

Figure 1: A Flipping Acrobot. The acrobot is displayed at 0.05 second intervals and are further separated into groups of eight for clarity. These groups should be read from left to right, and top to bottom.

Some of the movements created using the search technique are shown in Figures 1 and 2. The motion in Figure 1 is that of a gymnast or 'acrobot' which can bend forcefully at the waist in order to perform back flips and front flips, all the while maintaining balance. The foot drawn in Figure 1 has been added for cosmetic purposes; the foot in the underlying simulation exists only as a single point at the end of the leg. In order to be convinced of the difficulty of the resulting control problem, we encourage the reader to try the following experiment. While standing upright, place all the weight on the heels and attempt to maintain balance by bending only at the waist. Performing a sequence of flips is predictably even more difficult.

While the motion in Figure 1 was obtained by conducting a search using low-level control primitives, it is also possible to take advantage of existing high-level control primitives in order to conduct a control search at a macroscopic scale. In Figure 2, a search is conducted using several types of jumps as primitives. The goal is to determine a sequence of jumps which allow Luxo, the jumping lamp, to successfully negotiate some treacherous terrain. The animator defines the desired shape of the terrain, and the search algorithm then produces the necessary sequence of jumps in order to traverse it. Note that the planning necessary for this type of motion is more difficult than simply choosing the jump-size which could leap over an upcoming abyss. For traversing rugged terrain, the dynamic movements require advance planning in order to be successful. At present there are few known solutions for the planning of such motions.

The remainder of this paper covers various aspects of the proposed algorithm in greater detail. Section 2 provides a summary of related work from the fields of computer animation, robotics, control, and AI. Section 3 gives the details of the search algorithm itself. The search algorithm is used to plan control at both

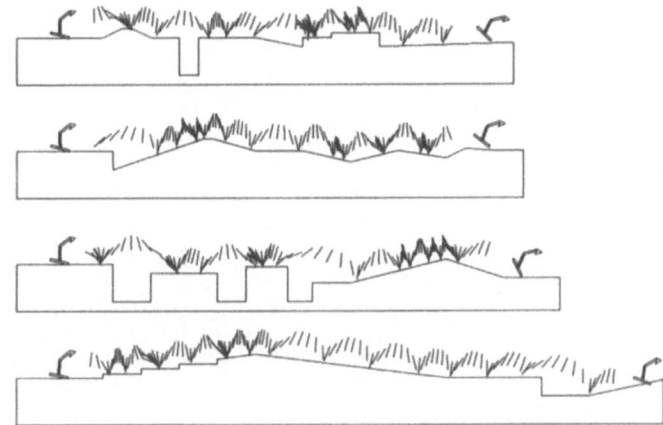

Figure 2: Luxo goes cross-country running. The position of the middle link or 'leg' of Luxo is shown every 0.1 seconds. The complete position of Luxo is given at the start and end of each motion, buffered by several skipped frames for clarity.

a low-level and high-level, discussed in sections 4 and 5, respectively. Lastly, conclusions and future work are presented in section 6.

2 Background

It is natural to draw upon work in control theory as a starting point for dealing with control problems in animation. Indeed, one of the motivations for this work was to attempt to tackle a problem which is receiving attention within the control community, namely that of controlling *underactuated* mechanisms. An underactuated mechanism is one which has fewer actuators than degrees of freedom. As an extreme example, we consider the *acrobot*, shown in Figure 3. The acrobot is a two-link robot with a single actuator placed at the connecing joint P_2 and effecting a torque between the two links. Point P_1 will be referred to as the *foot* and point P_3 as the *head*.

We work with the acrobot for two reasons. First, articulated figures such as humans are effectively underactuated because ankles only provide limited control over the global orientation of the body. Second, the acrobot serves as an example of an articulated figure that is difficult to control despite having very few degrees of freedom (DOF). Our contention is that the dynamic and unstable nature of a motion is a more important criterion than the the number of DOFs of an object in measuring the difficulty of controlling a movement. An illustrative example is

172

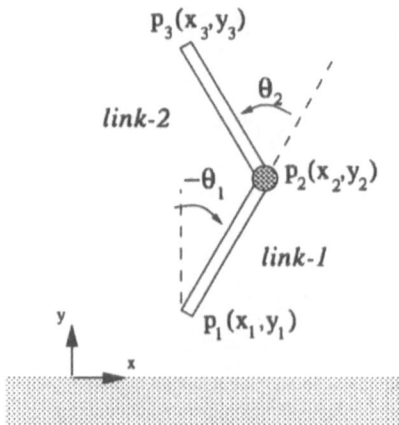

Figure 3: The acrobot.

to compare platform diving to swimming. Platform diving is arguably a more difficult motion to perform because of the timing and precision with which it must be executed.

The work of Hauser and Murray[HM90] first proposed a controller which could make an acrobot balance in place. In this case, the acrobot's foot is fixed to the ground using a frictionless, unactuated hinge. Bortoff and Spong[Bor92][BS92] use approximate linearization to produce slow movements among stable configurations. Their method is also shown to work on a real acrobot system.

Berkemeier and Fearing[BF92] attempt further types of motion with the acrobot and arrive at a controller capable of balancing, sliding, and hopping, subject to some constraints on the acrobot's physical design. The control for both balancing and sliding is successfully tested[BF94] using an inclined mechanism to reduce the effects of gravity. The hop is not implemented due to technical difficulties.

The challenge of controlling running motions for creatures with 'light-weight' legs has been successfully tackled and applied to animation by Raibert and Hodgins[RH91]. A variety of gaits are controlled for monoped, biped and quadruped creatures. The strategy for locomotion decomposes control into three separable components: (1) height control, (2) attitude control, and (3) speed control. Hodgins[HR90] also presents a control system to perform biped gymnastics, which is constructed by dealing with the takeoff, aerial, and landing phases as distinct control phases.

In some cases, controller design can be automated by using parameter optimization techniques. From the biomechanical literature, Pandy[PAH92] parameterizes the control history of a nonlinear dynamical system using a set of nodal points. Controllers based on stimulus-response rules are proposed by Ngo and Marks[NM93], who synthesize them using genetic algorithms. Sensor-actuator networks are introduced by Van de Panne and Fiume[vF93] to synthesize closed-loop locomotion control for a variety of simulated creatures equiped with binary sensors. Sims[Sim94] further uses genetic algorithms and a different type of control architecture to automate the generation of controllers capable of interesting behaviour. 'Virtual wind-up toys' are proposed by Van de Panne et al[vKF94] in order to examine the limits of open-loop, cyclic control signals in producing locomotion. Grzeszczuk and Terzopoulos [GT95] synthesize realistic locomotion for the animation of deformable physics-based animals in an aquatic environment, making use of simulated annealing techniques to produce the required control.

The search algorithm we present here is related to that presented in [vFV93], in which a search algorithm is used to plan turning motions for bicyclists and skiers. It is also loosely related to work on randomized path planning in configuration spaces.

3   The Search Algorithm

The search space for our problem consists of a series of sequential control decisions to be made at discrete instants in time. In the case of the acrobot, a control decision determines the desired position for joint p_2. The joint is driven towards the desired position over time using a proportional-derivative (PD) controller. The desired position is held constant for a chosen duration of $0.2s$, whereafter another control decision must be made. The choice of control duration should in general be correlated to the figure being animated and the type of movement being performed.

Our proposed approach for arriving at a sequence of successful control decisions is similar to those used in game-playing strategies, in that we evaluate the consequences of actions several stages into the future. For our animated figure, this corresponds to carrying out multiple simulations which explore the effects of different control sequences. Our particular strategy is a best-first search tree[Win84], exploring n stages into the future. With each stage having a duration of T seconds, this means motions have always been successfully planned nT seconds into the future. Once a plan has been found which is successful for the given planning window, a commitment is made to the first-stage control decision which is part of the successful sequence and the whole planning process is repeated again. An example search tree is shown in Figure 4.

Each node in the search tree represents the acrobot in a particular state at a particular point in time. New child nodes are generated by beginning in the state of the parent node, applying a chosen (constant) control input (denoted by u), and performing a forward dynamics simulation for a fixed-time interval (0.2s) to yield the state for the new node.

The simplest strategy to build a search tree is to simulate every possible control action at every branch point in the search tree. This requires the evaluation of $O(Nk^s)$ control actions in order to plan a motion for a total of N stages using

k decisions per stage and planning s stages in advance. Even with a small number of stages and control actions, this type of search rapidly becomes prohibitively expensive. There are two means which we shall use to address this. The first is to prune many branches of the search tree. Some of this happens naturally when the figure falls or does something similarly inappropriate. We introduce additional user-defined pruning functions in order to further eliminate exploration of clearly unpromising branches of the search tree. A second strategy to deal with the exponential nature of the proposed search method is to only require the success of a movement, and not its optimality. The search process can then be biased to pursue promising branches of the search-tree first.

Two choices must be made whenever carrying out a simulation to further expand the search tree. First, a starting node must be chosen. This should presumably be one which looks like it is part of a promising motion, so we shall define an evaluation function v to quantify how promising any given node is. Second, we need a method of choosing the control input u to apply. The method we employ is one of stochastically selecting the control input from a fixed, uniform distribution. Initial experiments to modify this distribution function according to what was previously successful in similar states have met with some success, although this is not discussed further here.

The algorithm which controls the development of the search tree is described with the pseudocode in Figure 5. The specific search tree shown in Figure 4 is created by the sequence of events documented in Figure 6. At each step, the actual scores for the nodes are given (Figure 6). The highlighted score indicates which node will be extended in the next step. For sorting efficiency, we store the tree nodes in a heap.

In the example tree, the current candidate input-histories are:

$$U_{cand} = \{(1.5, -2.2, -1.0), (-2.3, 1.5, 1.0), (-2.3, 1.5, 0.5)\}$$

These are obtained by tracing the possible directed paths from the root to each leaf. Some details of the algorithm are now examined in further detail.

3.1 Node Selection

The choice of which node of the search tree to expand is made using a user-defined evaluation function which evaluates the 'promise' of a node by examining the current state, the current search depth, and the current 'degree of previous exploration'. These factors are captures as follows:

$$v_{eval} = f(x) + g(n_{depth}) + n_{children} \cdot v_{retry}$$

where x is the state represented by the node; n_{depth} is the depth of the node in the tree; $n_{children}$ are the number of node children; v_{retry} is the penalty that is added for each node child; and f and g are user-specified functions. In the

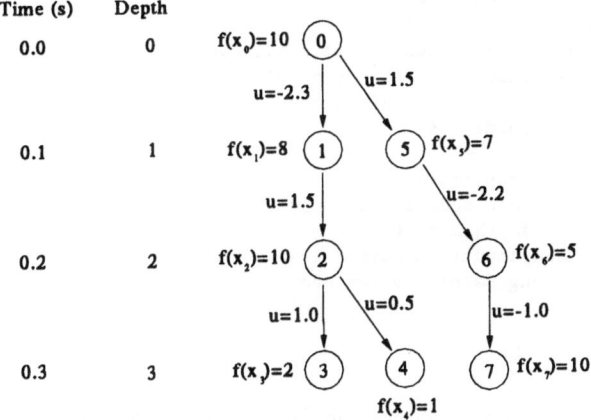

Figure 4: An example search tree.

example of Figure 4, we use the evaluation function

$$v_{example} = f(x) + n_{depth} + n_{children} \cdot v_{retry}$$

with $v_{retry} = -4$. The term $f(x)$ rewards being in a favorable state, such as one that is balanced for the acrobot. The term $g(n_{depth})$ rewards the growth of the search tree in depth. Lastly, the term v_{retry} ensures that the search distributes its efforts over currently promising motions.

3.2   Node Pruning

Many branches in the search tree can be pruned when the controlled object falls or enters an illegal or undesirable state. In the examples discussed in this paper, additional node-pruning functions, p, have been provided by the animator to further speed the progress of the search. While the development of these node-pruning functions admittedly requires some trial-and-error, we believe the development of node pruning functions can eventually be automated if we consider the following supporting argument. Once a sufficiently long sequence of successful motion has been synthesized, it becomes possible to answer questions of the form "Has a successful motion ever passed through a similar state before?". This type of query can then be directly used as a pruning function.

4   Results for Low-Level Control Synthesis

We use the proposed algorithm to generate cartwheeling, flipping and hopping motions for the acrobot. The evaluation and pruning functions are surprisingly simple and we obtain complex acrobot motions which are both new and entertaining.

```
1. best_node = choose_node(tree);
2. rand_input = generate_input();
3. new_node = simulate(state(best_node),rand_input);
4. new_node.score = evaluate(state(new_node),
                             depth(new_node));
5. if (test_prune(new_node)) {
      delete(new_node);
   } else insert(new_node,tree);
6. best_node.score = best_node.score + v_retry;
7. if (depth(tree) > depth_max) {
      trajectory = add_input(trajectory,tree,new_node);
      tree = child_along_path(tree,new_node);
   }
8. loop;
```

Figure 5: Pseudocode for the search controller.

Step	Node Scores							
	0	1	2	3	4	5	6	7
1	10							
2	6	9						
3	6	5	12					
4	6	5	8	5				
5	6	5	4	5	4			
6	2	5	4	5	4	8		
7	2	5	4	5	4	4	7	
8	2	5	4	5	4	4	3	13

Figure 6: Detail of progress for the example search tree.

A useful quantity to observe in the motion of the acrobot is the following, which defines the position of the centre of mass with respect to the acrobot foot:

$$cm_{offset} = x_{cm} - x_1,$$

where x_{cm} is the horizontal position of the center-of-mass; x_1 is as shown in Figure 3. We also define l as being the angular momentum measured in a counter-clockwise direction. General parameters for the simulations are given in Figure 7.

m_1, m_2	10 kg
l_1, l_2	1 m
I_1, I_2	0.8333 $kg \cdot s/m^2$
t_{sim}	0.001 s
$t_{interval}$	0.02 s
v_{retry}	-4.0
n_{depth}	20

Figure 7: Model parameters.

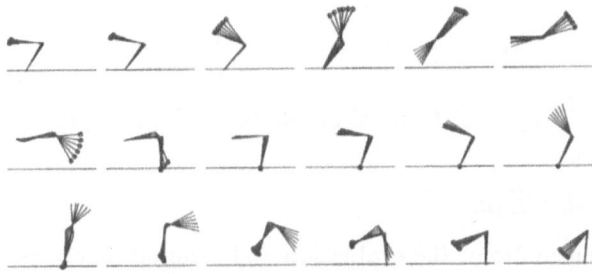

Figure 8: The cartwheel.

4.1 Acrobot Cartwheel

For a cartwheeling motion, the evaluation and pruning functions are:

$$
\begin{aligned}
v_{cartwheel} &= -l - 10 \cdot |cm_{offset}| + n_{depth}/10 \\
p_{cartwheel} &= (y_2 < 0.2) \vee \\
&\quad ((y_1 < 0.0) \wedge (y_3 < 0.0)).
\end{aligned}
$$

The evaluation function rewards negative angular momentum l; penalizes center-of-mass offsets $|cm_{offset}|$, and rewards simulation progress n_{depth}. The pruning function constrains the joint to be at least 0.2 m above the ground and ensures that only the end of one link may contact the ground at any instant in time. The result is a clockwise leg-over-arm motion as shown in Figure 8. We use $k_p = 50$ N/m and $k_d = 5$ $N \cdot s/m$ for the joint proportional-derivative (PD) constants.

The commanded joint angles and the actual joint angles for this motion are shown in Figure 9. Note that the control inputs define a step function, and the actual value of θ_2 is pulled toward the desired value by the PD-controller.

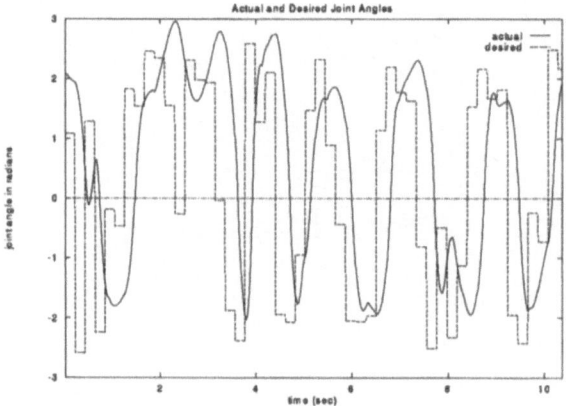

Figure 9: Control inputs to the joint angle.

4.2 Acrobot Flips

For somersaulting motions, the evaluation and pruning functions are:

$$
\begin{aligned}
v_{flip} &= -10 \cdot |cm_{offset}| + n_{depth} \\
v_{forward\ flip} &= -10 \cdot |cm_{offset}| + n_{depth} \\
p_{flip} &= (y_2 < 0.2) \vee (y_3 < 0.4) \\
p_{forward\ flip} &= (y_2 < 0.2) \vee (y_3 < 0.4) \vee \\
&\quad ((y_1 > 0.5) \wedge (l > 0.0)).
\end{aligned}
$$

The pruning function constrains the joint and the head to avoid contact with the ground. The evaluation function penalizes center-of-mass offsets and rewards simulation progress. Given these constraints, the flips naturally occur in the motions produced by the search algorithm. The flipping motions can be sustained indefinitely. Successful landing is attributed to the penalty on the center-of-mass offset, which drives the foot to be underneath the center-of-mass.

The frames in Figure 10 demonstrate a back-flip followed immediately by a forward-flip. To achieve the torque required for the flip, PD constants of $k_p = 200\ N/m$ and $k_d = 20\ N \cdot s/m$ are used. Higher-order flips (double, triple, etc.) are achievable by simply increasing the k_p of the actuator.

A motion with only forward flips uses the same pruning and evaluation functions as the normal flip with an additional constraint that whenever the foot is above 0.5 m, the angular momentum l must be positive.

Figure 10: A sequence of flips.

4.3 Acrobot Hop

The hop requires the largest number of pruning constraints in order for the search to be efficiently executed. The evaluation and pruning functions are:

$$
\begin{aligned}
v_{hop} &= n_{depth} \\
p_{hop} &= (y_2 < 0.2) \vee (y_3 < 0.4) \vee \\
&\quad ((y_1 > 0.0) \wedge (\dot{x}_1 < -0.1)) \vee \\
&\quad (y_1 > 0.4)
\end{aligned}
$$

The pruning function keeps the joint and head above the ground, permits only small backward velocities when the foot is in the air, and keeps the foot below $0.4\ m$ in the air. The evaluation function simply rewards temporal progress. To the best of our knowledge, the hopping motion can be indefinitely sustained. The PD-constants used here are the same as those for the flips.

Figure 11 shows a history of how simulation trials are allocated to different levels of the search tree (times of the motion) as the search algorithm proceeds. A negative slope in these graphs indicates a back-tracking behavior in the search. A steep positive slope indicates an easy motion to plan. Surprisingly, flip motions are the easiest to generate, followed by the cartwheel in difficulty, and then the hop. An increase in the number of pruning constraints has the effect of slowing down the search.

5 Results for High-Level Control Synthesis

The search technique can also be used to string together appropriate sequences of more complex control primitives. In this particular example, we shall deal with the motion of Luxo, a 3-link articulated figure with two actuators, as shown in Figure 2.

The motion primitives in this case are not constant control inputs, but rather the control histories necessary to execute complete jumps. A total of 5 different types of jumps are used in creating the motions shown in Figure 2. The job of

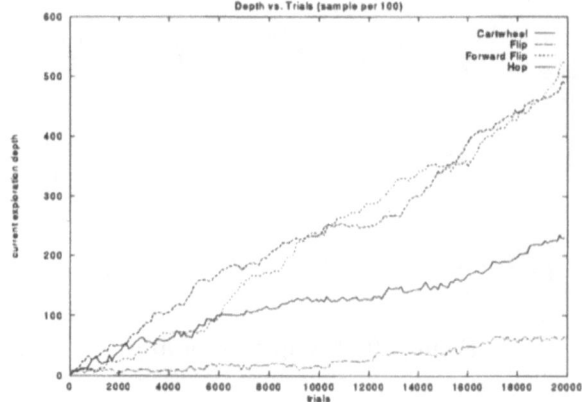

Figure 11: Progress depth per trial for different locomotion modes.

the search algorithm is then to produce an ordered sequence of these 5 types of jumps which can successfully negotiate the terrain. Each jump consists of a sequential series of three states, where each state is of a fixed duration (0.13 seconds) and holds the control inputs constant. As with the other articulated figures presented thus far, the control inputs are desired joint angles, which are fed to PD controllers that are used to generate actuator torques.

Executing a given jump primitive will not always produce the same motion. This is because the resulting motion is a function of the initial state and the environment as well as the applied control. For the examples shown, it is sufficient to plan ahead a maximum of 4 jumps. As with previous examples, the search is conducted using a best-first strategy.

The scoring function used to evaluate nodes is simply the distance travelled, as measured along the horizontal axis. The mechanism used to constrain the growth of the search tree consists of pruning search-tree branches leading to falls. A fall is defined as an undesired contact of a body part with the ground. In the given examples, the falls are sufficient to prune away 50 to 66% of the search tree. More of the tree could be pruned away by establishing a conservative upper bound on the distance that can be travelled in a jump. Branches which could not possibly obtain the current maximum distance, even with future maximum-size jumps can then be pruned. This then becomes a type of branch-and-bound algorithm.

The motions shown in Figure 2 took between 4.5 and 9.5 minutes to plan on a 90 MHz Pentium PC, where the simulation itself requires 0.41 real seconds for every simulated second. The final motions are dynamic in nature and exhibit considerable anticipation of the upcoming terrain.

It is possible that no solutions will be found for certain instances of terrain. There are several possibilites to remedy such situations, although all require additional search time. The first possibility is introduce additional types of jump primitives. The second is to allow some type of interpolation between existing control primitives so that the control space becomes continuous, as with the examples in section 4. The last possibility is to force the search algorithm to use a larger planning window, thereby doing a better job of avoiding getting trapped in dead-ends.

6 Conclusions

A new algorithm for the planning and execution of dynamic motions has been described and tested in simulation. It has been shown that various modes of locomotion can be produced using a decision-tree technique with simple pruning and evaluation functions. Examples of cartwheel, flip and hop motions are demonstrated for an unstable two-link figure, the acrobot. To our knowledge, this is the first successful hop control strategy for the acrobot that does not require over-rotation of one of the links, and the first successful control strategy for any kind of flipping.

Thus far, the application of the algorithm has been restricted to figures with effectively only one controllable input and a limited number of DOFs. While the motions may seem simplistic when characterized in this fashion, they are much more complex when the timing and instability of the motions are taken into consideration. This alternate definition of complexity needs to be considered in animation and is one that the proposed algorithm begins to address.

The search algorithm presented here cannot be used directly for closed-loop control. We are presently exploring the possibility of using the successful solutions as training data for producing a true closed-loop controller.

References

[BF92]   Matthew D. Berkemeier and Ronald S. Fearing. Control of a two-link robot to achieve sliding and hopping gaits. *IEEE Conference on Robotics and Automation*, 1:286–291, 1992.

[BF94]   Matthew D. Berkemeier and Ronald S. Fearing. Control experiments on an underactuated robot with applications to legged locomotion. *Proceedings, IEEE International Conference on Robotics and Automation*, pages 149–154, 1994.

[Bor92]   S. A. Bortoff. *Pseudolinearization Using Spline Functions with Application to the Acrobot*. PhD thesis, University of Illinois at Urbana-Champaign, 1992.

[BS92]   S. A. Bortoff and M. W. Spong. Pseudolinearization of the acrobot using spline functions. *Proceedings, 31st Conference on Decision and Control*, pages 593–598, 1992.

[GT95]   Radek Grzeszczuk and Demetri Terzopoulos. Automated learning of muscle-actuated locomotion through control abstraction. *Proceedings of SIGGRAPH '95, ACM Computer Graphics*, pages 63–70, April 1995.

[HM90]   J. Hauser and R. M. Murray. Nonlinear controllers for non-integrable systems: The acrobot example. *Proceedings, American Control Conference*, pages 669–671, 1990.

[HR90]   J. K. Hodgins and M. H. Raibert. Biped gymnastics. *International Journal of Robotics Research*, 2:115–132, 1990.

[NM93]   J. T. Ngo and J. Marks. Spacetime Constraints Revisited. *Proceedings of SIGGRAPH '93, ACM Computer Graphics*, pages 343–350, 1993.

[PAH92] M. G. Pandy, F. C. Anderson, and D. G. Hull. A parameter optimization approach for the optimal control of large-scale musculoskeletal systems. *Transactions of the ASME*, 114:450–459, November 1992.

[RH91]   Marc Raibert and Jessica Hodgins. Animation of dynamic legged locomotion. *Proceedings of SIGGRAPH '91, ACM Computer Graphics*, pages 349–358, 1991.

[Sim94] Karl Sims. Evolving Virtual Creatures. *Proceedings of SIGGRAPH '94, ACM Computer Graphics*, pages 15–22, 1994.

[vF93]   Michiel van de Panne and Eugene Fiume. Sensor-actuator networks. *Proceedings of SIGGRAPH '93, ACM Computer Graphics*, pages 335–342, 1993.

[vFV93] Michiel van de Panne, Eugene Fiume, and Zvonko Vranesic. Physically-Based Modeling and Control of Turning. *Computer Vision, Graphics, and Image Processing: Graphical Models and Image Processing*, Vol. 55, No. 6, November 1993, 507-521.

[vKF94] Michiel van de Panne, Ryan Kim, and Eugene Fiume. Virtual wind-up toys for animation. *Graphics Interface*, pages 208–215, 1994.

[Win84] Patrick H. Winston. *Artifical Intelligence*, 2nd Edition, Addison-Wesley, 1984.

Plausible Motion Simulation for Computer Graphics Animation

Ronen Barzel
University of Washington

John F. Hughes
Brown University

Daniel N. Wood
University of Washington

Abstract

Accuracy is the ubiquitous goal of dynamic simulation, in order to yield the "correct" motion. But for creating animation, what is really of interest is "plausible" motion, which is somewhat different. We discuss what we mean by *plausible* simulation, how it differs from "accurate" simulation, and why we think it's a worthwhile area to study. The discussion touches on questions of *physically plausible* vs. *visually plausible* motion, plausible simulation in a noisy or textured environment, and probability measures for motion, as well as issues for forward and inverse problems.

1 Introduction

Simulation is generally used in the context of a predictive model of behavior: given a precise description of a real-world situation, try to determine computationally what would really happen. When designing airplane parts, for example, accuracy of the model and of the simulation are critically important.

However computer graphics animation has different needs, requiring a slightly different outlook. In particular, we claim:

- For computer graphics animation we don't need a predictive model of what will happen. The creator of an animation decides a priori what is to happen: the simulation tool must make it happen in a way that seems real.

- Simulated motion often looks "sterile," because it lacks the variation caused by small details that are left out of the models. These are generally omitted because their inclusion would render the simulation computationally intractable, or because simulation methods for handling such detail are not known.

We thus introduce the idea of *plausible* motion: motion that could happen, given what is (un)known about the system. Many motions may be plausible for given conditions; this can give us latitude in creating or choosing a particular motion that is desired. To put it in different terms, the uncertainty arising from our imprecise knowledge of the system makes it reasonable to simulate the physics stochastically (i.e., with randomness in the simulation); we take this a step further and regard the variability implicit in such stochastic simulations as a source of further opportunities for control as well.

We have found that recasting the animation simulation problem domain to be one of plausible rather than accurate motion opens up a variety of interesting and promising directions for investigation. We will discuss some of these directions, and give some preliminary results. We hope to stimulate interest in an area that we have only just begun to explore.

We are not alone in studying approximations to dynamic simulation; indeed, several of the papers referenced later use approximations ("no friction", etc.), and others have made kinds of approximations that plausibly mimic rigid body dynamics while simplifying the necessary calculations [vO91], [BvO95]. But our main point is not that we can approximate, but that the unknowns of a simulation give us freedom to approximate in a way that helps us.

2 Thought Experiments

We discuss some simple thought experiments, to motivate the claims of the last section and to examine the notion of plausibility. The experiments lead to various conjectures about implementing and taking advantage of plausibility.

2.1 The Importance of Detail

Thought experiment: A Superball

Consider a typical CG simulation of a sphere released from rest above a ground plane: it bounces up and down above a single point on the plane.

Now consider a real-world superball that is held and released above a floor: it bounces and skitters every which way. Repeat the experiment; the ball will travel on a very different path, but the overall "character" of the skittering will be roughly the same.

There are a variety of factors that probably contribute to the skittering of a real-world superball: slight initial spin imparted when the ball is released, eccentricities in the shape of the ball, inhomogeneities in its mass distribution, non-horizontal floor plane, non-planar floor, and dirt and other particles on the floor.

Thinking about the bouncing ball, we observe:

- Simulations of CG models tend to look mechanical and sterile, no matter how accurate the computation. This is because the model is itself "sterile": a perfect flat plane and a perfect sphere.

- It would be hard to take into account all factors and imperfections to accurately model and simulate a real superball on a real floor. Furthermore, no matter how carefully we measure the superball and floor in question, there will be some uncertainty in the initial conditions (unless we build a precise mechanical release mechanism rather than simply dropping the ball by hand), which will lead to uncertainty in the resulting motion path.

- It doesn't matter exactly which motion path the ball takes if one is only concerned with the *appearance* of realism. Each real-world trial is different anyway. But it is essential that the path displays the same type of skittering that is caused by the imperfections in the real world.

It may be too hard to accurately *simulate* all the "details" of the real world. But we get a big win if we can *mimic* the details: we would make plausible, non-sterile motion.

Conjecture: We can mimic real-world imperfections by starting with the usual flat, smooth CG model, and introducing an appropriate amount of variability into the simulation process. This approach is well-known in the world of rendering: One provides *texture* to make models appear more realistic. Texture adds detail most effectively when the "character" of the detail is important, but the actual data in the detail is not (e.g., it matters that the wall is marble, but not where the veins in the marble lie).

2.2 The Futility of Accuracy

> **Thought experiment: Rolling Dice (a)**
>
> Consider rolling a die to see who plays first in a game of Monopoly. This extremely simple physical system—roughly, a cube and flat plane—is commonly considered to be a good source of random numbers.

Thinking about simulating a die roll leads us to two observations:

- Since behavior is random,[1] there's no point in trying to simulate it "accurately."

- A typical simulation of a rolling die would produce the same result each time it is run (for a given set of initial conditions). In some sense, to really be "accurate," a simulation should produce a different result each time it is run.

Since repeatability is a desirable property of computer programs, having a simulation truly produce random results is probably not ideal. More useful—though probably hard to compute—would be a simulation that reports (in some form) the space of possible results, allowing the user to choose a specific element as desired; the program could also choose one arbitrarily[2] or randomly.

> **Thought experiment: Rolling Dice (b)**
>
> Consider the following scenario: a pair of dice are on a table, showing seven; something knocks them to the floor, they end up showing "snake eyes." This is a plausible occurrence, but one that is hard to arrange or predict.

Suppose we want to create an animation of the above scenario. To produce a believable motion for the dice, simulation is a natural choice. But thinking about how to meet the final-state condition, we note:

- Since behavior is random, we can neither expect a predictive model nor expect to easily adjust the initial conditions to guarantee desired results.

- To create an animation, we don't need a predictive model, since we know what we want to have happen. But we do need a way to create a plausible motion.

One might imagine trying to create this animation by simulating it repeatedly with various parameter values—since the odds of "snake eyes" are 1:36, we'd expect that within, say, 50 tries we'd get the desired result.

But what if the director specified not only the initial and final scores of the dice, but also their positions? We now have a highly constrained (or multi-point boundary value) problem, for a highly unstable system.

Conjecture: The easiest way to create an animation of scenarios such as the above is to exploit the variability and instability within the system: At each moment when there is variability, can adjust the outgoing state within the bounds that are derived from the plausible set of incoming states and the instability in the system.

---

[1]More precisely: given the limits of precision in the initial conditions and the computation, and given the instability in the system, the results of this (or comparable situations) are provably indeterminate [HS92].

[2]Thus returning us to the usual behavior of simulation.

2.3   The Flexibility of Believability

Thought experiment: Baseball Hit

Consider a viewer in the bleachers watching a baseball[3] pitch, swing, and hit. Can the viewer guess where and how far the ball will travel—straight to the left fielder? over his head? inside the foul line? out of the park? Can the viewer measure how high the ball flies, or whether it travels in a parabolic arc?

To create an animation of a baseball, we can probably choose from a wide-range of trajectories—even ones that are physically infeasible—without compromising the believability (for example, have the ball "hang" in the air for a moment longer than it ought to, to increase the dramatic tension).

Again, making a few observations:

- People are not always terribly accurate predictors of motion. (Many novice outfielders have run forward to catch a fly ball only to have it pass over their heads.)

- In some cases, people are willing to accept surprising behavior by relying on unseen forces: in particular, the effects of wind are significant on balls hit a long way, and miscalculations and fielding errors can often be blamed on the wind.

- Believability depends on viewing angle. From the bleachers above home plate, the initial direction (towards left or right field?) is probably not as free to be adjusted as is the initial elevation (grounder, line-drive, or fly ball?), while from behind first base the opposite would be true.

Of course, there are limits to how much variation can be introduced before breaking the viewer's belief that the simulation is "real." For example, if the batter bunts, holding the bat still, it would be implausible for the ball to gain enough energy that it could fly to the outfield.

Conjecture: For computer graphics animation, we can in many cases introduce ad-hoc variation of motion without compromising believability.

3   Characterizing Plausibility

In the previous section we considered some intuitive notions about plausibility. We now attempt to characterize plausibility somewhat more precisely.

3.1   Sources of Variability

There are several factors that contribute to variability in a model and simulation:

- Numerical error in computation. The result of a solver is one element of the set of solutions accurate to within given tolerances—but there may be others.

- Approximations in the abstraction. (Are the bodies really rigid? How appropriate is the Poisson model of collision [KR66] or the Coulomb model of friction [Rei71]?)

---

[3] Any Europeans in the audience, consider instead kicking a football or soccer ball.

- Inaccuracy in the data. (How precisely do we know the mass? How accurate is the initial velocity?)

- Missing details in the model. (Is the ball really round? Is the floor really flat?)

These factors mostly cause continuous variability in the solution. But collisions introduce an entirely different class of variability: Each collision can non-linearly magnify all the other variabilities, producing macroscopic, discontinuous effects due to small changes in parameters.[4] Thus we have an additional source of variability:

- Instability in the system.

Conjecture: Since collisions can magnify invisible variations, in many cases it may be sufficient, for generating plausible motion, to neglect explicit consideration of the "primary" variations, and introduce ad-hoc variation of each collision instead.

Slightly abusing the English language, we refer collectively to the various sources of variability in a system as the *variabilities* of the system.[5]

3.2 Physical vs. Visual Plausibility

We consider a motion path to be *physically plausible* if it lies within the range of motions allowed by known error bounds on the above variabilities.

We consider a motion path to be *visually plausible* if it looks convincing. This is a weak definition, since it depends on a variety of perception and cognition factors, or more broadly, on who's doing the looking and in what context. But we can attempt to make some characterizations of visually plausible or implausible motion:

- In most cases, visual plausibility seems to require instant-to-instant "correctness." In our context, we can consider motion to be visually plausible if it lies within the range of motion allowed by arbitrarily chosen bounds on the above variabilities, so long as the end result looks convincing. Visual plausibility can allow temporal variation of parameters that would otherwise be considered to be constant (e.g., an object could possibly change mass slightly over time) .

- Visual plausibility may depend on the state of system and viewing parameters: If a ball approaches a surface perpendicularly, it should leave mostly perpendicularly. But if it arrives at, say, 47 degrees it can probably leave anywhere from 40 to 55 degrees without the viewer noticing—more if the ball is traveling directly away from the camera or if the camera is aimed along the wall thus confusing the viewer's ability to judge angles.

- Reliance on invisible forces can help provide visual plausibility, if the viewer expects that such forces might exist (e.g., wind effecting a baseball).

- Reliance on invisible forces can reduce visual plausibility, if the viewer doesn't expect such forces to exist.

---

[4]Indeed, Huberman and Struss [HS92] describe a simple billiard-table-with-obstacle system whose behavior is chaotic in large areas.

[5]The more obvious terms such as *variables* or *parameters* would suggest a model of the system that is more formal or complete than we wish to employ.

188

Figure 1: The set of plausible paths for a cannonball that bounces once. Here, the uncertainty in the initial conditions is very small, so the first arcs are nearly identical. Following the bounce, the subsequent arcs are many and varied.

- Visual plausibility depends on how well the viewer can see. Objects that are moving very fast, or are are very far away, or are obscured, or are poorly lit, provide extra opportunities for variability.[6]

In general, visual plausibility is a looser requirement than physical plausibility. But visual plausibility may occasionally be a stronger requirement: physical systems are sometimes non-intuitive, or behave unexpectedly due to invisible or otherwise unknown internal state.

What about the limits of visual plausibility? It would be interesting to learn how such things as viewing angle, speed, and impact angle affect viewers' impressions of plausibility, perhaps by conducting user studies. In general, however, it is likely to require the storytelling talent of human animators to know just how much implausibility or coincidence one can "get away with" in a given context.

Finally, note that we're not considering so-called "cartoon physics"—the Coyote walking off a cliff for several paces before falling, or Ricochet Rabbit's bullets chasing a villain around corners—to be within the realm of visual plausibility. The point of such gags is exactly their implausibility.

3.3 Motion Path Cones

The behavior of a system can of course be described as a path through state space or phase space [FW80]. We consider the plausible motion of a body to be a bundle of paths, or generalized cone, through state or phase space, as illustrated in Figure 1. The bounds of the cone are determined by the ranges of the variabilities in the model.

More precisely, a motion path cone starts at the region of phase space that describes the initial conditions (a region rather than a point, since we include error bounds or tolerances). We sweep out a volume by extruding the region over time, evolving it in keeping with physical law.[7]

Cones do not necessarily continue indefinitely: If friction slows down the object, it may come to rest, as in the case of the cannonball of Figure 1.

Whenever the path cone of a body intersects some other body so that they can collide, there is a branch point in the plausible motion. Thus there is a tree of cones, with "shadows" of obstacles in the parent cone.

The more detail or precision we have in the model, the narrower the cones. However, even with very narrow initial cones, the instability caused by collisions can quickly widen the cones farther down the tree. If the object is confined to some bounded region

---

[6]Thus to some extent, we can consider visual plausibility to be the same as physical plausibility: motion allowed by known tolerances—but based on the viewer's perception of the system, rather than the model-builder's knowledge.

[7]Note that the boundaries of the cone aren't necessarily determined by the conditions at the start; there may be continuously variable parameters such as atmospheric disturbance or gravity that can affect the boundaries.

of space, in many cases the cone may widen to cover all points of the space [KMS85].[8]

How does all this relate to simulation? A typical initial-value forward simulation chooses one path from within the tree of path cones. In thinking about simulations, it may often be worth remembering that any given solution has neighboring paths within the cones, that describe other plausible solutions. Although it is not in general feasible to compute all complete path cone trees—they can clearly grow too large and complex to represent, compactly or at all—in some cases computing a subtree might well be feasible and useful, as will be discussed below. If to find the "right" animation one must simulate repeatedly, then it might reduce the overall computation to compute the cone tree initially, and then simply pick a path that meets one's goals.

3.4 Probability and Plausibility

While a wide range of motion paths may be plausible, are they all really likely? We consider probabilities in conjunction with motion paths.

We start by introducing probability distributions as a model of underlying variability. For example, in a collision with a rough surface, the statistical variation in a normal vector might have a Gaussian distribution.

These underlying distributions induce probability distributions over each path cone. At each branching point in the tree of cones, we propagate probability by integrating the parent probability over the cross-section of the target area, to get the probability p of taking that branch. The probabilities in the child branch are scaled by p; the probabilities for paths not following that branch are scaled by $1 - p$.

Of course, in a continuous space of motion paths, the probability of any given trajectory is negligible (even if it's a pretty reasonable choice). This can be addressed by defining the probability *density* over the cone, and only assigning probability to *sets* of motion paths, by integrating the density over the range of paths in a set.

In discussing what makes a path acceptably plausible, it can be useful to take a Bayesian approach [HU93]. That is, if a viewer saw a given path, would the viewer's belief about the simulated world change? If, for example, one sees a ball dropped on a gravel driveway, and it took an odd bounce to the North, one might think nothing of it ("there was probably a stone that caught it just the wrong way"). But if it took seven odd bounces in a row, all to the North, one would begin to think that something was "rigged." From a Bayesian viewpoint, the implicit hypothesis that the gravel's normal vectors are uniformly distributed becomes less likely as one observes the string of unusual bounces.

Having a probability metric for path cones has the potential to be useful for minimizing computation. For example, in many cases, rather than compute an entire tree of path cones, it would be appropriate to compute only those that represent reasonably likely occurrences.

4 Applications

We discuss here a few ways in which the ideas of plausible motion can be applied.

---

[8]Although not necessarily all points of the phase space. For example, a billiard ball, bouncing about on a frictionless pool table with bumpers that absorb 10% of the energy on each collision will (with high probability) eventually pass very near to every point of the table, although only a small initial segment of its trajectory will be covered at a high speed.

4.1   Simulating with Texture

Perhaps the most basic idea discussed thus far is that for simulations to look realistic, they must add "texture" to the otherwise too-simple models, where we use the term "texture" in analogy with the texture-mapping commonly used in rendering: apparent detail added as an after-effect. Texture in image generation is produced by texture mapping of scanned images, by procedural textures, and by randomly-generated textures (among other methods), and we can do likewise. As per the conjecture of Section 3.1, we concentrate the texture in collision parameters:

- We can plausibly forward-simulate bouncing bodies by simply adding a certain amount of ad-hoc random variation to the initial conditions and to the normal vector associated with each bounce.

- We can perform experiments, e.g., measure real superball bounce directions, and use a statistical tabulation of the results as a source for distribution of variability, similarly to rendering's bidirectional reflection distribution functions or micro-facet slope distributions [FvDFH90].

- We can borrow directly from rendering, and use texture maps and bump maps—in many cases, the very maps that are used by the renderer. For example, we can vary the coefficient of restitution based on surface texture, and use the bumped normal for the collision.

We suspect that the best results will arise from combining randomness with stored or computed textures. For example, wherever there is a bump, widen the range of normals. Thus for a tile floor, with raised tiles bedded in grout, we might assign somewhat variable normals for the grout region, and substantially variable normals in the areas where the bump-map tells us that the normal is changing rapidly (i.e., on the curved edges of each tile).

In adding texture to simulations, we need to be careful not to add (too much) energy to the system, as this would likely destroy (visual) plausibility. This depends on whether there are active elements in the system, such as pinball machine bumpers.

4.2   Animation Control

By exploiting variability we have the potential to give animators direct-manipulation style control over animation, while automatically maintaining physical plausibility. We describe a few approaches:

- *Motion construction.* A program shows the user the next motion path cone for an object, given its current state and the various variabilities; the user chooses from within the cone. Thus the user builds the animation step-by-step.

- *Motion adjustment.* Given the motion path cones describing a particular path (which may have been computed by forward simulation or built step-by-step), the user can interactively manipulate the final position, and the program automatically propagates the necessary variation back up along the cone tree. The user might, in the course of doing this, come up against the cone boundaries. This is analogous to inverse kinematics (IK) limb manipulation with joint limits.

- *Constrained Motion adjustment.* The program finds the plausible solutions of a constraint problem (e.g., a two-point boundary-value problem such as "the ball bounces from here to there"), showing the user the set of path cones that all meet the constraints. The user can choose among them, again like manipulating an IK jointed limb that is fixed at both ends.

In the above cases, lacking an automatic metric for visual plausibility, we can simply provide the user with a knob or knobs to widen (or narrow) the ranges of the variabilities.

All the above could also compute and display the likelihood of each chosen solution, if we have probability distributions for each variable[9] (or, perhaps more informative, show the likelihood that, given such a motion-path, the user would believe the hypothesis that the chosen values for the variabilities are actually uncorrelated.)

The computation of motion path cones is reminiscent of the techniques in cone traced rendering [Ama84], and indeed, many of the ideas there have analogs in motion path cones.

4.3 Motion Synthesis

The motion synthesis problem, creating animation to meet desired goals, is often cast as an *inverse* simulation problem: given the desired end result, what initial conditions and forces should be applied?

Inverse problems can be very complex. For example, Tang et al. [TNM95] describe a simple system, in which one is to have the balls on a billiard table end up in a particular configuration, and the problem is to determine appropriate initial velocities. This is a daunting task,[10] made particularly difficult by the search for accurate solutions, which are highly unstable and sensitive to variation of the initial velocities.

From our point of view, slight errors in the initial velocity can be masked by using a system that allows for variabilities. At first glance, adding such variabilities is both good and bad: it increases the size of the solution space, but also increases the number of degrees of freedom to be searched.

We note that the degrees of freedom added by variabilities are not only in initial conditions, but are distributed throughout the simulation: we can "tune" each bounce. Thus to some extent, we can convert the difficulties of solving a two-point boundary value problem into a simpler one of leaping from stepping-stone to stepping-stone.

There is one further point to be made: it's tempting to say "Of course adding variability makes the problem easier—it lets us cheat to get the result we want!" But if the variabilities we include are physically plausible, then we are not cheating at all—the solution we get is one which, to the limits of our understanding of the system is one of the many plausible solutions that *could* arise. And if we're in the domain of visual plausibility, then it's OK to cheat!

5 Preliminary results

We have just begun to explore the ideas of plausible motion simulation. Our first steps have been to attempt to validate some of the conjectures for the simplest of test cases:

---

[9]One might imagine using this this type of system for non-animation applications; e.g., car crash reconstruction: what is the likelihood that a given scenario could happen? But this is a case where getting the correct answer can really matter, and as such our loose discussion of plausibility is not appropriate. (Also note that cars contain drivers, and are thus active volitional objects that can vary their behavior due to internal state, greatly complicating the problem.)

[10]Tang et al. describe an algorithm to reduce their roughly 10^{13} candidate solutions to only 10^6 trials that must be searched.

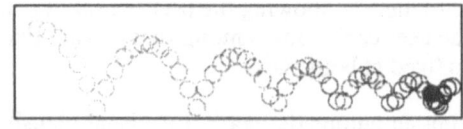

Figure 2: Simulation of a bouncing ball in a box, side view. *Top:* No texture added—the bounce is regular. *Bottom:* Collision normals are perturbed randomly up to 8 degrees.

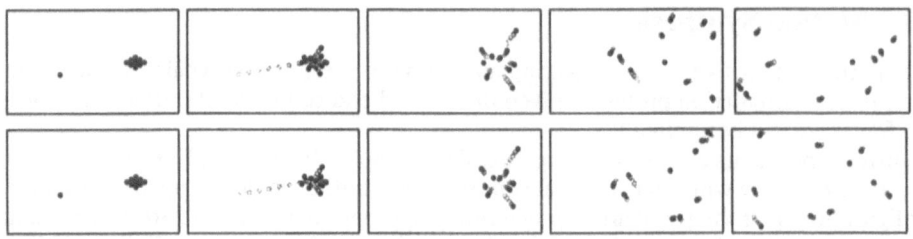

Figure 3: Simulation of a 9-ball pool break. *Top row:* "Accurate" solution. *Bottom row:* Collision normals are perturbed randomly by up to 8 degrees.

perfect spheres on flat surfaces. We report here the results of four preliminary experiments and what we have learned from them.[11]

The first two experiments are simple checks of the conjecture that adding random variability to the simulation can create plausible motion "texture," and moreover that we can do so by ad-hoc variation of collision parameters. The second two experiments test the conjecture that inverse problems are easier if we allow variability.

5.1 Bouncing ball

First, we simulated bouncing balls, as described in Section 2.1. Figure 2 shows a side view of one ball bouncing, with and without random texture.

The results of this test are straightforward:

- As expected, we found that adding a small amount of variation looked plausible and not as mechanical as the unperturbed control.

- The variation could be adjusted up to roughly 8 degrees without breakdown of plausibility.

The motion of this experiment, although interesting, instantly suggests the richness that could be added via texture mapping, so that we can have areas of gravel with higher variability, and so forth, as per Section 4.1. We have not yet implemented this, but expect it to work well.

---

[11] Animations are available online from: http://www.cs.washington.edu/homes/ronen

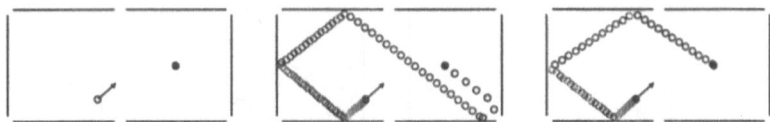

Figure 4: *Top left:* The problem: give the ball (black circle) an initial velocity so that ends up in the desired position with the desired velocity; there is no "accurate" solution on a table with friction. *Top right:* Introducing a variability of 2 degrees to collision normals allows two "five-rail" shots. *Bottom:* Increasing the variability to 5 degrees finds a simpler "three-rail" solution.

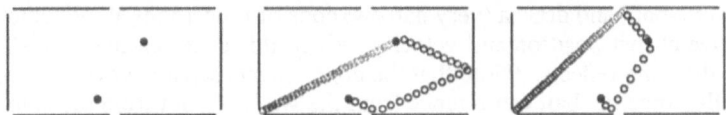

Figure 5: *Left:* A cue ball, and a target ball to sink in the corner pocket. *Middle:* Solution without perturbing normals. *Right:* Another solution introduced with 8 degree perturbation of collision normals.

5.2 Pool Break

Next we simulated billiard balls, in particular a "nine-ball break"—nine balls are arranged in a diamond shape, and a tenth ball is hit into them. As before, the collision normals could be subject to random variation (in the plane). The initial break is asymmetric. Figure 3 shows the results.

- In this case, the complexity of the underlying non-random system coupled with asymmetry in the initial conditions gives a plausible, non-mechanical feel, but it does so only once. When the simulation is repeated the results repeat exactly, quickly creating a mechanical feel.

- Adding roughly 10 degrees of random variation was completely unnoticeable in terms of the visual plausibility of the motion. But now the simulation is different each time, successfully keeping a "natural" feel.

From this we learn that in an already complex system, introducing extra variability "texture" does not harm the visual plausibility. This frees us to introduce variability into motion synthesis, as discussed in Section 4.3 and in the next two experiments.

5.3 One Pool Ball

We attempt a simple motion synthesis problem: The cue ball starts at rest; we strike it with the pool cue, and we want it to reach a given location traveling in a given direction (without "scratching" by entering a pocket).

Our simulation includes frictional losses as the ball rolls across the table, inelasticity in the collisions with the walls, and a maximum initial speed. These together effectively prune our search and make it far simpler than the problems considered by Tang et al. [TNM95], whose balls moved on a frictionless surface with no energy losses, and thus could continue bouncing forever.[12]

---

[12] Interestingly, having a more complex model simplifies the computation!

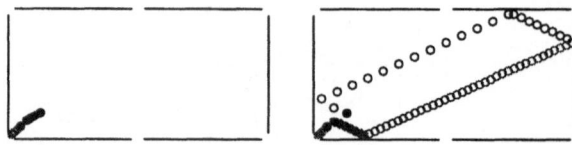

Figure 6: Two physically plausible pool shots. The one on the right is a much harder shot.

Our algorithm is a backwards search: we start at the desired end position and velocity of the cue-ball, and draw a (very narrow) cone of trajectories along which it must travel to arrive at that position and velocity. When this cone reaches a wall, the tree branches as the cone reflects. (Note that the cone reflects separately from each half of the long walls, since the ball can bounce from the walls but not from the side pocket.) The reflected cones include the variability of reflection, and therefore spread faster than the parent cone.

We search recursively, computing the required speed in each cone given the frictional table and collisions, and prune the search when the required speed exceeds a predefined maximum. All successful results (those where the cone encloses the ball, and the ball speed is below the maximum) are reported. For each match, we trace forward from the branch to the root of this cone tree, piecing together a sensible path. We start by connecting the cones roughly apex-to-apex, then perform a relaxation process to minimize the overall eccentricity of the collisions.

As illustrated in Figure 4, it is easy to encounter circumstances in which the "accurate" approach has no solution at all. But adding as little as 2 degrees of variation at collisions makes it easily soluble.

For this test, the variability approach works well: allowing a small amount of variation per collision quickly builds up enough controllability, due to magnification at subsequent collisions, that the cones eventually encompass the solution. As we mentioned before, this isn't solving the problem by "cheating," it's finding a solution that is plausible within the stated limits of knowledge of details in the model.

5.4 Two Pool Balls

Finally, we consider a more complex problem: given a cue ball and a target ball, we must "sink" the target ball into a chosen pocket, by giving the cue ball an initial velocity.

We use the same algorithm as used in Section 5.3, but here we start with a cone from the pocket, and have branch points additionally when a cone encounters the target ball. Some results are shown in Figure 5.

Notice that in this case, the instability of the ball-to-ball collision allows many solutions, even without perturbing normals: (ignoring rotation) the cue ball can send the target ball towards, say, the East, by hitting the target on its west side; the cue ball can be headed in any direction from due East (direct hit) to almost vertical (glancing hit).

When we introduce variability into the problem, we do find many new solutions. However, these solutions tend to be on the fringes of acceptability—situations such as the right of Figure 5, in which the "accurate" solution would scratch, while the variability allows one to *just barely* make the shot by using the end of the rail. This result is perhaps somewhat disappointing, but not surprising in retrospect: the wide spread of incident cue angle at the collision overshadows the benefits of the small additional spread variation we introduce.

Figure 7: A collision with random normal perturbation. *Left:* incident at 5.1 degrees, plausibly reflected at 6.84 degrees. *Right:* incident at 5.1 degrees, implausibly reflected at -2.3 degrees.

In using our solver, we see that many solutions (in both the "pure" case and the one with variability) are, although physically plausible, certainly in the realm of the remarkable. Consider, for example, the two shots shown in Figure 6. The first, in which the cue ball hits the target ball and sends it directly into the pocket, is the sort of shot that anyone can make. The second, in which the cue-ball hits four rails and finally grazes the target ball, causing it to roll slowly into the corner pocket, might have been executed by a well-tuned machine (or by Minnesota Fats), but the viewer might still describe the shot as "remarkable." We conjecture that two factors contribute to the second shot's being surprising:

- Can a pool table really support that kind of precision? Along the lines of the discussion of Section 3.4, if the table was marble we might believe that all the angles will work out exactly as needed; but for a felt-covered table, we'd expect the random effects to make it impossible for anyone to deliberately make the shot.

- Can a pool player really hit the ball with that kind of precision? Given the instability of the system, among all possible initial conditions, the measure of those that lead to sinking the target ball at the end is almost vanishingly small.

If we want to eliminate the "Minnesota Fats solutions" from our solver, a general approach would be to prune based on probability, as discussed in Section 3.4: Before descending each branch of the path cone tree, integrate the probability over that cone, and make sure it remains above threshold; and for the candidate solutions, compute the Bayesian probability to make sure that the variabilities along the way are behaving in a manner consistent with our expectations of their probability distributions.

A more specific approach to eliminating surprising solutions for this problem is to simply place an arbitrary limit on the spread of incident angles for the ball collision, to rule out grazing shots. This is a situation where visual plausibility is stricter than physical plausibility, as discussed in Section 3.2.

5.5 Additional Results

To quantify the effects of introducing variability into the inverse problems of Sections 5.3 and 5.4, we ran them on a series of random trials, and accumulated statistics. The table lists the average number of solutions of a given length, for the "accurate" solution, and for 5 and 10 degrees of normal perturbation:

# bounces:	1	2	3	4	5	6	7
"accurate":	0.04	0.09	0.07	0.05	0.01	0.00	0.00
5 degrees:	0.21	0.52	0.88	1.18	0.43	0.00	0.00
10 degrees:	0.32	1.00	2.14	1.92	0.44	0.00	0.00

ONE BALL

"accurate":	2.16	3.66	2.34	0.70	0.18	0.04	0.00
5 degrees:	2.23	4.68	3.64	2.33	0.63	0.00	0.00
10 degrees:	2.42	5.89	6.21	3.51	0.72	0.00	0.00

TWO BALLS

As expected, for the one ball case, there were rarely any "accurate" solutions, and adding variability increased the number of solutions found. For the two ball case, increasing the variability mostly helps in finding longer solutions. In both cases, the maximum speed and friction of the table ruled out most any solutions with six or more collisions.

Finally, we came across occasional situations in which our small normal perturbation yields visually implausible results, illustrated in Figure 7: Although it was generally fine for collision normals to be perturbed, for a nearly-perpendicular collision, occasionally the ball would fail to cross the centerline of the collision; lacking any spin, this is implausible. This points out the need for care in choosing limits on plausibility. We suspect that some of the ideas of qualitative physics [Bob85] will be of use for this.

6 Conclusion

Computer graphics animation systems do not need to be predictive modelers of the physical world. Instead, they have the quite distinct task of being *plausible mimickers* of the physical world, while at the same time providing flexibility and controllability for animators. We believe that

- *detail* in motion, just like the detail in geometry and in light-reflection models, is an essential characteristic of effective mimicry,

- randomness can often provide effective motion detail, and

- the ability to select from a distribution can help provide effective controllability.

The addition of variable detail to generate plausible motion has complimentary effects: on the one hand, it eliminates the need to accurately model and simulate the detail; on the other hand, it enlarges the space of possible motion paths that one may consider, and, at least for the approaches discussed in this paper, requires that we consider cones of motion paths rather than single paths, thus enlarging the work done in simulation. In trade for this added work, there is a new controllability in the generated paths, making the solving of inverse problems more tractable.

Limitations, Future Work

All of the ideas presented in this paper are preliminary, and the examples are all deliberately simple. For more complex systems, the notions we discussed may need to be drastically reorganized, for example with some sort of "factorization" of complex systems into simpler parts, each of which may be amenable to plausible simulation.

We have also only discussed rigid bodies and passive motion. Will active or volitional motion complicate or break the ideas we've described? Will deformable or fluid body interactions add new kinds of variability that are more difficult to describe or control? We find such questions intriguing, and intend to do further research on the topic.

Acknowledgments

The authors are grateful to Leslie Kaelbling for helping us make sense of our intuitive notions of Bayesian probability. We would like to dedicate this paper to the late Minnesota Fats (Rudolf Wanderone Jr., d. Jan 18, 1996).

References

[Ama84]   J. Amanatides. Ray tracing with cones. *Computer Graphics*, 18(3), 1984.

[Bob85]   Daniel Bobrow. *Qualitative Reasoning About Physical Systems*. MIT Press, 1985.

[BvO95]   Bart Barenbrug and Kees van Overveld. All you need is force: a constraint-based approach for rigid body dynamics in computer animation. In D.Terzopoulos and D.Thalmann, editors, *Proceedings: Computer Animation and Simulation '95*, pages 80–94. Springer Computer Science (Springer: Wien, New York), 1995. ISBN 3-211-82738-2.

[FvDFH90] J. Foley, A. van Dam, S. Feiner, and J. Hughes. *Computer Graphics: Principles and Practice*. Addison Wesley, 2nd edition, 1990.

[FW80]   Alexander L. Fetter and John Dirk Walecka. *Theoretical Mechanics of Particles and Continua*. McGraw-Hill, Inc., 1980.

[HS92]   Bernardo A. Huberman and Peter Struss. *Chaos, Qualitative Reasoning, and the Predictability Problem*. MIT Press, 1992.

[HU93]   Colin Howson and Peter Urbach. *Scientific Reasoning: The Bayesian Approach*. Open Court Publishing Company, 1993.

[KMS85]   S. Kerckhoff, H. Masur, and J. Smillie. A rational billiard flow is uniquely ergodic in almost every direction. *Bulletin of the Americal Mathematical Society*, 13(2):141–142, Oct 1985.

[KR66]   C.W. Kilmister and J.E. Reeve. *Rational Mechanics*. American Elsevier Publishing Company, 1966.

[Rei71]   Arnold L. Reimann. *Physics: Mechanics and Heat*. Barnes and Noble, 1971.

[TNM95]   Diane Tang, J. Thomas Ngo, and Joe Marks. N-body spacetime constraints. *Journal of Visualization and Computer Animation*, 6:143–154, 1995.

[vO91]   C. van Overveld. An iterative approach to dynamic simulations of 3-d rigid body motions for real-time interactive computer animation. *The Visual Computer*, 7:29–38, 1991.

Motion Synthesis By Example

Alexis Lamouret and Michiel van de Panne
Department of Computer Science
University of Toronto

Abstract: A technique is proposed for creating new animations from a set
of representative example motions stored in a motion database. Animations
are created by cutting-and-pasting together the example motion segments as
required. Motion segments are selected based upon how well they fit into a
desired motion and are then automatically tailored for a precise fit. Various
fundamental problems associated with the use of motion databases are outlined. A prototype implementation is used to validate the proposed concepts
and to explore possible solutions to the aforementioned problems.

Keywords: computer animation, motion capture, motion reuse, motion
database

1   Introduction

Building tools for character animation has long been a difficult business. The
problem of helping animators in their job is ill-defined in many ways. Just
how does an animator communicate a set of desired motion characteristics to
a software tool? How does the tool inform the animator of possible constraints
or compromises in achieving a desired motion? This paper investigates the
possibility of generating motions-by-example: the animator provides the tool
with a series of sample motions for the character. This *motion database* can then
be used to generate further motions of the same style. Such an animation tool
is aimed precisely at automating the predictable aspects of motions, whatever
they may be.

Like much of science, many approaches to animation have been deconstruc-
tionist, seeking to build models of motion by breaking it down into its constituent
components. This has yielded mechanical models to which the laws of physics
are applied and which must be controlled using a simulated musculature[1, 5, 13,
7, 12, 9, 10]. The idea behind such *physics-based animation* is to automatically
constrain animated motions to be physically plausible. It has since been noted
by many that this is a necessary, but not sufficient condition for producing *natural* motion. In order to obtain desired natural motions, we additionally need to
choose control actions which are also 'natural'. This, unfortunately, has proved
to be a difficult problem to solve.

Recent advances in motion capture technology have made it the animation
method of choice in a variety of situations. By allowing acted human movements
to be directly mapped onto an animated character, the creation of a desired

motion is direct and instantaneous. Recent work has focussed on how to edit and manipulate the motion data in order to make it more adaptable and reusable[14, 11, 4]. These efforts provide methods of post-processing the motion capture data. The animator can use a series of semi-automated tools to alter and tailor a chosen segment of motion capture data to meet particular desired constraints.

Kinematic models of motion capture the essence of a particular type of motion (e.g., walking) and attempt to parameterize it in a useful way[2, 3, 6, 8]. For example, kinematic models of walking typically let the animator directly control the speed, stride-length, and direction of the walking gait. The motion models are typically constructed and tuned by extracting important characteristics from real motion data. The synthesis of kinematic motion models is a fairly complex procedure, making it non-trivial to develop new motion models.

In order to arrive at a more flexible model of character motion, we propose to use a large set of representative motions together with techniques for tailoring these motions to make them fit new situations. In effect, the proposed technique consists of sampling a phenomena and being able to reconstruct new instances of the phenomena using these sample points. In our case, the phenomena represents a type of character motion and the new sample points represent this type of character motion executed in a new environment.

A brief example will serve to illustrate the fundamentals of the proposed technique. Consider a human walk across variable terrain. Sample walk sequences across variable terrain are stored in a motion database and used as the basis for constructing motion across a new instance of variable terrain. For each stride, the database is queried for the stride which best represents the previous action under similar circumstances. The criteria for the best-fit involves a match of the current state of the body, as well as a match of the terrain. Once found, the best-fit step is adapted to precisely fit its current use and the entire process is repeated for the next stride.

While building a motion database may in reality be infeasible for a variety of reasons, the preliminary results are sufficient to show its promise. Unlike previous techniques for altering motion-capture data, the proposed technique performs most of the work of motion synthesis through the intelligent choice of a similar motion among a set of examples.

2 Motion Databases: Problems to Overcome

A motion model seeks to represent the following function in as general a way as possible:

$$x \times e \times s \rightarrow m$$

where x is the present state [1] of the character, e is the state of the environment, s is the style of motion (e.g., big steps or bent knees), and m is a motion history of finite duration (e.g., one stride for a walking gait). The function domain thus consists of the conditions which cause the choice of a particular motion instance. A motion database provides a set of discrete samples of this function, $\{m_1...m_n\}$,

---

[1]state = position + velocity. configuration = position only

and their associated preconditions, namely the starting state, the condition of the environment, and the chosen style (if any). The motions and their preconditions serve as prototypical examples in the construction of new motion instances. Any example motion m_i can be adapted to fit new circumstances, yielding a tailored motion, m_i^*.

Many issues arise in the construction and use of a motion database. The following list is a brief exploration of some of them.

1. *What duration should the stored sample motions have?*

   The database consists of a series of example *motion primitives*. Motions of a cyclic nature, such as walking or hopping, have an obvious choice of granularity, namely a single cycle. Other types of motion may not be so easy to break into constituent motion primitives.

2. *What distance metric should be used to define the fit of a motion?*

   A best-fit motion primitive chosen to be appended to a current motion should satisfy several possibly-conflicting preconditions. The starting state (position and velocity) should be a good match with the current state of the character. Similarly, the state of the environment should also be a good match. Lastly, if the style of motion is also made a parameter, it needs to be part of the matching criteria. The distance metric must weight these factors appropriately. It should be efficient extracting the best-fit motion from the set of motion examples.

3. *Once chosen, how can the best-fit motion primitive be adapted to precisely fit the current sitation?*

   The required C^0 continuity of the initial state (position and velocity) as well as environmental constraints prevent a direct cut-and-paste of a best-fit motion into the final motion. Recent techniques do not directly address the problem of how to modify a motion to satisfy constraints involving interaction with the environment. The reconstruction technique should preserve the original motion characteristics as much as possible.

4. *How can a motion database be kept to a minimal size?*

   There are many possible approaches to reduce the size of a motion database. All of them involve eliminating redundancy in the data. One potential method consists of only adding sample motions to a database when they pass a redundancy test. Another would be to use compression techniques which take advantage of existing similarities between motion samples. Alternatively, the existing database could be resampled, the existing motion samples being replaced by a new, minimal number of optimally-placed motion prototypes. Lastly, the separability of motions can be exploited. For example, perhaps upper and lower body motions for humans can be carried out largely independently of each other, thereby allowing them to be individually matched and spliced together to produce a final motion.

Statistical correlations can perhaps serve as an indicator of which joint movements can be treated independently.

Another intriguing possibility is that of being able to take a single continuous stream of motion capture data, perhaps several hours worth collected from a person going about everyday activities, and to produce a reduced, minimal- size motion database from this data.

5. *How can ambiguous actions in the database be dealt with?*

If for a given precondition (state, environment, and style of motion) multiple motions exist in the database, what should be done? The database can be considered to be inconsistent, in effect storing multiple responses to a single query. All of the responses are in principle satisfactory, allowing for an arbitrary choice among them.

6. *How can higher-level planning be carried out using the motion primitives?*

Many actions require advance planning and anticipation. For example, carrying out a jump may require effecting preparations for the jump several steps in advance in order to build the necessary momentum. While a motion database helps define the immediate capabilities of a character, it does not provide a means of ordering the motion primitives to achieve a given goal. Planning techniques thus need to be developed which can use a motion database to achieve higher-level goals.

3 A Prototype System

As an initial investigation into the feasibility of the proposed method, we have implemented a motion database for 'Luxo', a planar 3-link articulated figure capable of a dynamic hopping behaviour. The 5 degrees of freedom of Luxo are shown in Figure 1. While it is easy to dismiss this figure as having a trivial number of degrees of freedom, its movements over variable terrain are dynamic and unstable, making it surprisingly difficult to animate using physics-based methods. By analogy, many human motions in sports are considered difficult because of their dynamic nature and the importance of the timing of the movements, rather than the number of degrees of freedom used in executing the movement.

3.1 The Motion Database

The motion samples for Luxo are generated using physics-based animation. In our case, the use of physics-based animation proved to be a convenient source of motion data. Five different types of control actions are defined, each of which causes a different style of hop to be executed. The total number of possible motions is much larger than the limited set of five control choices because the motions are also very sensitive to (a) the initial conditions for the hop, and (b) the state of the environment. A decision-tree technique is used to plan the control actions as Luxo travels across variable terrain. This technique simulates the effect of control decisions several steps into the future, much like a

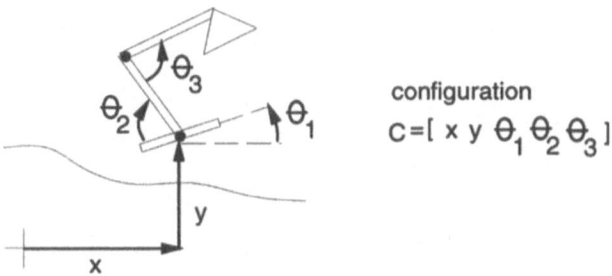

Figure 1: Luxo

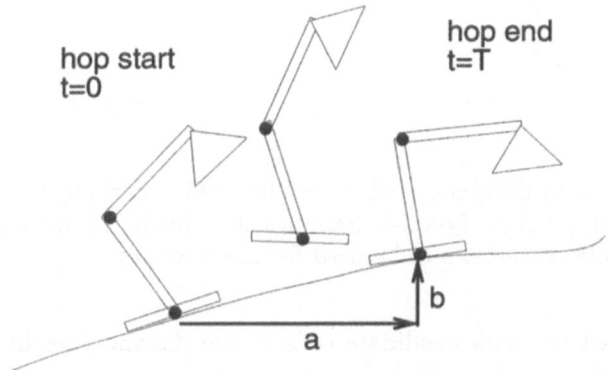

Figure 2: Measuring hop distance (a) and hop height (b).

game-playing algorithm and produces successful plans for Luxo leaping across variable terrain. However, the necessity of carrying out multiple simulations makes generating a physics-based animation considerably more expensive than the proposed synthesis-by-example technique.

The choice of primitive for Luxo is straightforward – it consists of a single hop. The start and end of hops are defined by the controller responsible for generating the motions. The result of a single sequence of physics-based animation is thus broken into multiple motion primitives, each of which serves as an entry in the motion database.

Being able efficiently search for the matching preconditions is important. Therefore, the motion samples are stored in a structured fashion. In order to simplify the search, the jumps are classified according to the state of the environment, rather than according to their initial states. In the case of Luxo, this is implemented using a two-dimensional table, composed of the length, a, and height b of the jump, measured as shown in Figure 2. The database can therefore be divided in cells, as shown in Figure 3.

During the search for the matching preconditions, the terrain variations are used to restrict the candidate motions as follows. The current terrain to be

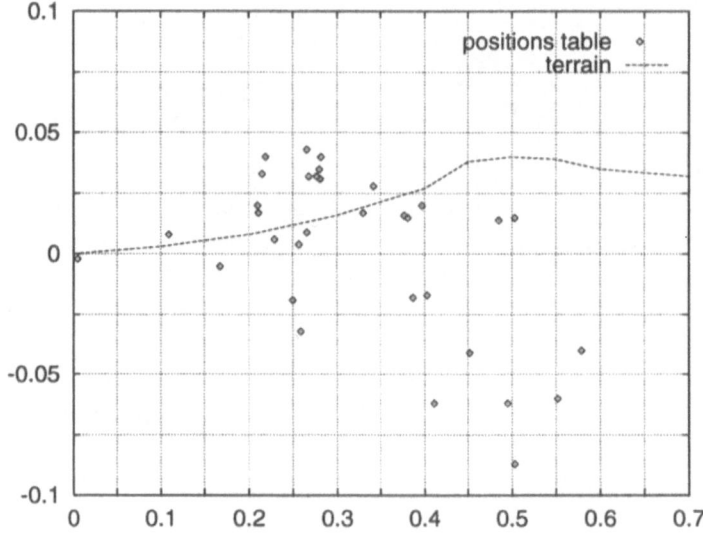

Figure 3: A motion database with hops classified according to jump distance (x-axis), and jump height (y-axis). Samples close to the shown terrain instance might be suitable candidates to be used for the next hop.

traversed is used to mark candidate cells in the distance/height classification table. This is done with a simple intersection test as shown in Figure 4. This quickly reduces the number of motion samples to search according the present 'state' of the environment. In the prototype implementation, issues of compression, redundant motion samples, and higher-level planning are not dealt with at present.

Figure 4: Using the terrain variation to restrict the candidate motions

3.2 The Distance Metric

As described earlier, deciding on the suitability of a motion instance induces matching several preconditions, including the continuity of the motion as well as its suitability given the terrain. Further user specifications might also come into effect, such as a preferred hop style. A database query retrieves the motion corresponding to the following minimum distance over the candidate samples m_i:

$$d_{min} = min_{\{m_i\}}(d_{state} + k_1 d_{env} + k_2 d_{user})$$

where

d_{state} measures the compatibility of the initial state
d_{env} measures the compatibility of the environment (terrain)
d_{user} measures the compatibility with particular user specifications
k_1, k_2 adjust the relative importance of the terms

Various metrics are possible to measure d_{state}, the distance between two states. A straightforward approach is to calculate an L_2 norm on $x^i - x^*$:

$$d_{state} = \sum_{j=1}^{N} \lambda_j (x_j^i - x_j^*)^2.$$

where $x = \{x_j\}_{1 \leq j \leq N}$ is the state vector, $x = [c, \dot{c}]$ with c the configuration vector shown in Figure 1. $\{x_j^i\}$ and $\{x_j^*\}$ thus represent the initial state vector for the ith sample in the database and the current state vector, respectively.

Unfortunately, this is also a misguided approach, as the choice of state vector is not unique and furthermore can do a bad job of measuring the possible correspondence of two states. An improved scheme is the mass-distance metric proposed in Figure 5:

$$d_{state} = \sum_m M_m \|p_m^i - p_m^*\|^2$$

Here, a point-mass distribution is created to approximate the real mass distribution of the articulated figure. p_m^i are the points taken on the creature for the initial state of the ith sample in the database, and p_m^* on the current state. The square of the dislocation of these point masses, weighed proportionately by their mass is used as a distance metric which is independent of the choice of state vector.

One item yet to be addressed is that of matching velocities. It is possible to have two creatures be in an identical position but having different velocities. As seen before, comparing the state vectors is misguided. We currently deal with velocities to a limited extent, by also including an evaluation of the mass-distance metric for the immediately preceding configurations of the articulated figure. A more accurate way to take the dynamics of the hops into account could

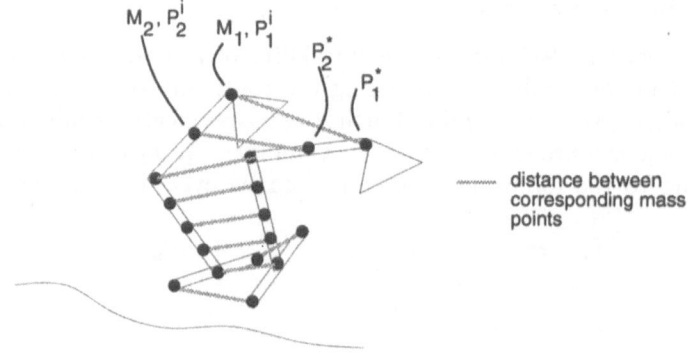

Figure 5: The mass distance metric

be to compare a relatively larger number of positions, possibly with decreasing coefficients as we go further away from the current state.

The d_{env} term is calculated using the square of the distance between the true landing point for a sample hop and the closest landing point in the given environment. An example of the necessary type of translation is shown in Figure 7, which will be discussed in further detail shortly.

The d_{user} term may be introduced, to take particular user specifications into account. In our current implementation this term is used to introduce a preferred hop length.

3.3 Adapting the Best-fit Motion

Once a best-fit motion primitive has been found, it needs to be adapted to be continuous with the previous motion as well as to precisely enforce any necessary constraints imposed by the environment. The adapting process is best illustrated by viewing the trajectory in the configuration space, as shown in Figure 6. The specifics of an adapation of a Luxo hop are shown in Figure 7.

First, the adaptation necessary to make the starting state, $x(0)$, match the final position of the existing motion, x_f, is determined: $\Delta x_1 = x_f - x(0)$.

Second, an adaptation to make the final position of the motion properly match the given terrain constraints is determined: $\Delta x_2 = x_c - x(T)$, where T is the duration of the motion primitive, $x(t)$. For Luxo, this involves finding the minimal displacement such that the terrain contact configuration matches that found in the sample motion. This includes ensuring the contact of specific points with the terrain as well as maintaining the same relative angle of the base with respect to the terrain. The adaptations carried out at $x(0)$ and $x(T)$ should by their nature be specific to the character being animated, as the types of constraints which need to be satisfied will depend on the character.

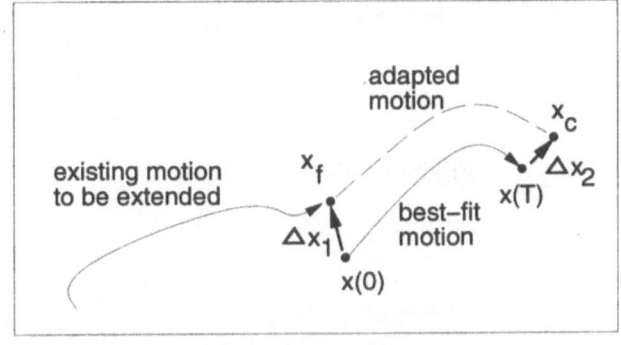

Figure 6: Adapting the best-fit motion.

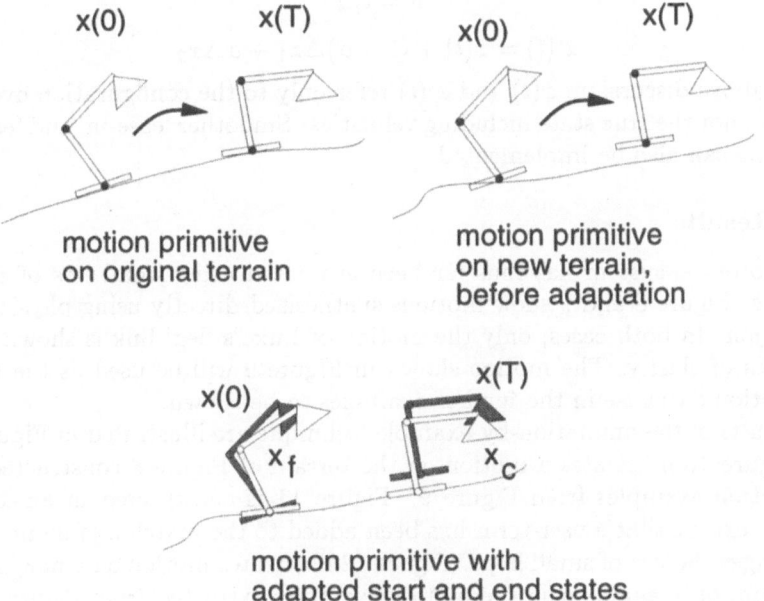

Figure 7: Adapting a Luxo jump.

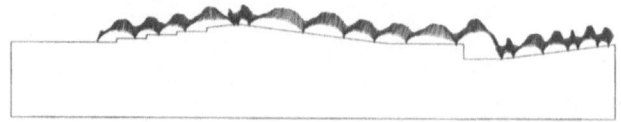

Figure 8: Motion Dataset 1

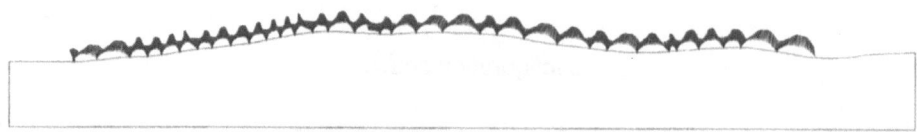

Figure 9: Motion Dataset 2

The final adapted motion is defined by gradually phasing in or out the adaptations over the time-duration T:

$$\alpha = t/T$$

$$x'(t) = x(t) + (1 - \alpha)\Delta x_1 + \alpha \Delta x_2$$

In the above discussion, $x(t)$ and $x'(t)$ refer only to the configuration over time, and thus not the true state including velocities. Smoother 'ease-in' and 'ease-out' functions can also be implemented.

3.4   Results

The prototype system has thus far been evaluated using small sets of example motions. Figure 8 and 9 show motions synthesized directly using physics-based animation. In both cases, only the motion of Luxo's 'leg' link is shown for the purposes of clarity. The motion shown in Figure 9 will be used as the basis of our motion database in the further examples to be shown.

Results of the animation-by-example technique are illustrated in Figures 10–12. Figure 10 illustrates a motion on the terrain of Figure 8 constructed using the motion examples from Figure 9. Figure 11 is constructed in an identical fashion, except that a user-term has been added to the matching function which encourages the use of small hops. Figure 12 illustrates motion on a new instance of terrain, once again using the motion examples extracted from Figure 9.

While subjective judgement of the resulting motions reveals them to be missing some of the fluidity of the original motions, the motions nevertheless appear quite plausible to the eye. Figure 13 shows a detail of the original, physics-based animation of Figure 8. A detailed view of the synthetic motion across the same terrain is shown in Figure 14. The synthetic motion is in this case somewhat smoother than the actual motion.

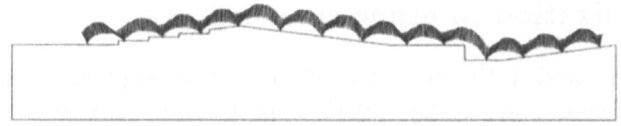

Figure 10: Output on terrain 1 with dataset 2, big hops

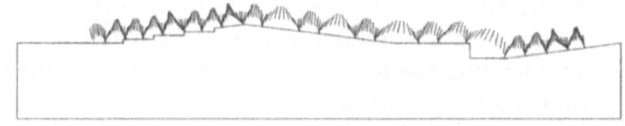

Figure 11: Output on terrain 1 with dataset 2, small hops

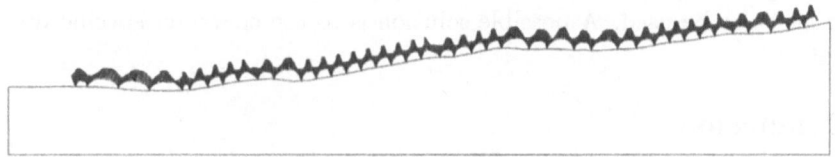

Figure 12: Output on terrain 3 with dataset 2

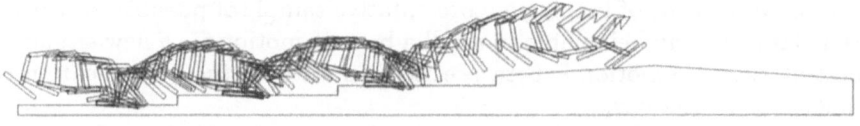

Figure 13: Detail of original motion (dataset 1).

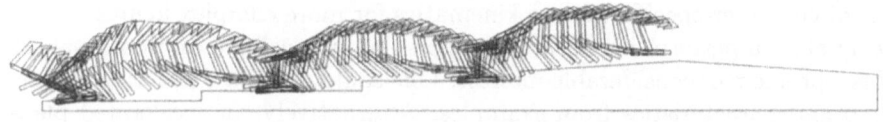

Figure 14: Detail of synthetic motion (dataset 2 applied to terrain 1).

4   Generalization to other creatures

The model presented in the previous sections can be applied to various kinds of articulated creatures, providing that they meet certain requirements.

First of all, we must consider quasi-cyclic kinds of motion, such as hopping, running or walking, in order to be able to find a coherent primitive. Motions not having any contact constraints, such as swimming or flying, are easier to deal with, and thus will not be discussed in this section.

We expect the generalization of our technique to running monopeds and bipeds to be relatively simple. We consider the motion primitive to start and end with the occurence of a new ground contact. As before, the adapting process can proceed by blending the modifications required to fit the start and end states to the previous motion and the terrain.

Biped walking, however, proves to be a more difficult problem, because of the existence of double-stance phase. While the distance metric used to choose the best fit may remain the same, a more complex algorithm for adapting it to the terrain needs to be used. A possible solution is to use character-specific inverse kinematics.

5   Conclusions

The idea of directly modelling motion has long existed in the form of procedural animation. Similarly, the idea of adapting existing motion data to fit new situations has also recently seen considerable interest. We have speculated that it is possible to build animation systems which can 'animate by example'. The proposed framework is one of keeping a representative sample of possible motions in a motion database and being able to recall a best-fit motion for a new situation. The best-fit example motion is then precisely adapted to the new situation by applying small corrections.

A variety of subproblems of the animation-by-example technique were examined. Many of the problems to be solved are related to those of machine learning, where the goal is to learn a compact representation of a function by correctly generalizing from a series of examples (supervised learning). The subproblem of adapting a motion for a precise fit is specific to animation. Although the adaptation problem is relatively simple for our chosen examples, it will require the use of character-specific inverse kinematics for more complex figures.

Being able to perform higher-level motion planning using a motion database remains a problem of considerable interest. One could imagine extracting higher-level motion characteristics from examples. Alternatively, an accelerated planning technique could operate by composing together the primitives found in a motion database.

In order to keep a motion database to a reasonable size, a variety of compression strategies are possible. By extracting correlations between components for a movement, it should be possible to recognize, for example, that head motion is largely independent of leg motion during walking and should therefore be treated separately. An ideal system would be able to extract a compact, irreducible set of example motions given a large pool of motion data.

In conclusion, this workshop paper proposes that the idea of animation-by-example is an interesting and desireable feature for animation tools of the future. It is hoped that the ideas presented here will inspire further discussion at the workshop.

References

[1] N. I. Badler, B. Barsky, and D. Zeltzer. *Making Them Move.* Morgan Kaufmann Publishers Inc., 1991.

[2] R. Boulic, N. M. Thalmann, and D. Thalmann. A global human walking model with real-time kinematic personification. *The Visual Computer*, 6:344–358, 1990.

[3] A. Bruderlin and T. W. Calvert. Interactive animation of personalized human locomotion. *Proceedings of Graphics Interface*, pages 17–23, 1993.

[4] A. Bruderlin and L. Williams. Motion signal processing. *Proceedings of SIGGRAPH '95, ACM Computer Graphics*, pages 97–104, 1995.

[5] J. K. Hodgins et al. Animating human athletics. *Proceedings of SIGGRAPH '95, ACM Computer Graphics*, pages 71–78, 1995.

[6] M. Girard. Interactive design of computer-animated legged animal motion. *IEEE Comptuer Graphics and Applications*, 7(6):39–51, June 1987.

[7] R. Grzeszczuk and D. Terzopoulos. Automated learning of muscle-actuated locomotion through control abstraction. *Proceedings of SIGGRAPH '95, ACM Computer Graphics*, pages 63–70, 1995.

[8] H. Ko and N. I. Badler. Straight line walking animation based on kinematic generalization that preserves the original characteristics. *Proceedings of Graphics Interface '93*, pages 9–16, 1993.

[9] J. T. Ngo and J. Marks. Spacetime constraints revisited. *Proceedings of SIGGRAPH '93*, pages 343–350, 1993.

[10] K. Sims. Evolving virtual creatures. *Proceedings of SIGGRAPH '94, ACM Computer Graphics*, pages 15–22, 1994.

[11] M. Unuma, K. Anjyo, and R. Takeuchi. Fourier principles for emotion-based human figure animation. *Proceedings of SIGGRAPH '95, ACM Computer Graphics*, pages 91–96, 1995.

[12] M. van de Panne and E. Fiume. Sensor-actuator networks. *Proceedings of SIGGRAPH '93*, pages 335–342, 1993.

212

[13] M. van de Panne, R. Kim, and E. Fiume. Virtual wind-up toys for animation. *Proceedings of Graphics Interface '94*, pages 208–215, 1994.

[14] A. Witkin and Z. Popovi'c. Motion warping. *Proceedings of SIGGRAPH '95, ACM Computer Graphics*, pages 105–107, 1995.

Appendix :
Colour Illustrations

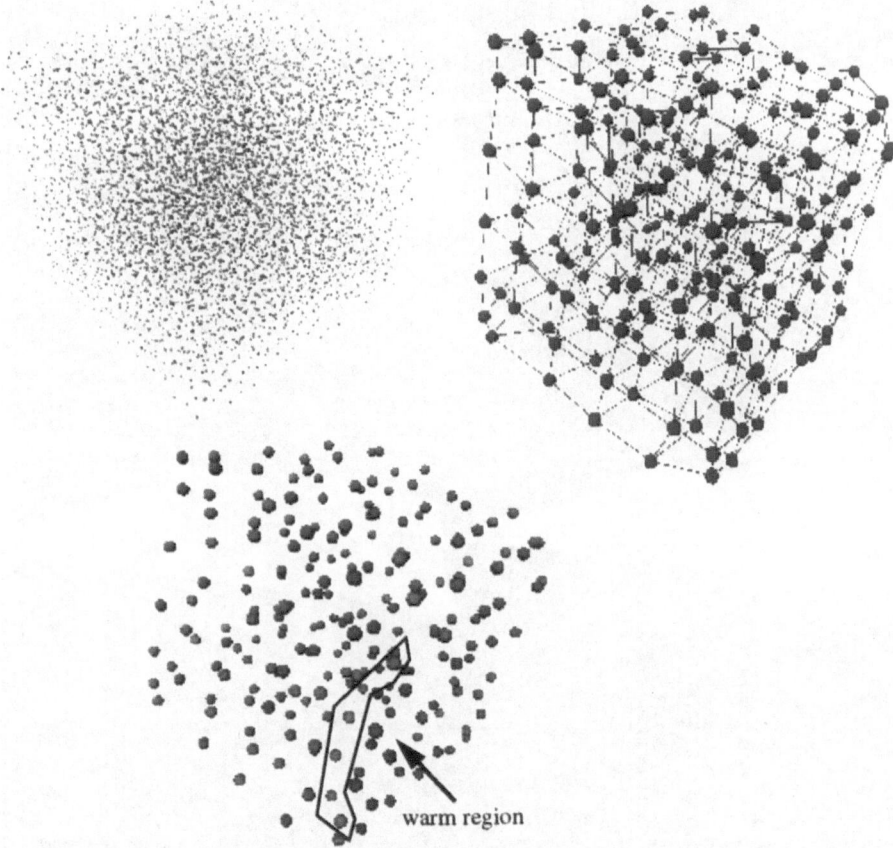

Discretization and property mapping example (Balmelli et al., Figs. 6, 8)

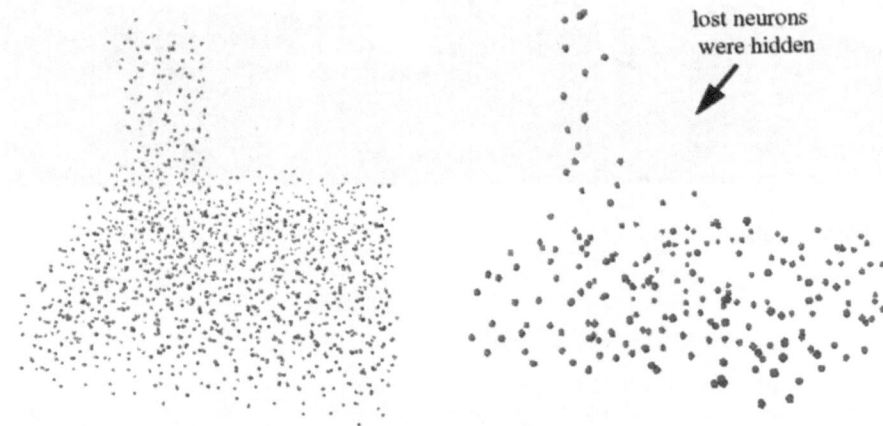

Hiding of neurons using property mapping (Balmelli et al., Fig. 9)

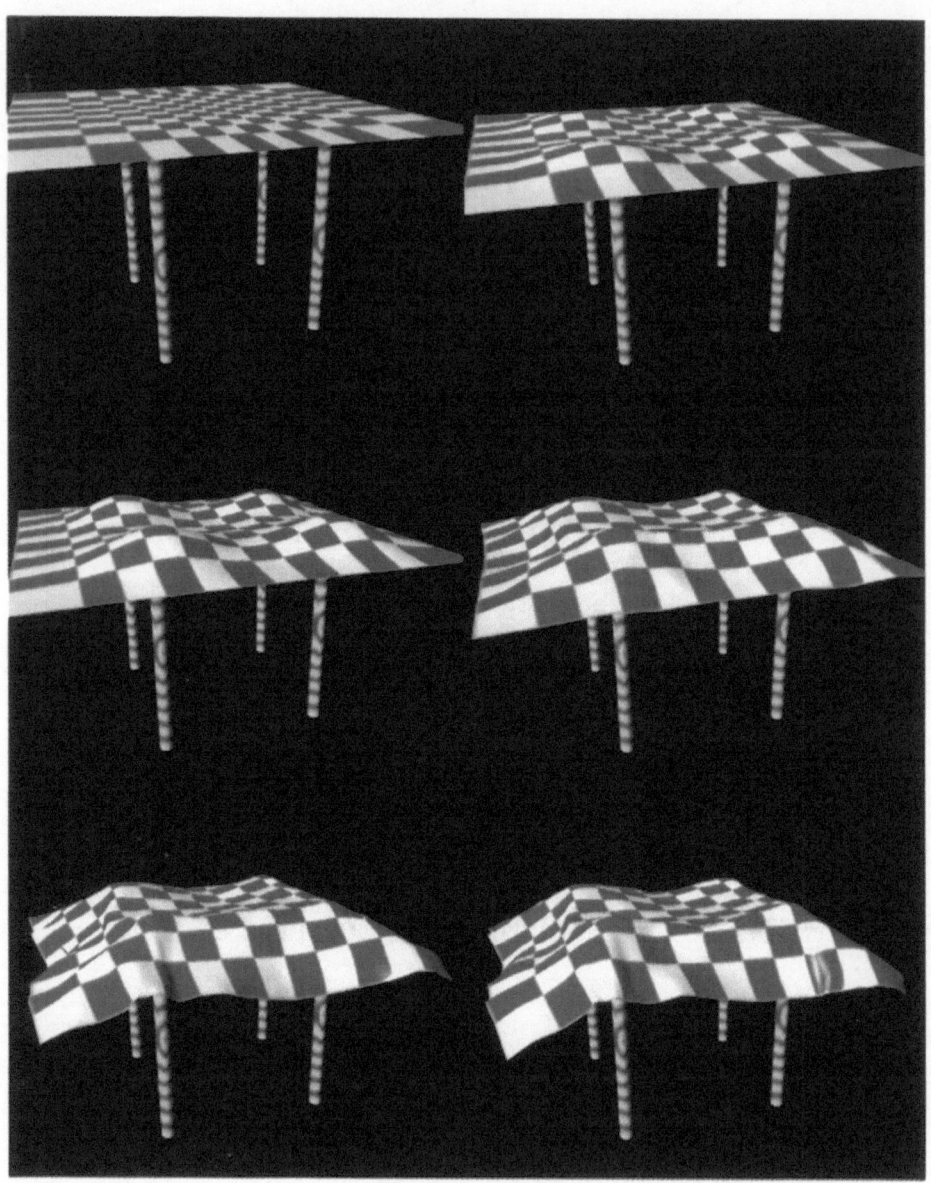

(Hutchinson et al.)

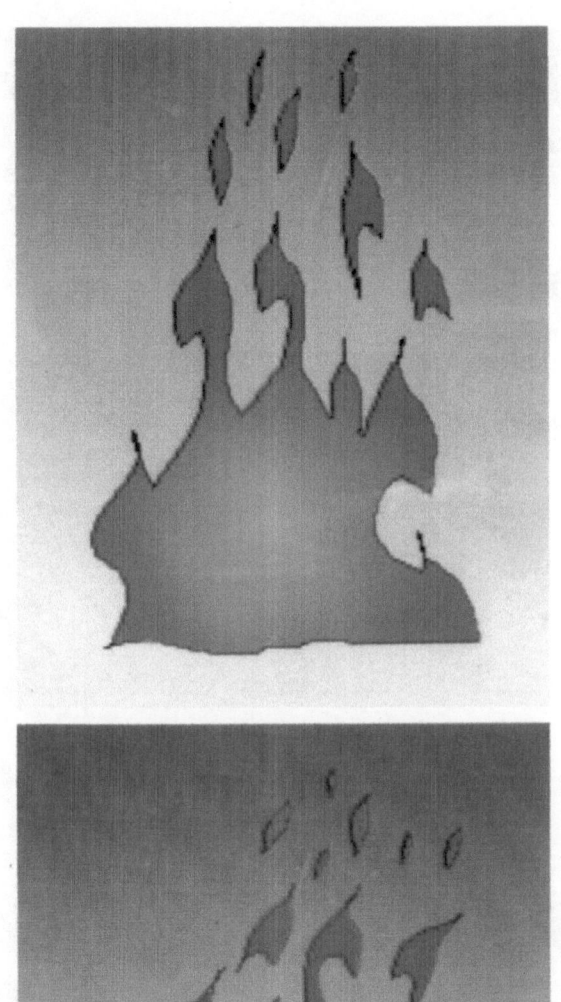

(Yu and Patterson)

Performed and converted postures of a soccer motion (Molet et al., Fig. 10)

Without special twisting
evaluation

Comparison of postures obtained with and without special twisting evaluation for
shoulders and knees (Molet et al., Fig. 12)

Fig. 5

Fig. 15

Fig. 16

The keyframes (events) for four
reference movement cycles:
(a) SW (b) LW (c) SRH (d) LRH
(Guo and Robergé, Fig. 5)

A movement sequence from
standing to running
(Guo and Robergé, Fig. 15)

A walk in the clouds
(Guo and Robergé, Fig. 16)

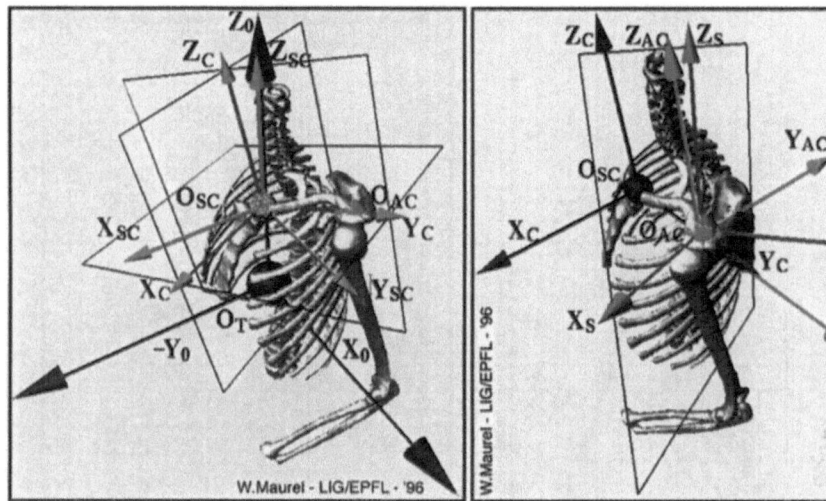

Sterno-clavicular joint (Maurel et al., Table 5.1)

Acromio-clavicular joint (Maurel et al., Table 5.2)

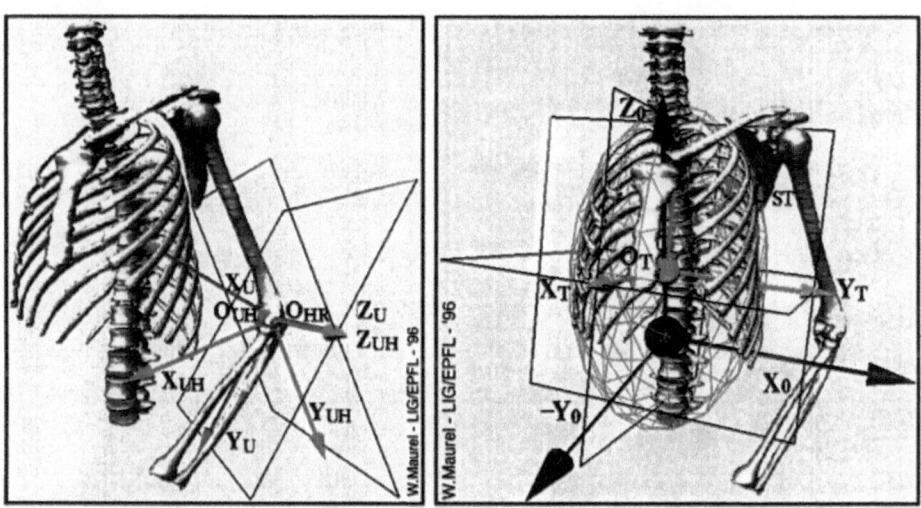

Ulno-humeral joint (Maurel et al., Table 5.4)

Scapulo-thoracic joint (Maurel et al., Table 5.6)

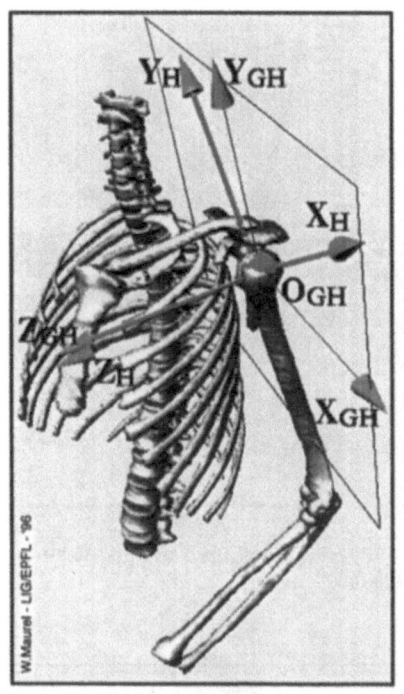

Gleno-humeral joint (Maurel et al., Table 5.3)

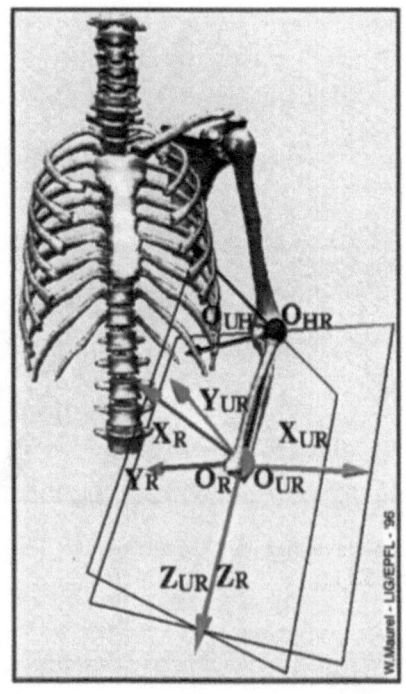

Ulno-radial joint (Maurel et al., Table 5.5)

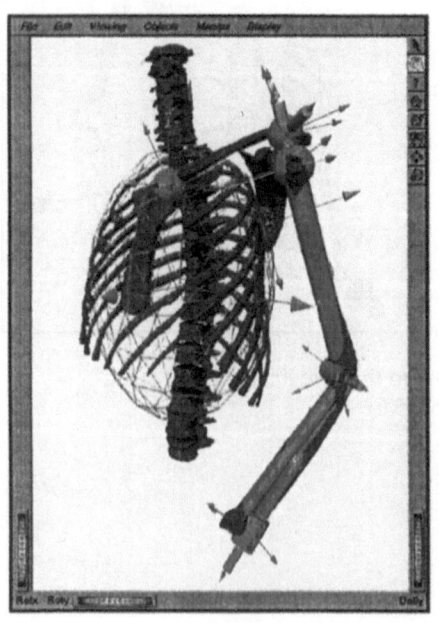

Joint frames modeling (Maurel et al., Fig. 8)

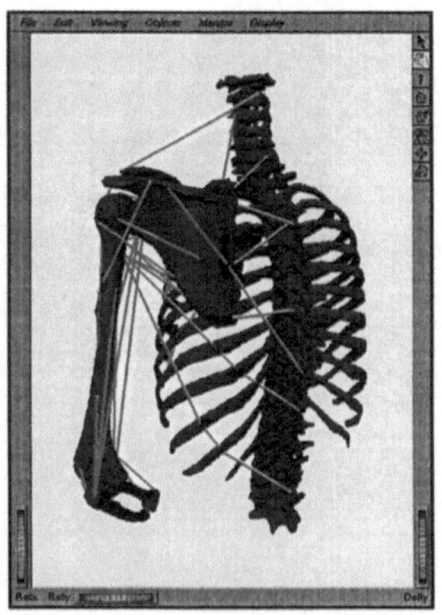

Muscle topology (Maurel et al., Fig. 10)

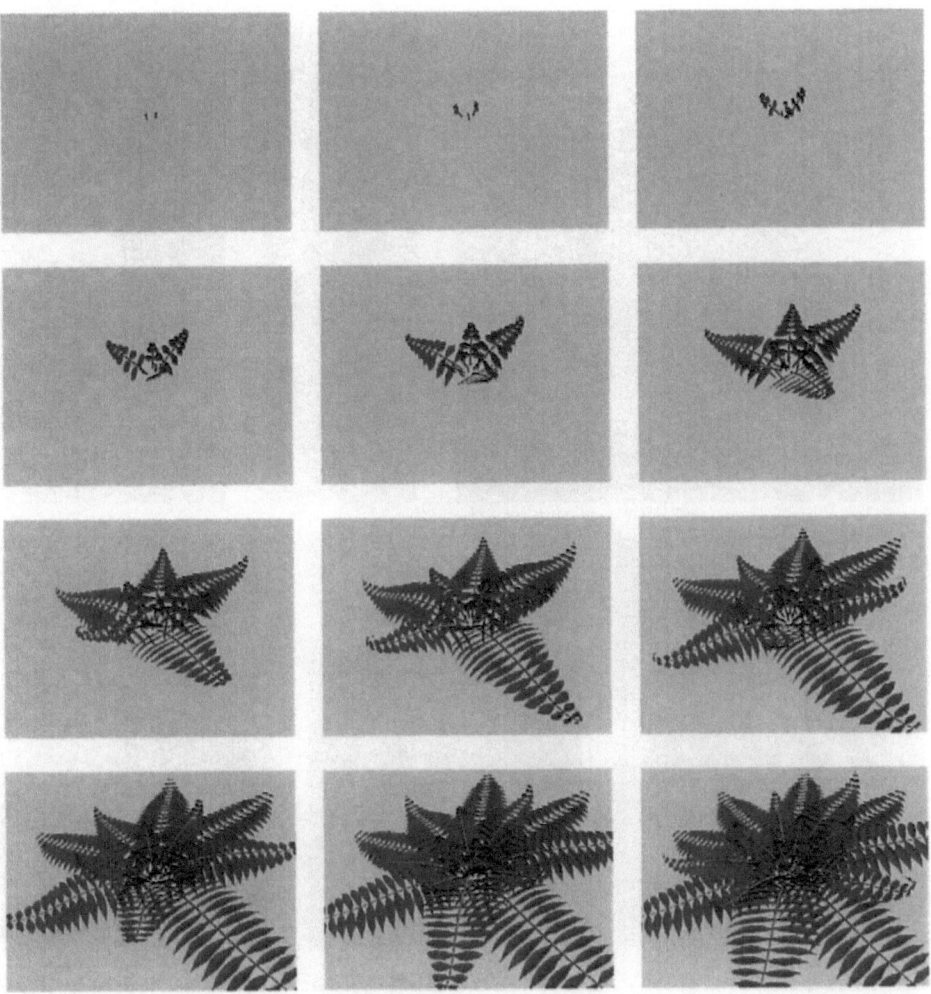

Example frames of an animation with embedded keyframing. The growth of the twigs and leaves starts at different times, each leaf uses its local time for growing (Lintermann and Deussen, Fig. 11)

224

Some examples of static models generated by the modeller (Lintermann and Deussen, Fig. 12)

(Beneš)

SpringerEurographics

Martin Göbel, Jaques David, Pavel Slavik, Jarke J. van Wijk (eds.)
Virtual Environments and Scientific Visualization '96

Proceedings of the Eurographics Workshops in Monte Carlo, Monaco, February 19-20, 1996

and in Prague, Czech Republic, April 23-24, 1996

1996. 169 partly coloured figures. VIII, 324 pages.

Soft cover approx. DM 118,–, öS 826,–

ISBN 3-211-82886-9

Selected papers from this year's Workshops on Virtual Environments and on Visualization in Scientific Computing are included in this volume. The papers on VE discuss Virtual Environment System architecture, communication requirements, synthetic actors, crowd simulations and modeling aspects, application experience in surgery support, geographic information systems, and engineering and virtual housing systems.

Contributions from the Visualization workshop are presented in four groups: volume rendering, user interfaces in scientific visualization, architecture of scientific visualization systems and flow visualization.

Xavier Pueyo, Peter Schröder (eds.)
Rendering Techniques '96

Proceedings of the Eurographics Workshop in Porto, Portugal, June 17–19, 1996

1996. 197 figures. X, 294 pages.

Soft cover approx. DM 120,–, öS 840,–

ISBN 3-211-82883-4

27 contributions treat the state of the art in Monte Carlo and Finite Element methods for radiosity and radiance. Further special topics dealt with are the use of image maps to capture light throughout space, complexity, volumetric stochastic descriptions, innovative approaches to sampling and approximation, and system architecture.

The Rendering Workshop proceedings are an obligatory piece of literature for all scientists working in the rendering field, but they are also very valuable for the practitioner involved in the implementation of state of the art rendering system certainly influencing the scientific progress in this field.

 SpringerWienNewYork

P O Box 89, A-1201 Wien • New York, NY 10010, 175 Fifth Avenue
Heidelberger Platz 3, D-14197 Berlin • Tokyo 113, 3-13, Hongo 3-chome, Bunkyo-ku

SpringerEurographics

Bodo Urban (ed.)
Multimedia '96

Proceedings of the Eurographics Workshop in Rostock, Federal Republic of Germany,
May 28–30, 1996
1996. 71 figures. VII, 178 pages.
Soft cover DM 85,–, öS 595,–, US $ 67.00
ISBN 3-211-82876-1

Theoretical concepts and specific applications for handling multimedia data, still and motion pictures
on the net, WWW and multimedia, collaborative multimedia, and multimedia and education are dealt
with in this volume. The reader will profit in getting up-to-date information about current trends in mul-
timedia/hypermedia services and applications in open distributed environments.

Remco C. Veltkamp, Edwin H. Blake (eds.)
Programming Paradigms in Graphics '95

Proceedings of the Eurographics Workshop in Maastricht, The Netherlands, September 2–3, 1995
1995. 41 partly coloured figures. VIII, 172 pages.
Soft cover DM 85,–, öS 595,–, US $ 59.00
ISBN 3-211-82788-9

Philippe Palanque, Rémi Bastide (eds.)
Design, Specification and Verification of Interactive Systems '95

Proceedings of the Eurographics Workshop in Toulouse, France, June 7–9, 1995
1995. 153 figures. X, 370 pages.
Soft cover DM 118,–, öS 826,–, US $ 95.00
ISBN 3-211-82739-0

Martin Göbel (ed.)
Virtual Environments '95

Selected papers of the Eurographics Workshops in Barcelona, Spain, 1993,
and Monte Carlo, Monaco, 1995
1995. 134 partly coloured figures. VII, 307 pages.
Soft cover DM 108,–, öS 756,–, US $ 85.00
ISBN 3-211-82737-4

SpringerWienNewYork

PO Box 89, A-1201 Wien • New York, NY 10010, 175 Fifth Avenue
Heidelberger Platz 3, D-14197 Berlin • Tokyo 113, 3-13, Hongo 3-chome, Bunkyo-ku

SpringerEurographics

Demetri Terzopoulos, Daniel Thalmann (eds.)
Computer Animation and Simulation '95
Proceedings of the Eurographics Workshop in Maastricht, The Netherlands, September 2–3, 1995

1995. 156 partly coloured figures. VIII, 235 pages.

Soft cover DM 89,–, öS 625,–, US $ 69.00

ISBN 3-211-82738-2

Riccardo Scateni, Jarke J. van Wijk, Pietro Zanarini (eds.)
Visualization in Scientific Computing '95
Proceedings of the Eurographics Workshop in Chia, Italy, May 3–5, 1995

1995. 110 partly coloured figures. VII, 161 pages.

Soft cover DM 85,–, öS 595,–, US $ 69.00

ISBN 3-211-82729-3

Patrick M. Hanrahan, Werner Purgathofer (eds.)
Rendering Techniques '95
Proceedings of the Eurographics Workshop in Dublin, Ireland, June 12–14, 1995

1995. 198 partly coloured figures. XI, 372 pages.

Soft cover DM 118,–, öS 826,–, US $ 98.00

ISBN 3-211-82733-1

Martin Göbel, Heinrich Müller, Bodo Urban (eds.)
Visualization in Scientific Computing
1995. 150 figures. VIII, 238 pages.

Soft cover DM 118,–, öS 826,–, US $ 85.00

ISBN 3-211-82633-5

Wolfgang Herzner, Frank Kappe (eds.)
Multimedia/Hypermedia in Open Distributed Environments
Proceedings of the Eurographics Symposium in Graz, Austria, June 6–9, 1994

1994. 105 figures. VIII, 330 pages.

Soft cover DM 118,–, öS 826,–, US $ 79.00

ISBN 3-211-82587-8

 SpringerWienNewYork

PO Box 89, A-1201 Wien • New York, NY 10010, 175 Fifth Avenue
Heidelberger Platz 3, D-14197 Berlin • Tokyo 113, 3-13, Hongo 3-chome, Bunkyo-ku